Honoring the memory of
Winton M. Blount
(1921-2002)
for his generous support of programs and exhibitions
at the Folger Shakespeare Library.

He was a man. Take him for all in all,
I shall not look upon his like again.
Hamlet (1.2.195-196)

This volume has been published in conjunction with the exhibition, *Elizabeth I, Then and Now,* presented at the Folger Shakespeare Library,® Washington, DC, from March 21 through August 2, 2003, on the occasion of the 400th anniversary of the death of Elizabeth I.

Gail Kern Paster
Director

Richard Kuhta
Librarian

Rachel Doggett
Andrew W. Mellon Curator of Books and Exhibitions

The exhibition and the catalogue have been funded by The Winton and Carolyn Blount Exhibition Fund and The Andrew W. Mellon Publication Fund of the Folger Shakespeare Library.

Sponsors for the Folger Shakespeare Library *Elizabeth I, Then and Now* celebration:

American Airlines;
American Express Company;
Artex;
British Airways;
British Tourist Authority;
Christie's;
Chubb Group of Insurance Companies;
GM Foundation;
Heart of England;
PEPCO;
Arthur Sanderson and Sons North America Ltd.;
Union Station, Washington, DC;
Visa, U.S.A., Inc.;
WETA.

Distributed by University of Washington Press, Seattle and London.
ISBN 0-295-98323-X

Photographs by Julie Ainsworth and Tom Wachs.

Design by Studio A, Alexandria, VA

Printing by Balding + Mansell, Norwich, England

Contents

Foreword

It is unusual for a Folger Shakespeare Library exhibition to focus on the life of a single individual. But the occasion of the 400th anniversary of Elizabeth I's reign is momentous, and the life in question one of historically great significance and accomplishment. Perhaps most important, the Folger's rich materials on Elizabeth allow us to portray her in stunning detail, as this catalogue makes clear.

This exhibit begins with the firm assumption that Elizabeth I remains a figure of charismatic power in British and American culture. Hence the subtitle "Then and Now." Films on Elizabeth have been a Hollywood staple from early days. The most recent example, the 1998 film starring Cate Blanchett, shows Elizabeth—in a radically simplified but nonetheless visually striking moment—deciding to take charge of her own public persona. The film marks the moment through her sudden, almost violent application of heavy, chalk-white makeup. She is transformed in an instant from vulnerable young woman to other-worldly icon—the Virgin Queen. But the real queen's charisma was also evident early in her reign, as her nation—reeling from the shock of dynastic uncertainty and post-Reformation religious tensions—looked to her as a central figure of stability and responded gratefully when she offered herself as a figure of popular understanding. If the accident of her birth made her a monarch, the force of her personality has made her a legend. Certainly, one result of her long reign in historical terms is that Elizabeth so completely personifies sixteenth-century England that an exhibition, like this one, devoted to her life truly encompasses the full range of the dazzling culture that takes her name.

In the materials displayed in the exhibit and more fully investigated in this wonderful catalogue written by Georgianna Ziegler, Head of Reference at the Folger, and her scholarly collaborators, we see Elizabeth as affectionate stepdaughter and censorious cousin, as humanist prince adept in several languages, as wily partner in complicated courtship dances that left her resolved not to marry, as powerful and often capricious patroness, and as private person. She was the center not only of national culture but also of a vibrant court culture with complex ritual practices such as elaborate New Year's gift exchanges and summertime progresses through the countryside. Her wardrobe expressed a personal desire for splendor but, as the prince of a small European nation with imperial ambitions, Elizabeth was obliged to display herself magnificently on public occasions. The many portraits which survive of her—one of the most splendid being the 1579 Sieve Portrait which is the centerpiece of this exhibition—suggest the complex interplay between Elizabeth's canny politics of self-display and her powerful vanity.

This catalogue is an expressive reflection of the Folger's rich holdings in materials relating to Elizabeth I collected over many years, first by the library's founders Henry Clay Folger and Emily Jordan Folger and later by important acquisitions such as parts of the Loseley Collection (1938–1954). We are happy to have the opportunity to convert these materials into the stuff of a compelling exhibition and catalogue. I wish to thank not only Georgianna Ziegler for her devotion over several years to curating the exhibition and masterminding the catalogue, but to others on the Folger staff who have worked long and hard on this ambitious, multifaceted project of celebrating Elizabeth. They include Rachel Doggett, Janet Field-Pickering, Janet Griffin,

Richard Kuhta, Garland Scott, Anita Sperling, and Sharon Stanczak—colleagues whose creativity, vision, enthusiasm, and sheer capacity for hard work have brought a four hundredth anniversary vision radiantly to life. All of us at the Folger wish to honor the inspiration of Werner Gundersheimer, my predecessor as director, in the planning and conception of this endeavor. We are very grateful as well to Karen Hastie Williams, Chair of the Folger Library Committee, for her strategic wisdom and to Deborah Dingell for joining the Elizabeth cohort with timely support and influential counsel.

Sharing our enthusiasm for commemorating Elizabeth has been a group of wonderfully supportive sponsors. We have been especially grateful to the British Embassy for their ongoing counsel and encouragement, and wish to thank Sir Christopher Meyer and his excellent staff, especially Pauline Morgan. Union Station in Washington, D.C., generously gave the Folger use of their magnificent West Hall for a panel exhibition complementing the larger exhibition in the Folger's Great Hall. The British Tourist Authority and the Heart of England, Great Britain's most ambitious tourism organizations, provided crucial early support for "Elizabeth I: Then and Now," by underwriting the panel exhibit at Union Station and the exhibition brochure. British Airways has served as the official airline of the exhibition by providing transportation for guest artists and lecturers from the United Kingdom. American Airlines helped to guarantee the exhibition's success by providing domestic transportation for staff and visiting artists. WETA drew wide public attention to the exhibit through their generous on-air promotional efforts. Among corporate sponsors, we wish to thank Chubb Insurance for their lead sponsorship of the exhibition's opening night gala, *The Queen's Revels*. The General Motors Foundation also participated generously in *The Queen's Revels* and helped us to honor Elizabeth by hosting a reception for her political descendants in America—the women members of Congress. The American Express Company funded the exhibition's acoustiguides to greatly enhance the visitors' experience. Visa, a long-time Folger Corporate Guild member, provided early unrestricted support to the effort. Christie's, working closely with Folger staff, brought the Elizabeth celebration to their exhibition space in New York City and publicized the exhibit in a Christie's catalog. PEPCO, generous underwriter of the Folger Consort's *Shakespeare and Elizabeth* concerts, enabled us to present the music of Elizabeth's times to an enthusiastic public.

The Folger is deeply grateful to these supporters for their understanding and appreciation of our goals in this exhibit—to celebrate the life and achievements of a uniquely gifted female ruler by the public viewing of books, letters, documents, artifacts, and costumes closely associated with her. In its rich array of texts and objects, our exhibit seeks to convey the wonder of Elizabeth I —her stunning imaginative and political power over her contemporaries—even as it demonstrates the political and biographical complexity of her life and times.

Gail Kern Paster

Director

Acknowledgments

The idea of celebrating Elizabeth I came to me about five years ago when my colleague, Rachel Doggett, designed a display of Elizabeth-related items for our annual Acquisitions Night. I remember being stunned by seeing so many colorful and interesting objects together and thinking that it would be fun to do an exhibition to honor the 400th anniversary of Elizabeth's death. 2003 seemed suitably far away in 1998. As usually happens, I discovered much more about the depth of our collection when I began reviewing books and manuscripts to include in the exhibition. It became clear that the Folger Library has the largest collection of Elizabeth-related material in the United States. I had been interested in Elizabeth I for quite awhile, and fortunately after three years of working on this project, I still find that like Cleopatra, "Age cannot wither her, nor custom stale/ Her infinite variety." In the post-Feminist moment, we may admire her today as a competent politician, a woman who put her career first over her personal desires, who decided —against the pleading of male counselors and Parliamentarians—that she couldn't "have it all." But Elizabeth would not have described herself in that way. If asked, she would probably wonder why and say that she was just following the legacy of her father and grandfather and trying to rule in the best interest of her country.

Exhibitions are really collaborative efforts and many people have helped make this one possible. First I would like to thank the wonderful group of scholars who brought their areas of expertise to the essays in this catalogue: Peter Blayney, Sheila ffolliott, Heidi Brayman Hackel, Barbara Hodgdon, Carole Levin, and Janel Mueller. Visiting historians Vincent Carey and Paul J. Hammer kindly read and commented on two of the essays. Paul was also helpful with transcriptions, as were my colleagues Heather Wolfe and Dever Powell. In addition, Heather has provided a very useful listing of manuscripts at the Folger with Elizabeth's signature. My colleague Erin Blake supplied important details about several of the art objects, and our rare book cataloger, Ron Bogdan, helped with some translating from early Spanish. Steven May generously provided his expertise on Elizabeth's writings and her court. This catalogue owes its beauty to the magnificent work of our photographers, Julie Ainsworth and Tom Wachs, and to the skill and imagination of designer, Antonio Alcalá of Studio A. The exhibition itself would not be possible without the behind-the-scenes organization of our Reading Room staff, under the direction of Elizabeth Walsh, and of our assistant Susan Scola. It would not even take place without the hard work and creativity of the Folger's Conservation Department: Frank Mowery, Linda Blaser, Linda Hohneke and Rhea Baier. Our talented consultant, Esther Ferington, created the brochure, the poster exhibition, and the Acoustiguide script. It was a pleasure to work with all of these colleagues and friends, and I am deeply grateful to them.

Georgianna Ziegler

E R

HONI·SOIT·QVI·MAL·Y·PENSE·

S
P Q
R

SEMPER EADEM

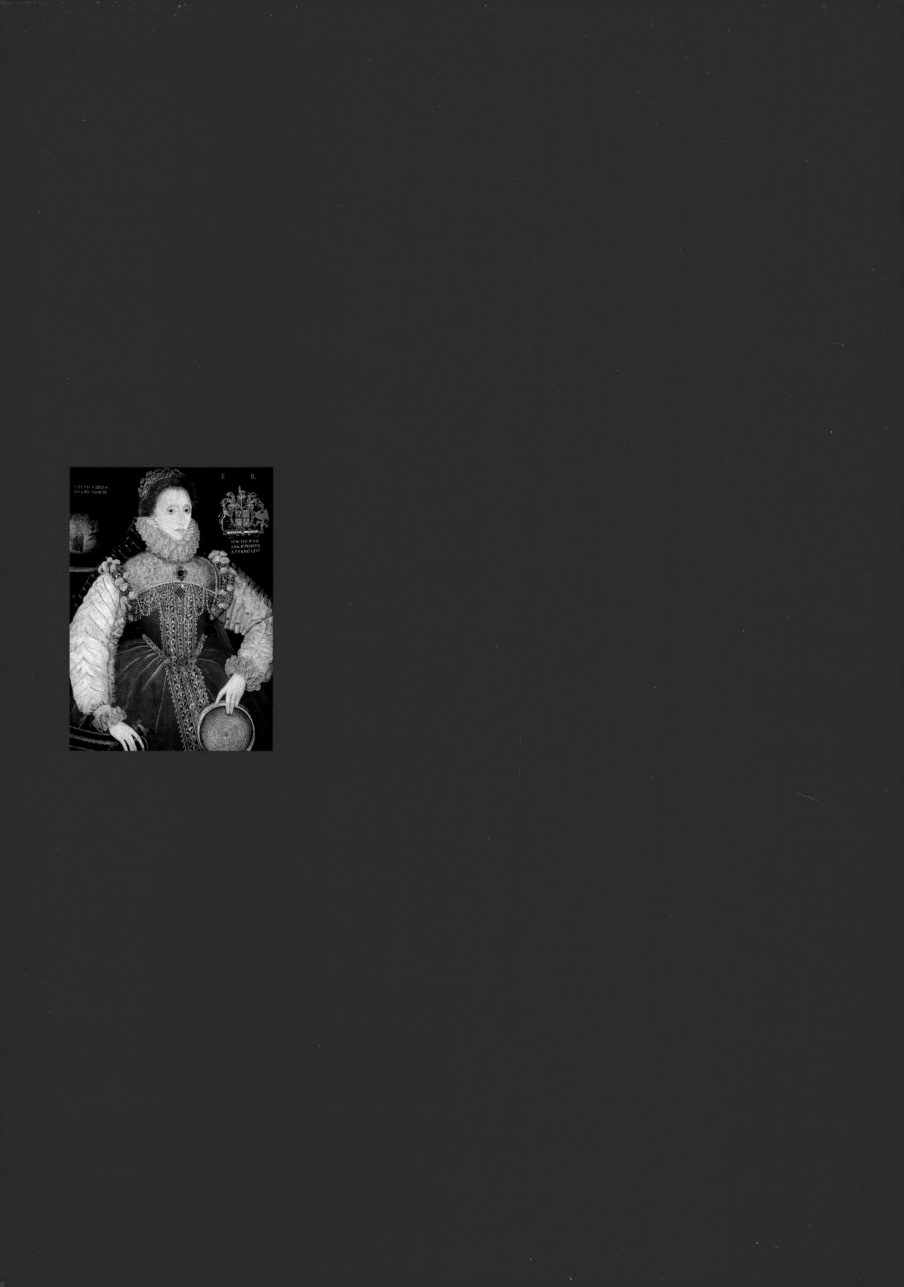

Compiled and edited by
Georgianna Ziegler

Elizabeth I
THEN AND NOW

The Folger Shakespeare Library
Washington, DC 2003

Distributed by University of
Washington Press
Seattle and London

Introduction to the Life and Reign of Elizabeth I[1]
Carole Levin

HENRY VIII WAS CONVINCED THAT FOR HIS DYNASTY TO BE SECURE and his country safe he must have a son to follow him as king. But his daughter Mary was the only child from his marriage to Catharine of Aragon who survived infancy. Henry's advisors assumed that the Pope would annul the marriage and that Henry would negotiate another politically advantageous one that would yield an heir. The situation was more complex, however. Catharine's nephew, the Holy Roman Emperor, did not want his aunt insulted by having her marriage declared invalid, and Henry meanwhile had fallen in love with a lady at court, Anne Boleyn.

In 1533, after years of stalemate, Parliament declared the Church of England separate from Rome, and Thomas Cranmer, archbishop of Canterbury, proclaimed Henry's marriage to Catharine null and void. Henry now openly acknowledged his marriage to the pregnant Anne Boleyn. Every soothsayer Henry consulted assured him that the child would be a son, but on September 7, 1533, Anne Boleyn gave birth to a daughter, Elizabeth. Although Henry did eventually have a son to succeed him, Edward's reign has been largely overshadowed by Elizabeth's long and far more successful one.

Less than three years after Henry married Anne Boleyn he had her executed for adultery. His third wife, Jane Seymour, gave him the son he wanted, but she died soon afterwards. Although Henry married three more times, none of these marriages produced children. Even so, both Mary and Elizabeth were declared illegitimate. Near the end of his life, Henry did make a will declaring that if Edward were to die without heirs the throne would pass to Mary. If Mary were to die without heirs, then Elizabeth would succeed. Henry excluded the descendants of his older sister Margaret, who had married James IV of Scotland, designating instead the descendants of his younger sister Mary should Elizabeth have no heirs. Ironically, it would be Margaret's granddaughter Mary, Queen of Scots, who would cause such anxiety during Elizabeth's reign, and her son James who would succeed Elizabeth on the throne.

As a young princess, Elizabeth received an excellent humanist education within the reformed tradition. She studied classics, history, theology, philosophy, and the other sciences that comprised

---

John Norden (1548–1625?), *Speculum Britanniae.* London: Eliot's Court Press, 1593. STC 18635 c.1, sig. A2v.

the advanced curriculum of the day. She also learned to play musical instruments and to dance, ride, and hunt.

When Henry VIII died at the end of January 1547, Edward succeeded to the throne. The younger of Edward's maternal uncles, Thomas Seymour, soon involved Elizabeth in a scandal by considering marriage to her after the death of his wife, Catharine Parr, the widow of Elizabeth's father. In the fall of 1548, Seymour engaged in other unwise and illegal activities as well, including piracy and coining false money. He even attempted to kidnap his nephew Edward, which led to his arrest on the charge of high treason. Seymour was executed in March 1549, but the fifteen-year-old Elizabeth kept her own counsel and protected her servants and her own reputation.

If Elizabeth was in danger during her brother's reign, her situation became perilous when Edward died in July of 1553. Elizabeth managed to stay aloof from the attempt to subvert the succession in favor of her cousin Lady Jane Grey and offered her congratulations to her Catholic half-sister Mary when she triumphed. But while she participated in Mary's coronation, Elizabeth refused to convert wholeheartedly to Catholicism causing Mary, who feared that Elizabeth would be the focus of Protestant dissension, to be more and more distant. When Thomas Wyatt led a rebellion against Mary's proposed marriage with Philip of Spain, some proclaimed Elizabeth the natural alternative. Although Elizabeth protested she knew nothing about the rebellion, Mary had her imprisoned in the Tower.

Meanwhile Mary married Philip in July 1554 and formally restored papal authority. In February 1555 she began the persecution of heretics, and by the time of her death in November 1558, around three hundred people had been burned to death. Elizabeth feared for her life and her place in the succession, but the country experienced a surprisingly smooth transition. There were fears, however, that Elizabeth's reign would be short and stormy.

Because she wanted to emphasize national unity, Elizabeth decided that the beginning of her reign was not the time to settle old scores or to let others do so for her. She wanted England to be strong and independent, with as broadly based a religious settlement as possible. She also wanted to be surrounded by those she could trust, and one of her first acts was to appoint William Cecil as her Principal Secretary. Elizabeth had a long and fruitful partnership with Cecil, whom she eventually made Treasurer and Lord Burghley. When Cecil died in 1598, his final advice to his son Robert was "to serve God by serving the Queen." Her other loyal servants included Sir Francis Walsingham; Sir Christopher Hatton; Thomas Radcliffe, the earl of Sussex; John Whitgift, appointed Archbishop of Canterbury in 1583; and Sir Robert Dudley, eventually earl of Leicester, for whom Elizabeth had strong feelings and with whom she had a special relationship for many years.

From the beginning of her reign, Elizabeth's Council and Parliaments beseeched her to marry. They were eager for Elizabeth to have a son and settle the succession, and many of them found the idea of an unmarried woman ruling unnatural. Despite her affection for Dudley, the Queen did not want to marry him or anyone else. Yet, during the first twenty years of her reign she was involved in marriage negotiations with many of the royal houses of Europe, including France and the Holy Roman Empire. There was no concensus, however, about whom she should marry. The Hapsburg Archduke Charles and the French Valois princes were all Catholic as well as foreign; Elizabeth showed no interest in Erik of Sweden or the Earl of Arran of Scotland. Meanwhile, her favorite, Robert Dudley, was deeply mistrusted, especially after the mysterious death of his first wife, Amy Robsart, in 1560.

It is difficult to know if Elizabeth ever seriously considered marriage. She knew she would give up a great deal of power if she did marry, but if she didn't she would have to name an heir and she was afraid of the dissension that might result. Her Council and Parliament pressured her to marry, but Elizabeth would not, even though her Protestant subjects were horrified by the idea that the Catholic Mary Stuart might assume the English throne.

The issue of religion also confronted Elizabeth as soon as she became queen. After the constant changes the English people had seen over the previous decades, Elizabeth wanted a compromise with outward conformity and hoped she could avoid persecuting people for their beliefs. In 1559 Parliament defined England's official religion through the Act of Uniformity, which abolished the mass in favor of services in English. But while the theology was Protestant, the service also retained some Catholic elements, and the wording of the liturgy allowed people to understand Communion in a variety of ways. Elizabeth, as Supreme Governor of the Church of England, believed that the Religious Settlement was completed and that there should be no more changes, but many radical Protestants wanted a more thorough reform of the Church.

As Elizabeth's reign progressed, she was pressured by both Puritans and Catholics. When Edmund Grindal became Archbishop of Canterbury in 1575, he and Elizabeth had serious conflicts over groups of radical Protestants coming together and "prophesying." Elizabeth worried that such groups could lend themselves to seditious practices. In 1577, when Grindal refused to stop these meetings, Elizabeth suspended him from exercising the duties of his office as archbishop. The conflict between them only ended with his death in 1583, and her next archbishop, John Whitgift, was far more supportive of her point of view. Elizabeth had hoped that Roman Catholicism would die out naturally, but enthusiasm for it strengthened instead. Her cousin, Mary Stuart, queen of Scotland, was the clear Catholic alternative to Elizabeth, but her reign in Scotland was short and troubled. Her marriage to her cousin Henry Stuart, Lord Darnley, had produced a son, James, but Mary had grown disgusted with Darnley's behavior. He was murdered in 1567. Only a few months later Mary married James Hepburn, Lord Bothwell, suspected by most of Scotland of Darnley's murder. In 1568 the country rose up in rebellion forcing Mary to abdicate and flee to England where her presence complicated the issue of the succession even more.

Soon after Mary's arrival in England, Elizabeth insisted on an examination of the murder of Lord Darnley. One of the commissioners was Thomas Howard, duke of Norfolk, a cousin to Elizabeth on her mother's side. Although no formal conclusion was reached by the commissioners, the infamous Casket Letters, said to be the correspondence between Mary and Bothwell, were given to them, and Norfolk declared himself appalled by Mary's letters. Privately, however, Norfolk was in negotiations to marry Mary once she obtained a divorce from Bothwell; he hoped eventually to be king of both Scotland and England.

Elizabeth believed that Mary was a threat to her security, a conviction she held even more strongly when some of the great lords in the north of England rebelled in 1569. The rebellion was crushed, but the Pope, in a show of support, excommunicated Elizabeth in 1570, releasing her Catholic subjects from loyalty to her. In 1571, Norfolk was involved in another plot, this time with Ridolfi, an agent of the Pope. He planned to marry Mary and have Elizabeth assassinated.

Resisting Parliament's calls to execute Mary, her cousin and an anointed queen, Elizabeth did agree to Norfolk's execution in 1572.

For a decade and a half, Mary stayed under house arrest. Elizabeth refused to permit Mary to leave England while Mary continued to plot against her cousin. The final act in this long melodrama took place in 1586 when a young gentleman named Sir Anthony Babington wrote secretly to Mary. He had yet another plan to place Mary on the English throne once Elizabeth had been assassinated. Mary wrote back to Babington enthusiastically supporting his plot. But neither of them was aware that Sir Francis Walsingham not only knew of their secret means of communication but could break their cipher. Walsingham even added a postscript to one of Mary's letters asking for the names of all the conspirators. Once Babington had happily complied, the conspirators were arrested and Mary was tried for treason.

Mary claimed that Elizabeth and her government had no right to try her, an anointed queen of Scotland. While Elizabeth herself may have concurred with this view, her advisors did not, and Mary was tried and found guilty. Even then, Elizabeth was deeply reluctant to sign Mary's death warrant. Both France and Scotland sent emissaries to beg for Mary's life. Mary's son, James VI of Scotland, was not at all sure he was willing to lose Elizabeth's good will and his potential place in the English succession, so he was less emphatic than the French emissary. When Elizabeth did sign the death warrant, she told her secretary, William Davison, not to send it on although she must have been aware that once it was signed it would indeed go into effect. Mary was executed the next day.

Mary left her claim to the English throne not to her son James but to Philip of Spain. England's relations with Spain had been tense for some time before Mary's death. The Spanish were upset by privateers such as Francis Drake, who saw picking off Spanish treasure ships as a patriotic duty. When Drake returned to England in 1580, Elizabeth's share of the take was about £160,000, half of the total. While Burghley advised placating the Spanish and returning the money, Elizabeth listened to Leicester's and Walsingham's advice instead and ignored the Spanish protests.

In the Netherlands, where Protestants were being persecuted, William of Orange and his followers were attempting to throw off Spanish rule, and Philip II had promised rewards to anyone who would kill this enemy of Spain. When William was assassinated in 1584, Elizabeth reluctantly agreed to intervene and to take the Dutch under her protection. She sent English troops to aid them in their fight against Spain, hoping that if the Dutch had a stronger position Philip would be forced to grant them religious freedom. Philip, however, perceived Elizabeth's move as an act of war.

Philip readied an Armada to sail against England in 1587, but a successful raid by Drake delayed the sailing until the following year. As England prepared to fight the Spanish fleet, Elizabeth traveled to Tilbury to review her troops and gave her famous speech assuring them that, having "the heart and stomach of a king," she truly valued her subjects. Philip's plans to conquer England and return it to the Catholic faith were thwarted by English ships and seamen and by the weather. The Armada was scattered and defeated.

The defeat of the Armada was a great victory for England, but the 1590s were a difficult decade. The English feared that Philip would build a new and stronger fleet and would try again to conquer England; indeed he did send further fleets in 1596 and 1597 but they were driven back by storms. As the end of Elizabeth's reign approached, the great victory of 1588 and the rich cultural achievements of the age were tempered by difficulties elsewhere. Problems with Ireland deepened, and poor harvests and inflation contributed to a general sense of insecurity as the century drew to a close.

Elizabeth lost many of the advisors on whom she had depended in the years after the Armada. She was greatly saddened by Leicester's death in 1588. Walsingham died two years later, and although Burghley survived until 1598, he was frail and turned much of his work over to his son Robert. The younger Cecil and Leicester's step-son Robert Devereux, earl of Essex, competed for influence with the Queen. The glamorous Essex flirted with Elizabeth and was intensely jealous of anyone else at court who gained favor. He insisted that he be sent to Ireland to attempt to keep order there, and Elizabeth gave him an enormous force and great financial support for the expedition. It was, however, a disaster. After spending a lot of money and knighting many of his men, Essex refused to engage the Irish in battle. In a panic, he rushed back to court without leave to explain to Elizabeth himself what had happened. Furious over the disastrous campaign, she had him confined to his house and investigated. Cleared of disloyalty, he was nonetheless found guilty of misgovernance in Ireland, suspended from his offices, and banished from court. In November 1600 Elizabeth refused to renew his monopoly on sweet wines, a disaster for Essex as he was deeply in debt.

Essex became increasingly wild and uncontrollable, turning Essex House into a gathering place for adventurers disallusioned with Elizabeth and her government. Convinced that his enemies at court wanted to have him murdered, Essex decided that he and his allies should seize the court. But when Essex and two hundred followers marched through London, none of the populace joined them. His followers melted away, and Essex bolted back to Essex House but soon after surrendered. Less than two weeks later he was tried and found guilty of treason. Elizabeth treated the rebels with leniency, letting most of them off with fines, but Essex and four others were executed.

The same year as the Essex rebellion, Elizabeth delivered her "Golden Speech" before her final Parliament, declaring her great love for her subjects. At the beginning of 1603 Elizabeth's health began to fail and she died on March 24. She had never named a successor, claiming that God would take care of England. Had Elizabeth died earlier there might well have been bloodshed and civil war. In 1603, however, Elizabeth's cousin, James VI of Scotland, could peacefully ascend the throne of England.

1 The classic study of Elizabeth I is still John Neale's *Queen Elizabeth I* (1934; Garden City and New York: Anchor Books, 1957). More recently, Wallace MacCaffrey crowned his career of work on Elizabeth with his biography, *Elizabeth I* (London and New York: E. Arnold, 1993). For more on her life as well as her political rule, see Anne Somerset, *Elizabeth I* (New York: St. Martin's Press, 1992). For a more critical view, see Christopher Haigh, *Elizabeth I* (London and New York: Longman, 1988). For some of the more specialized works on Elizabeth, see scholarship by Susan Doran, Susan Frye, Helen Hackett, Norman Jones, and Carole Levin.

AFFLICTORVM   CONSERVATRIX

SEMPER EADEM

ELISABE   D G   ANGLIÆ

VERBV   TIA

IVS   TI   TIA

DEI

Æ B   Æ

Queen Elizabeth's Books
Heidi Brayman Hackel

AS PART OF THE CELEBRATIONS ON THE DAY BEFORE ELIZABETH'S CORONATION in January 1559, the citizens of London presented their queen with an English Bible, which she warmly accepted: "how reverently did she with both her hands take it, kiss it, and lay it upon her breast," having already "promised the reading thereof most diligently."[1] Elizabeth participated in the ritual presentation of books throughout her life both as giver and as recipient, laying to her breast a veritable library of books but also at times refusing to engage in such ceremonies of obligation. Her devotion to the Bible, which Elizabeth enacted for the citizens of London, clearly extended to a deep and abiding connection to books both secular and sacred. Starting as a child, Elizabeth read widely in several languages, translated classical and contemporary works, kept a commonplace book, and accepted scores of dedicated books. Elizabeth's physical embrace of the Bible was matched by her material engagement with books as a girl. Not only did she write texts, she also made books, writing in her own adolescent italic hand and stitching decorative covers. Yet, despite leading a life with unprecedented access to books, Queen Elizabeth "does not seem to have preserved very many" of the nearly 200 printed books dedicated to her; the contents of her library are, ultimately, "as enigmatic as the rest of her personality."[2] What does survive is a fragmentary record of a queen's various and sustained connection to books—both as intellectual vessels and as precious objects—throughout her life.

RECEIVING AND REFUSING BOOKS

Elizabeth's earliest connection to books came in the form of dedications in both printed books and manuscript volumes. Perhaps as early as the year of her birth, certainly before she could read, the young princess shared a dedicatory address with her parents.[3] Over the course of her lifetime, nearly 200 printed books were dedicated to her, roughly the annual output of the English presses during much of her reign. Even so, one of her subjects felt this show of loyalty insufficient: "And doth not she daily deserue to haue books dedicated in the highest degree of honor to her Highnesse?"[4] Though not daily, Elizabeth was named in the dedications of a stunning range of

George Vertue. Elizabeth I. Engraving after painting by Isaac Oliver [London, ca.1732]. Bd.w. STC 18348.2

books printed in English, Welsh, Latin, Greek, French, Italian, and Anglo-Saxon: herbals and histories, travel narratives and marriage guides, alchemical treatises and religious polemics, epic poems and shorthand manuals.[5] If printed books announced their dedications widely and in part defined themselves by their patrons, manuscript volumes might solicit the queen's attention in a more intimate fashion. Produced in unique copies, such books have also surely disappeared in great numbers; the tally of printed books addressed to the queen, therefore, must be far smaller than the total number of books presented to her. One such uncounted book is a small oblong volume, elegantly bound in vellum and tooled in gold, written by Esther Inglis, one of the finest calligraphers of the period.[6] A discourse on faith addressed in French "To the most high and powerful Princess Elizabeth, Queen of England," this 1591 volume is a quiet companion to Edmund Spenser's *Faerie Queene* published the year before and dedicated "To the Most High, Mightie and Magnificent Empresse" Elizabeth.

In addition to printed and manuscript volumes dedicated by their authors or publishers, the queen also received books every year as New Year's gifts from her subjects.[7] In the first year of her reign, for instance, the gift rolls record the presentation of copies of *Ecclesiastes, De la Vie de la Morte*, the *Aeneid* in English, a map and Ptolemy's tables in Italian, the works of Flavius Josephus in Greek, fourteen song books, and one unnamed book. The attention to these books as ornate physical objects reveals both their ceremonial and economic value. The gift of *Ecclesiastes*, for example, is described as "Oone booke couered with purple vellat garnished and clasped with Siluer and giult of Ecclesiastes"; a few years later, Sir George Howard gave her "a book containing thoffice of the Armery, covered with blak vellat, and bound with parssarmoryne of silver, with two plates of silver." Extant books from these gift rolls include a set of nine heraldic manuscripts given to Elizabeth between 1568 and 1580 as "poore presente[s]" by Sir Gilbert Dethick, Garter King of Arms.[8] Covered in crimson velvet with ties of gold thread and gold braid adorning the edges, these beautiful books contain paintings of 294 coats of arms. Kept in the Royal Library through the reigns of the early Stuart kings, these quarto volumes were stamped with King Charles I's royal monogram and probably sold during the "Commonwealth Sale" of books from the Royal Library.

These gifts in purple, crimson, and black velvet bindings accord well with Elizabeth's appreciation of the aesthetics of bookbindings. Her favoring of velvet and fabric bindings seems to have been an olfactory as well as a visual and tactile preference, for Lord Burghley provided specific instructions when officials from Cambridge University sought to present a book to the queen: "they must have regard, that the book had no savour of spike, which commonly bookbinders did seek to add, to make their books savour well. But that her Majesty could not abide such a strong scent." The Vice-Chancellor responded by presenting her with a Greek New Testament in folio bound in red velvet. The course of this New Testament, like that of the Dethick volumes, exemplifies the difficulties in tracing Elizabeth's books and uncovering her reading. Still present in the royal collection in the early seventeenth century, it was given away in 1642, only to return in 1660 before finding its way by the early eighteenth century to Queen's College in Oxford.[9]

Along with the dispersal of her books, a further difficulty in reconstructing Elizabeth's life as a reader is the frequent absence of evidence about her response to dedicated books. As the dance of negotiations surrounding the presentation of the New Testament at Cambridge suggests, unsolicited dedications were not always welcomed by the monarch. A remarkable record of a writer's expectations and the queen's rebuff survives in the accounts of Richard Robinson, a citizen of London and minor translator and editor in the last quarter of the sixteenth century.[10] In the 1590s, Robinson made a series of presentations to high-placed persons, for which he expected financial "Comfort" but received none. His most ambitious presentation was to Queen Elizabeth herself:

I presented yt vnto youre Highnes on all Sainctes day beeyng Saturnday the first of November Anno 1595 at Richmond youre Maiestie then goyng to ye Chappell in ye morning.[11]

"Vtterly disapoynted," "vnregarded, and vnrewarded," Robinson chronicles the response of the queen to his unsolicited dedication. Elizabeth's Master of Requests thanks Robinson on the queen's behalf for his "good will" but reminds Robinson that the queen "sett [him] not on worck" and therefore would not "pay [him] any wages."[12] In the absence of Robinson's account, scholars might assume Elizabeth's reception of the book and guess at her patronage of its author or even her reading of his text. Her successor, King James I, was no more receptive to unsolicited dedications, rejecting one such volume by accounting it "rather a dishonour" and insisting that he could not "with patience looke upon their dedication to mee."[13] Clearly one cannot assume, then, that a dedicatory bid for patronage necessarily signals the acceptance, much less the reading, of a book.

READING BOOKS

Sir Thomas North, when dedicating his translation of Plutarch's *Lives* to Elizabeth, denied its suitability for her and asked only for her guardianship of it, naming her subjects as its intended audience: "though this booke be no booke for your Majesties selfe, who are meeter to be the chiefe storie, than a student therein, and can better understand it in Greeke, than any man can make it in Englishe: yet I hope the common sorte of your subjects, shall not onely profit them selves hereby, but also be animated to the better service of your Majestie."[14]

Elizabeth did, in fact, demonstrate her facility with Plutarch's Greek by translating his essay "On Curiosity" twenty years later. Richard Mulcaster, similarly uneasy about soliciting the queen as a reader of his *Positions* (1581), proposed that she might "take only some taste of any one title, of smallest inscription" of his pedagogical treatise, and from it, judge the whole book as one might judge a lion by its paw. Any more royal time spent reading his book would, he feared, open him to accusations of being "injurious to the common weale."[15]

Richard Mulcaster's concerns aside, one of the ways in which Elizabeth represented herself to the commonweal was as a reader. In a speech to Parliament in 1585, Elizabeth acknowledged her many responsibilities as a reader: "I am supposed to have many studies . . . And yet, amidst my many volumes, I hope God's book hath not been my seldomest lectures."[16] While Elizabeth was often portrayed as a Protestant heroine holding a Bible,[17] her classical learning and secular reading were celebrated as well. William Camden attested that Elizabeth "read or wrote something every day," while Bathsua Makin later reported that "Mr. *Ascam*, her Tutor, used to say, She read more *Greek* in a day then many of the Doctors of her time did *Latin* in a week."[18] This classical emphasis of her reading was publicized early in her reign by the printing of her commonplace book as part of a tiny miscellaneous volume titled *Precationes privatae. Regiae E. R.*[19] Organized along humanist principles and entirely in Latin, *sententiae* from the queen's reading are classified under the categories of Governance, Justice, Pity, Advice, Peace, and War. Among the cited authorities are Socrates, Plato, Plutarch, Quintillian, Seneca, Livy, Pliny, Cicero, Augustine, and Erasmus; most insistent, though, are quotations from the Bible. Elizabeth's handwritten inscription on the flyleaf of a tiny New Testament suggests that her practice of gathering these sayings was integral to her reading of scripture: "I walke many times into the pleasant fieldes of the holye scriptures, Where I plucke vp the goodlie greene herbes of sentences by pruning: Eate the[m] by reading: Chawe the[m] by musing: And laie them vp at length in the hie seate of memorie by gathering them together: that so hauing tasted thy sweetenes I may the lesse perceaue the bitternes of this miserable life."[20] Though she attributes this quotation to Augustine, Elizabeth clearly reflects here on the method, regularity, and comforts of her own pious reading as a queen. In scope and organization, the *Precationes privatae* positions its author as an educated Christian prince at home with many books. Elizabeth's court, too, had a reputation for bookishness, which Raphael Holinshed chronicled by imagining a foreigner entering the court and thinking "himselfe to come into some publike schoole of the universities, where manie give eare to one that readeth."[21]

Just such a foreign visitor to the Royal Library at Whitehall in 1598 remarked upon the variety of books "all . . . bound in velvet of different colours, though chiefly red, with clasps of gold and silver; some have pearls, and precious stones, set in their bindings."[22] Dispersed since Elizabeth's reign, this magnificent and doubtless revealing collection no longer survives as a coherent library.[23] Further, the royal arms on a binding, which might otherwise identify a copy as a monarch's, did not yet indicate royal property or even connection before James I.[24] A recent survey of English monarchs and their books assesses an eighteenth-century catalogue of the Royal Library, concluding that "perhaps 300 at the utmost" of the 1600 books associated with Queen Elizabeth were "definitely hers." Contrary to expectations, this list yields "not much of a literary harvest" and "remarkably little foreign literature."[25]

MAKING BOOKS, WRITING TEXTS

If we cannot know finally whether Elizabeth read many of the books dedicated to her or extant in the Royal Library, scholars can be certain about Elizabeth's engagement with a handful of surviving books. Among the most evocative artifacts from Elizabeth's life are three calligraphic manuscripts that she created as a young girl: English translations of Marguerite de Navarre's *Le Miroir de l'âme pécheresse* and John Calvin's *Institution Chrétienne* and a translation into Latin, French, and Italian of Catharine Parr's *Prayers, or Meditations*.[26] New Year's gifts for her father and stepmother, each one displays her translation copied in her own hand and decorated with an embroidered cover. All three volumes share striking similarities in design, color, and materials. Worked on canvas in a stitch now called plaited Gobelin, the three covers feature a central monogram honoring the recipient framed by four pansies in the corners. Even more than 450 years later, one can sense the vibrancy of the original covers with their careful interplay of red, blue, and silver silk thread. While the volume presented to Catharine Parr in 1544 displays her initials alone, the more ambitious covers of the two 1545 gifts form a pair, celebrating the king and queen with the interlaced letters spelling "HENRY KATHERIN." Stitched in purple and yellow thread, the pansies in the corners of all three volumes may be Elizabeth's signature; she claimed the flower as a favorite, and its potential pun on the French "pensée" (or "thought") suggests wit and cleverness behind these dutiful covers.[27]

Elizabeth's translation of the *Miroir*, given to Catharine Parr in 1544, has especially attracted scholars' notice. A meditation on the soul's relation to God, "The Glass of the Sinful Soul," as Elizabeth titled it, shows off the princess's education and feminine accomplishments even as its mistakes reveal her anxiety and anger at her father. With its royal female lineage and its ornate presentation, the volume seems to have been a self-conscious bid for protection and status within an extraordinarily complex and perilous family network.[28] Like her later embrace of the Bible before her coronation, these gifts reveal Elizabeth's use of books as powerful symbols.

As she produced both texts and books, Elizabeth displayed her facility with modern and classical languages, her range of reading, and her sensitivity to the beauty of books. Though Elizabeth seems not to have made needlework gifts as queen,[29] she did own decorative manuscript volumes. In her forties, she acquired a multilingual girdle prayer book written on vellum, which featured gold clasps, inset rubies, gilt initials, and miniatures by Nicholas Hilliard, and she embroidered the cover of a miniature New Testament with Latin mottos and aphorisms: "[CO]ELUM PATRIA" ("Heaven [is my] Fatherland"), "SCOPUS VITAE X[RIST]VS" ("Christ the Guardian of life"), and "CHRISTVS VIA" ("Christ is the Way").[30] Even more than the embroidered monograms on the gifts she stitched as a girl, these sayings display the meaning of the text on its covers. Like her preference for velvet bindings, the exquisite handiwork on these two tiny books conveys too the queen's appreciation for books as treasured objects.

As her embroidered New Testament suggests, Elizabeth was not fond merely of beautiful covers. As a princess, she praised the "invention of letters" as "the most clever, excellent, and ingenious" of the arts and sciences.[31] Described as "an immensely productive writer" by her modern editors, Elizabeth wrote letters, prayers, speeches, translations, and poems, starting at age eleven and perhaps even earlier.[32] Her translations alone span more than half a century from 1544 to 1598 and demonstrate her mastery of Latin, Greek, French, Italian, and Spanish. She translated from a range of genres—devotional literature, theological treatises, literary theory, essays—as she tackled authors as diverse as Seneca, Boethius, Petrarch, and her own stepmother Catharine Parr.

While most of Elizabeth's translations survive only in manuscript and while her handwrought treasures likely remained within royal circles during her lifetime, some of Elizabeth's texts circulated in print. Her poetry was widely enough known for George Puttenham in *The Arte of English Poesie* (1589) to proclaim it "the most bewtifull and gorgious" of all English poetry, asserting that her Muse "easily surmounteth all the rest that haue written before her time or sence."[33] Other contemporaries, too, described her as a "poet of the highest rank," praise that survived after her death.[34] Despite its pervasive metaphor of incest and its uneasy relevance to Elizabeth's family history, her translation of the *Miroir* appeared in print five times between 1548 and 1590. Another collection of prayers of doubtful authorship was styled as the Queen's Prayer Book.[35] Finally, there were books that Elizabeth never handled that accrued value because of their evocation of her. Andrew Willett's *Synopsis papismi, that is, A generall viewe of papistrie* (1594), for instance, opens with a dedicatory epistle to Queen Elizabeth. In the epistle in one extant copy, which seems never to have been owned by the queen though it bears the royal arms, Elizabeth's name and references to her are overpainted in gold, so that "Most gracious and dread Soueraigne" and "O noble Queene" shimmer in gilt on the printed page.[36] Such a book, while likely never seen by Elizabeth, might still belong to the category of the queen's books most broadly defined, for it imagines her as its ideal reader. Published to impress her and handwrought to celebrate her, this book hints at the range of Elizabeth's intellectual and material influence on books during her reign. And, like so many of the books closest to Elizabeth—those written and stitched by her, kissed and embraced by her—this book is more precious and beautiful because of its association with her.

1 Richard Mulcaster's account of this scene is reprinted in *Elizabeth I: Collected Works* (hereafter *Works*), ed. Leah S. Marcus, Janel Mueller, and Mary Beth Rose (Chicago: University of Chicago Press, 2000), 55.

2 T. A. Birrell, *English Monarchs and their Books: From Henry VII to Charles II*, Panizzi Lectures 1986 (London: British Library, 1987), 24, 26.

3 Giles du Wés, *An introductorie for to lerne to rede, to pronounce, and to speake Frenche trewly* (London, 1533?), S4r.

4 Thomas Churchyard, *The Worthines of Wales* (London, 1587), A2r.

5 For a comprehensive list of printed dedications, see Franklin B. Williams, Jr., *Index of Dedications and Commendatory Verses in English Books before 1641* (London: Bibliographical Society, 1962). Elkin Calhoun Wilson includes manuscripts as well in his annotated list of nearly 250 books presented to Queen Elizabeth (*England's Eliza*, [Cambridge, MA: Harvard University Press, 1939], 413–58).

6 "Discovrs de la foy. Escrit à Lislebovrg par Esther Langlois, Françoise, M.D.XCI." HM 26068, Henry E. Huntington Library, San Marino, California. Wilson's list does not include this manuscript. See Georgianna Ziegler, "'More Than Feminine Boldness': the Gift Books of Esther Inglis," in *Women, Writing and the Reproduction of Culture*, ed. Mary E. Burke, et al (Syracuse: Syracuse University Press, 2000), 19–21. Lisa M. Klein discusses another Inglis manuscript presented to Elizabeth, who declined to reward Inglis's husband for it and passed it along to Christ Church, Oxford ("Your Humble Handmaid: Elizabethan Gifts of Needlework," *Renaissance Quarterly* 50 (1997), 474–75).

7 I am very grateful to Steven May for sharing with me his list of books given to Queen Elizabeth as New Year's Gifts.

8 These nine volumes, which recently came up for sale, are described in the Sotheby's catalogue for the auction of December 18–19, 1986.

9 David Pearson, "A Binding Presented to Queen Elizabeth I by Cambridge University, 1578," *The Book Collector* 49 (2000), 547, 550.

10 British Museum Royal 18 A. lxvi, ff. 5–13. For a full transcript, see George McGill Vogt, "Richard Robinson's *Eupolemia* (1603)," *Studies in Philology* 21 (1924): 629–48.

11 Robinson f. 8r; Vogt 637.

12 Robinson f. 11r, Vogt 643; Robinson f. 8v, Vogt 638.

13 Daniel Featley, *Cygnea Cantio* (1629), C3r. Quoted by Franklin B. Williams, Jr., "An Index of Dedications and Commendatory Verses," *The Library* 5th ser., 12 (1957), 14.

14 Reprinted in Clara Gebert, *An Anthology of Elizabethan Dedications and Prefaces* (New York: Russell, 1966), 52–53.

15 Mulcaster's letter appears in Gebert's anthology, 55–57.

16 Quoted in Patrick Collinson, *Elizabethan Essays* (London: Hambledon Press, 1994), 88.

17 John N. King, *Tudor Royal Iconography: Literature and Art in an Age of Religious Crisis* (Princeton: Princeton University Press, 1989), 104.

18 Jennifer Summit, *Lost Property: The Woman Writer and English Literary History, 1380–1589* (Chicago: University of Chicago Press, 2000), 165; Lisa Gim, "'Faire Eliza's Chaine': Two Female Writers' Literary Links to Queen Elizabeth I" in *Maids and Mistresses, Cousins and Queens: Women's Alliances in Early Modern England*, ed. Susan Frye and Karen Robertson (Oxford: Oxford University Press, 1999), 185.

19 The commonplace entries occur in the middle third of the book (Fiir–Kvir), which is briefly described in *Works* 135n.

20 Quoted in King, 109.

21 *The Chronicles of England, Scotlande, and Irelande* (1577), I, 197.

22 Quoted in H. M. Nixon and M. M. Foot, *The History of Decorated Bookbinding* (Oxford: Clarendon Press, 1992), 41–42.

23 For a succinct history of the Royal Library, see Cyril Davenport, *Royal English Bookbindings* (London: Seeley, 1896), 5–6.

24 R. R. Holmes, ed., *Specimens of Royal Fine and Historical Bookbinding selected from the Royal Library, Windsor Castle* (London: Griggs, 1893), ii–iii.

25 Birrell, 24–25.

26 Elizabeth's translation of *Le Miroir* is reproduced from the original at the Bodleian Library in Marc Shell's *Elizabeth's Glass* (Lincoln, NE: University of Nebraska Press, 1993); the other two manuscripts are held by the Scottish Record Office and the British Library. For discussions of these embroidered books, see Klein; Margaret H. Swain, "A New Year's Gift from the Princess Elizabeth," *Connoisseur* (August 1973), 258–66; and Susan Frye, "Sewing Connections: Elizabeth Tudor, Mary Stuart, Elizabeth Talbot, and Seventeenth-Century Anonymous Needle-workers" in *Maids and Mistresses*, 165–82. Elizabeth's Latin translation of Bernardino Ochino's *De Christo sermo*, now held by the Bodleian Library, was a gift for her brother, Edward, in 1547 (Shell, 291–92).

27 Klein, 477–78.

28 For these views on "The Glass," see Frye, 169; Anne Lake Prescott, "The Pearl of the Valois and Elizabeth I: Marguerite de Navarre's *Miroir* and Tudor England" in *Silent But for the Word: Tudor Women as Patrons, Translators, and Writers of Religious Works*, ed. Margaret Patterson Hannay [Kent, OH: Kent State University Press, 1985], 69; and Klein, 477–79.

29 Frye, 169.

30 *Works* identifies the prayer book (311–12, n1); see King for a description of this New Testament (109).

31 *Works*, 11.

32 *Works*, xi.

33 Quoted by Summit, 164.

34 Summit, 164–65.

35 *Christian prayers and meditations* (1569), several of which appear in *Works* 143–63 as the Queen's.

36 RB 79715, Henry E. Huntington Library, San Marino, California.

Next page:
After John de Critz.
Elizabeth I Oil on panel.
After 1620. FPb66

ELISABETH

Catalogue of the Exhibition
Georgianna Ziegler

DIEV ET MON DROIT

Coronation

ELIZABETH I WAS TWENTY-FIVE YEARS OLD WHEN SHE CAME TO THE THRONE in 1558. She was a mature young woman, well-educated and already politically astute, who had inherited the better qualities of her father, King Henry VIII. Two things probably kept Elizabeth alive during the reign of her Catholic sister, Mary: her own wits and outward subservience to Mary, and her popularity with the people of England. When Mary died on November 17, 1558, Elizabeth was ready to take over. Since Parliament was in session, they officially declared her queen later that day. She immediately chose as her chief counselor, William Cecil, and together they selected a new council and set up her household. Included among the new officeholders was Elizabeth's old friend, Robert Dudley, now Master of the Horse. Mary was buried with due respect and formality in December, and a month later on January 14, Elizabeth rode through the streets of London to receive the tribute of her people. The next day, January 15, 1559, she was crowned.

The details of the street festival have come down to us in a little book—now known to have been written by Richard Mulcaster—printed eight days later, and giving an eye-witness account: *The Quenes Maiesties Passage through the Citie of London to Westminster the Day before her Coronacion.* These details may be fleshed out with information from other documents. It appears that the Londoners left nothing to chance, for they had formed a committee to organize the pageants and decorations as early as December 7.[1] While not aware of all the details, Elizabeth herself became involved when she ordered Sir Thomas Cawarden, Master of the Revels, to lend certain costumes to the city for the occasion. Her warrant is at the Folger Library, as well as an indentured note listing the costumes to be delivered the day before the festival and returned on January 16, the day following the coronation, evidently for use in a masque at court.[2]

Although there are no illustrations, Mulcaster provides a colorful account of the queen's passage through London, accompanied by "gentlemen, Barons, and other the nobilitie of thys realme, as also with a notable trayne of goodly and beawtiful ladies." The proceedings began at 2 PM on January 14 when the queen was carried in a large litter from her apartments in the Tower to the east side of the city at Fenchurch, where a child delivered in verse London's welcome of

Renold Elstracke. Queen Elizabeth enthroned. Engraving in Robert Glover, *Nobilitas politica vel ciuilis* (London, 1608). STC 11922, c.3, p.110.

"blessing tonges" and "true hertes." The five pageants emphasized Elizabeth's legitimate claim to the throne, her own virtuousness, and her association with Protestantism. The first pageant occurred at Grace Church Street. Here on three stages, one above the other, sat persons representing Henry VII and his queen Elizabeth of York; Henry VIII, their son, and Anne Boleyn, mother of Elizabeth; and at the top, Elizabeth herself. The whole pageant was decorated with red and white roses and represented "The vniting of the two houses of Lancestre and Yorke." As Elizabeth of York had brought an end to the civil wars by marrying Henry of Lancaster (Henry VII), so their granddaughter, Elizabeth, "might maintaine the same among her subiectes."[3] The noise of the crowd was so great that Elizabeth had difficulty hearing the child who was interpreting the pageant, so she had to ask for an explanation. Indeed, noise from the excited crowds proved to be a constant problem throughout the progress, leading the queen to ask for silence or for explanations on more than one occasion.

Children seem to have been the main performers in the pageants, possibly because their lighter weight enabled them to stand on the scaffolding. In the second pageant at Cornhill, a child representing the queen sat in "The seate of worthie gouernance," upheld by Virtues—Pure religion, Love of subjects, Wisdom, and Justice—who trampled various Vices underfoot.[4] In addition to explanatory verses recited by a child at each stop, the pageant scaffoldings were covered with signs and printed matter in English verse and Latin prose explaining the allegory. At the third stop in Soper Lane, eight children represented the Beatitudes from *Matthew*, chapter 5. (They may have worn the "viii cappes & hattes of cloth of gold" listed among the garments on loan.[5]) Each of these qualities—meekness, mourning, mildness, hunger for righteousness, mercy, cleanness of heart, peace, and wrongly persecuted—were applied to the queen in her past

Elizabeth I. *Whereas you have in youre custodie and charge certen apparrell as officer for our Maskes and Revelles . . .* ([London], January 3, 1558/59). Folger MS L.b.33.

experience. "Therfore trust thou in god, since he hath helpt thy smart/That as his promis is, so he will make thee strong."[6]

As the queen passed along Cheapside, the city "waites" or minstrels sang, and "out at the windowes & penthouses of euerie house, did hang a number of ryche and costlye banners and streamers." She smiled when she heard someone mention her father, "old king Henry the eight." The queen inquired ahead what the next pageant would be, and when she learned that she was to be given a Bible, she would have sent one of her knights on ahead to receive it, but held back when realizing that she would spoil the show. First, the Recorder of the City, on behalf of the Lord Mayor and other officials, presented the queen with a red satin purse, embroidered with gold, containing 1,000 gold marks, as a token of their good will toward her and in hope of hers in return. Elizabeth replied, "I wil be as good vnto you, as euer quene was to her people." When she finally reached the fourth pageant, she saw two hills, one "cragged, barreyn, and stonye," and one "freshe" and "grene," representing a ruined republic and a flourishing commonwealth. From a cave between the two appeared old man Time with his scythe followed by his daughter Truth, holding the true word, or the Bible. This was let down towards a child who gave it to Elizabeth's knight. Elizabeth herself took the Bible in both hands, kissed it, held it up, then laid it on her breast, indicating how important the English Bible—symbolic of the Protestant church— was to her.[7]

On her way to the fifth pageant at Fleet Street conduit, the queen passed by Ludgate and Fleet Bridge. The final pageant represented the biblical prophetess Deborah as a queen, sitting beneath a date palm tree, "bewtified with leaues as grene as arte could deuise." The image was meant to remind the queen "to consult for the worthie gouernment of her people, considering god oftimes sent women nobly to rule among men, as Debora which gouerned Israell in peace . . . & that it behoueth both men & women so ruling to vse aduise of good counsell."[8]

As she progressed towards the city gate at Temple Bar, the queen stopped to hear the petition of an orphan child at St. Dunstan's, asking her to remember the poor, and she declared "her gracious mynde toward their reliefe." Two giants representing Albion and Britain at Temple Bar produced verses summarizing the pageants, and saying:

Therfore goe on O Queene, on whom our hope is bent,
And take with thee this wishe of thy towne as finall,
Live long, and as long raigne, adourning thy countrie,
With vertues, and maintain thy peoples hope of thee.[9]

Mulcaster particularly remarked on Elizabeth's interaction, not only with participants in the pageants, but also with individuals from the crowds that surged around her—simple folks such as the poor woman who gave her a sprig of rosemary, other women who pressed on her countless bouquets, or the old man who wept to see her.[10] Elizabeth must have been aware of the political advantages of showing herself to the people and interacting with them in what we would now call a "media event." She continued to travel among her subjects for the remainder of her long reign, recognizing that the support of the people secured her position. Nevertheless, when one reads the accounts, it is difficult not to believe that her feelings towards them were genuine, and that she was moved by their outpouring of welcome and love.

The coronation itself occurred on Sunday, January 15, 1559, a day held to be propitious by the mathematician and astrologer John Dee.[11] Elizabeth had three costumes for the occasion, two of them inherited from her sister, Mary. One of these—the mantle of estate and kirtle (gown) she had worn the previous day—were made of cloth of gold, the mantle trimmed with ermine. A new bodice and sleeves were made to fit Elizabeth. Yards and yards of gold, silver, purple and crimson cloth were provided to clothe the members of the coronation procession, from the Lords Chamberlain and Treasurer, down through thirty-nine ladies and other women, Elizabeth's jesters—William and Jane Summer—and various yeomen and henchmen. Even Elizabeth's horse was issued "clothe of golde tissue for coveringe of a Sadle and harnes."[12] The route to Westminster Abbey was lined with blue cloth, which the crowds tore up for souvenirs afterwards. During the ceremony, Elizabeth was presented with three crowns: St. Edward's crown, and the imperial crown—both used for the coronations of her brother and sister—and a third crown made for Elizabeth, possibly from one worn by her mother, Anne Boleyn.[13]

Elizabeth's Protestant leanings affected the ceremony. According to the ancient rite of coronation, the actual anointing should be performed by the Archbishop of Canterbury. That seat was not filled, however, after the death of Reginald Pole, and the other senior bishops were either too old or too closely tied with the Catholic Church to be useful. Finally, Bishop Oglethorpe of Carlisle officiated, and Elizabeth was duly proclaimed and anointed queen. This ceremony was followed by mass, which was served without raising the host and with reading of the Epistle and Gospel in English and Latin—two of Elizabeth's Protestant innovations that were abhorred by the bishops. It seems likely that her own chaplain, George Carew, officiated for this part of the service.[14] At some time during the proceedings, the coronation pardon was read in Latin, but Elizabeth excepted from it all those who had dealt unkindly towards her during Mary's reign.[15]

After all the formalities were finished, Elizabeth proceeded back to Westminster Hall for a great banquet that went on from 3 o'clock in the afternoon until 1 o'clock the next morning.[16] Most importantly, the new queen had been crowned in the sight of and proclaimed by her people. Mulcaster summarized the event as a kind of theatrical performance with London "a stage wherin was shewed the wonderfull spectacle, of a noble hearted princesse toward her most louing people, & the peoples exceding comfort in beholding so worthy a soueraign."[17]

1 On Mulcaster, see David M.
   Bergeron, "Elizabeth's Coronation
   Entry (1559): New Manuscript
   Evidence," *English Literary
   Renaissance*, 8 (1978): 4; and
   Richard DeMolen, "Richard
   Mulcaster and Elizabethan
   Pageantry," *Studies in English
   Literature* 14 (1974): 209–21.
   The members of the committee,
   commissioned by the companies
   of the city, were: "Richard Hilles,
   M.P. and a Merchant Taylor,
   Lionell Duckett, a Mercer . . . ,
   Francis Robinson, a Grocer, and
   Richard Grafton, a chronicler and
   printer." (DeMolen, 211).

2 Bergeron, 7. The warrant is Folger
   MS L.b.33; the list is Folger MS
   L.b.109.

3 *The Quenes Maiesties Passage
   through the Citie of London . . .*, ed.
   James M. Osborn (New Haven:
   Yale University Press, 1960), sig.
   Aiir, Aiiir, Bir. All quotations are
   from this facsimile edition.

4 *Passage*, sig. Biiiv.

5 Bergeron, 6.

6 *Passage*, sig. Ci–Civ.

7 *Passage*, sig. Ciiv, Ciiir, Eiiir,
   Ciiiv, Ciiiir, Ciiiiv.

8 *Passage*, sig. Diiir, Diiiir.

9 *Passage*, sig. Diiiiv, Eir, Eiv.

10 *Passage*, sig. Eiiir–Eiiiv.

11 David Starkey, *Elizabeth* (London:
    Chatto & Windus, 2000), 263.

12 Janet Arnold, "The 'Coronation'
    Portrait of Queen Elizabeth I,"
    Burlington Magazine 120 (Nov.
    1978), 736, 737.

13 Arnold, "'Coronation' Portrait," 732.

14 See William P. Haugaard,
    "The Coronation of Elizabeth I,"
    Journal of Ecclesiastical History, 19
    (1968), 164.

15 Starkey, 273.

16 Paul Johnson, *Elizabeth I*
    (London: Futura, 1976), 69.

17 *Passage*, sig. Aiiv.

*Passage of our most drad
Soveraigne Lady Quene
Elyzabeth through the citie of
London to westminster the daye
before her coronacion*
[London: Richard Tottill, the
xxiii day of Ianuary 1559]
STC 7590

Renold Elstrack (1570–1630?)
Queen Elizabeth enthroned
Engraving in Robert Glover,
Nobilitas politica vel ciuili
London: William Jaggard, 1608
STC 11922, c.3

Great Britain. Office of
the Revels
*ffor work of the Revelles the
saconde day of Ianuary in the
fyrste yere of the reygne of . . .
elyzabethe*
[London, 1558/59]
Folger MS L.b.111

Great Britain. Office of the
Revels
*The note indented of suche
garmentes as are this present
xiijth of Ianuary 1558 deliuered
by Sir Thomas Carden*
[London, 1558/59]
Folger MS L.b.109

Great Britain. Sovereigns.
Elizabeth
*Whereas you have in youre
custodie and charge certen
apparrell as officer for our
Maskes and Revelles*
[London], January 3, 1558/59
Folger MS L.b.33

Great Britain. Sovereigns.
Elizabeth
Warrant, January 29, 1592
To John Fortescue, Master of
the Wardrobe
With an Elizabethan sixpence
attached to the signet
Folger MS V.b.55

Elizabethan Coins
Various denominations.

Georg Braun (1540/41–1622)
Londinum, from
Civitates orbis terrarum
Cologne, 1572–1618
ART 229985.1

George Vertue (1684–1756)
Eliza Triumphans
London, 1742
Engraving after painting attrib-
uted to Robert Peak, ca.1601
ART File E43 no.48, c.1

The.holie.Bible.

ELISABETH·D·G·ANGLIÆ·FRANCIÆ·ET·HIBERNIÆ·REGINA·FIDEI·DEFENSOR·ETC·

Non mé pudet Euangelij Christi.
Virtus enim Dei est ad salutem
Omni credenti Rom. 1.

Private Prayers

ELIZABETH NEVER COMPLETELY SPELLED OUT HER PERSONAL RELIGIOUS BELIEFS, in part perhaps because she was trying to maintain a delicate balance between her Protestant and Catholic subjects, and with various European heads of state. But she also felt strongly that her own religious beliefs, as well as those of others, were a personal matter. In later years, Francis Bacon recalled that she did not like "to make windows into men's hearts and secret thoughts."[1] Evidence indicates that Elizabeth was pious and a staunch Protestant, though not completely aligned with either the Lutherans or the Calvinists.[2]

"First in the morning she spent some time at her devotions,"[3] and a service was held in her chapel once a week. The large folio edition of the 1568 Bishops' Bible presented to her by Matthew Parker, archbishop of Canterbury, would have graced her chapel with its red velvet binding and silver-gilt hardware. She insisted on maintaining a silver cross and two candlesticks on her chapel altar, and she liked to have her priests serve in proper vestments, details that were scorned by more sober Protestants at the time. Indeed, Elizabeth went even further with her delight in polyphonic music, a form abandoned by most Protestants in favor of the singing of psalms in unison. She supported thirty-two adult men and twelve boy singers in her chapel, as well as two of the most outstanding composers of early English sacred music: Thomas Tallis and William Byrd. She even overlooked the fact that both were secret Catholics, and allowed them to dedicate their *Cantiones Sacrae* to her in 1575,[4] though the English Protestant church had pretty much given up the use of Latin in its services.

Richard Day's 1569 book, *Christian Prayers and Meditations*, contains a woodcut frontispiece showing Elizabeth kneeling at private prayer. In the presence of God, whom she called "my Lord and my King," and "my highest Emperor," she has removed her crown and placed it on the prie-dieu above a little open prayerbook, with the sword of justice at her knees. Roy Strong suggests that this woodcut may be based on a design by Levina Teerlinc, artist and Gentlewoman of the Privy Chamber, from 1558 to 1576.[5] John King has called attention to the prominent placement of the book over the sword in this woodcut, as in other portraits of Elizabeth, presenting "the image

Franz Hogenberg. Engraved portrait of Elizabeth. *The holie Bible*. (London, 1568). STC 2099 c.3, title page.

INDEX, IN QVO INITIVM
& numerum vniuscuiusque canti-
onis lector reperiet.

FINIS.

1589.

Londini, apud Thomam East typographum
in vico Aldersgate.

CONTRATENOR.

Liber primus
SACRARVM CANTIO-
num Quinque vocum.

*Autore Guilielmo Byrd Organista
Regio, Anglo.*

Excudebat Thomas Est ex assigna-
tione Guilielmi Byrd.

Cum priuilegio.

Londini. 25. Octob. 1589.

Elizabeth Regina.

2.PARALIPOM.6.
*Domine Deus Israel, non est similis tui Deus in cœlo & in terra,
qui pacta custodis & misericordiam cum seruis tuis, qui ambu-
lant coram te in toto corde suo.*

To the Christian Rea-
der, zeale and knowledge in true
and harty prayer through
Christ Iesus.

Dauid, a Prophet and
a prince, to whom
the lord had done ma-
ny, great, & singular
benefites, bethought
him selfe, not so much
to increase thë by vse,
as to require them by
thankes. He there-
fore, willing as a Prophet, & able as a prince,
but not able in deede, though willing so to
doe, opened his good hart, and said: *Quid re-
tribuam Domino?* What reward shall I geue vnto
the Lord? Being resolued, he answered: I will
receaue, I will call, and I will pay. *Psal.116.*

Doe thou the like (Christia Reader) which
art as farre indebted as euer he. And seeing
that Iesus Christ him selfe calleth, saying:
Come vnto me all you that labor, and are laden,
and I will refresh you. *Mat.11.* Answere thou,
I come, Lord Iesu, I come. I come, and will
pay my vowes, promissed to thee in the presence of all thy people, euen in the Courtes
of thy house, when I was receaued into the
houshold of faith.

I come, and will pray and prayse thee for al
thy benefites. I come, and will harken to thy
blessed word, and keepe the same. I come, and
will receaue y cup of saluation, at thy holy table, in remembrance of thy death, to thanksge-

---

A Godly Medytaci
on of the christen sowle, concer-
ninge a loue towardes God and
hys Christe, compyled in frenche by lady
Margarete quene of Nauerre, and aptely translated into Englysh by the
ryght vertuouse lady Elyzabeth
doughter to our late soueyayne
Rynge Henri the viij.

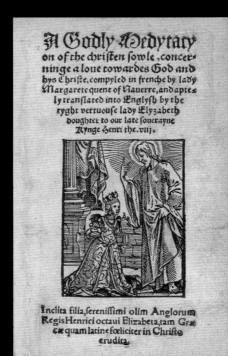

*Inclita filia, serenissimi olim Anglorum
Regis Henrici octaui Elizabeta, tam Græ-
cæ quam latine fœliciter in Christo
erudita.*

of a cautious queen who in her own life adopted the pose of a ruler who prefers reading the book symbolic of divine wisdom and mercy to wielding the sword of military and judicial power."[6] The image shows the queen in a private moment and an intimate space, with a book perhaps of her own prayers—which is what Day's collection purports to be—or her French psalter, or another little book containing her prayers in Latin, *Precationes Privatae* (1563), which recent scholarship suggests may have been published "as a public demonstration of gratitude to God for her recovery from a near-fatal case of smallpox in October 1562."[7] There is no way of knowing for sure whether the prayers printed in the 1569 edition of Day's book were in fact *by* Elizabeth, but a hand-colored copy of the book at Lambeth Palace, in which the form of address in some of the prayers was printed in the first person, appears to have been Elizabeth's own copy, given her by Day.[8]

In 1544 when she was eleven, Elizabeth translated Marguerite de Navarre's long poem, *Le Mirror de l'âme pécheresse* (1531), as *The Glass of the Sinful Soul*, wrote it out carefully, and embroidered a special binding as a present for her stepmother, Queen Catharine Parr, herself a devout Protestant. Though Elizabeth writes modestly to Catharine that she "translated this little book out of French rhyme into English prose, joining the sentences together as well as the capacity of my simple wit and small learning could extend themselves,"[9] nevertheless, the English Reformer and writer, John Bale, interested in the political significance of the translation, had it printed four years later with his own dedication and conclusion, under the title *A Godly Medytacyon of the christen sowle . . . compyled in frenche by lady Margarete quene of Naverre, and aptely translated into Englysh by the ryght vertuouse lady Elyzabeth.*[10] The title page woodcut shows a crowned woman holding a book and kneeling before Christ. The Latin inscription beneath identifies the figure as Elizabeth, daughter of Henry VIII, learned as much in Greek as in Latin, most happily in Christ. John King has suggested that she represents the type of "the Woman of Faith, with Bible in hand," a figure popular among Protestants.[11]

Obviously pleased with Catharine Parr's reception of her gift, Elizabeth followed it up the next year, 1545, with a translation into Latin, French and Italian of Parr's newly-published, *Prayers or Meditations*, this time as a gift for her father, Henry VIII, which showcased Elizabeth's own educational advancement. Elizabeth continued to translate religious and moral texts throughout her life, sometimes when she was in need of consolation. These included Ochino's *Sermo de Christo*; book one, chapter one of Calvin's *Institutes* ("How we ought to know God."); and Boethius's *De Consolatione Philosophiae*. Later in life she wrote a draft of a prayer on the defeat of the Spanish, dating from 1588 or the 1590s; a prayer for the Cadiz expedition, 1596; a prayer for the sailing of the Azores expedition, commanded by Essex, in 1597; and stanzas in French that seem to be a rough translation from a long religious poem in English, now lost.[12]

One of the most interesting books of private devotion associated with Elizabeth is a handwritten collection of prayers in several languages. The tiny volume was decorated by Hilliard with miniatures of herself and the Duc d'Alençon, whom she was courting around 1579 when this book was made. The handwriting uses "a distinct style for each language," and William Haugaard and

---

Top: William Byrd. *Liber primus sacrarum cantionum quinque vocum.* (London, 1589). STC 4247 c.1, Contratenor, title page.

Center: Queen Elizabeth at Prayer. Woodcut in Richard Day, *A booke of Christian prayers* (London, 1578). STC 6429, title page verso.

Bottom: Marguerite de Navarre. *A godly medytacyon of the christen sowle.* Trans. Princess Elizabeth. (Wesel, 1548). STC 17320, title page.

others have accepted that the prayers were likely composed by Elizabeth and written out by her, though some recent scholars have questioned the authenticity of the handwriting.[13] Such a tiny books, about 2 by 3 inches, were the sort that women often hung from a chain at the waist, so as to have them handy for private reflection. Known as "girdle books," most were psalters, New Testaments or prayer books. Elizabeth's contained six lengthy prayers; the first and last were in English, while the others were in French, Italian, Latin, and Greek, all languages in which she was fluent.

Haugaard has pointed out that "the theological and devotional expressions, taken as a whole, would have been appropriate within any of the Christian communities of Europe," though there are places where Elizabeth shows her Reformation roots, in particular her feelings that God has taken special care of her and has set her vocation.[14] In these prayers, she draws heavily on Biblical texts, especially the Psalms, but it is interesting also to note the ways in which she voices her relationship with God. Her strength and power she acknowledges as coming from Him:

Of nothing has Thou made me not a worm, but a creature according to Thine own image; heaping all the blessings upon me that men on earth hold most happy; drawing my blood from kings and my bringing up in virtue; giving me that more is, even in my youth knowledge of Thy truth, and in times of most danger, most gracious deliverance; pulling me from the prison to the palace; and placing me a sovereign princess over Thy people of England. And above all this, making me (though a weak woman) yet Thy instrument to set forth the glorious Gospel of Thy dear Son Christ Jesus.[15]

These words recall the great difficulties she encountered as a young woman when imprisoned and questioned by her sister, Mary Tudor, because of her religious beliefs. When Elizabeth came to the throne, after Catholic Mary, she was praised for giving back the English Bible—"the glorious Gospel of Thy dear Son Christ Jesus"—to the people.

In the language of her prayers, Elizabeth establishes a personal relationship with God, humbling herself before Him while maintaining a sense of her earthly position which she owes to God. She may be a "weak woman," His "humble servant," and "handmaid," but she is also God's instrument. Continuing the female imagery, she thanks God in the French prayer for giving her "the honor of being mother and nurse of Thy dear children . . . Preserve therefore the mother and the children whom Thou hast given her; thus shall we serve Thee better still to the good of Thy poor Church."[16] In the Latin prayer that follows, she implores, "Give me, Thy handmaid, a teachable heart, so that I may know what is acceptable in Thy sight." Using the exaggerated language of the period, she prostrates herself as a suppliant before God, asking for guidance and instruction, that "with the help of Thy wisdom, may I so assist others that I not harm myself, so rule others with the scepter that I may rule myself by Thy Word."[17] It is evident that what she sees in God is the wisdom, patience, understanding, and forgiveness of a great ruler, that she humbly hopes to emulate as an earthly ruler, guided and supported by Him.[18]

Late in her reign, during a reply to Parliament (1586), Elizabeth spoke of the great mercies of God towards her, using a female image of folded and embroidered cloth that harks back to those embroidered bindings she had made as a girl: "And yet must I needs confess that the benefits of God to me have been and are so manifold, so folded and embroidered one upon another, so doubled and redoubled towards me, as that no creature living hath more cause to thank God for all things than I have."[19]

1 Quoted in Carole Levin, *The Heart and Stomach of a King: Elizabeth I and the Politics of Sex and Power* (Philadelphia: University of Pennsylvania Press, 1994) 180, n25.

2 See Susan Doran, "Elizabeth I's Religion: the Evidence of her Letters," *Journal of Ecclesiastical History*, 51 (2000): 718–19.

3 Edmund Bohun, *The Character of Queen Elizabeth* (1693) quoted in Paul Johnson, *Elizabeth I: a study in Power and Intellect* (London: Futura, 1976), 198.

4 Johnson, *Elizabeth I*, 204–5.

5 Roy Strong, *Gloriana: the Portraits of Queen Elizabeth I* (London: Thames & Hudson, 1987), 56.

6 John N. King, *Tudor Royal Iconography* (Princeton: Princeton University Press, 1989), 115.

7 Elizabeth I, *Collected Works* (hereafter *Works*), ed. Leah S. Marcus, Janel Mueller, and Mary Beth Rose (Chicago: University of Chicago Press, 2000), 135, note 1.

8 Samuel C. Chew, "The Iconography of *A Book of Christian Prayers* (1578) Illustrated," *Huntington Library Quarterly*, 8 (1944–45): 293; William Keatinge Clay, Preface, to *Private Prayers, Put Forth by Authority during the Reign of Queen Elizabeth.*, ed. William Keatinge Clay, The Parker Society, vol. 37 (Cambridge: Cambridge University Press, 1851), xix–xxi; Patrick Collinson, "Windows in a Woman's Soul," in *Elizabethan Essays* (London: Hambledon Press, 1994), 92.

9 Quoted from Marc Shell, *Elizabeth's Glass: with "The Glass of the Sinful Soul" (1544) by Elizabeth I, and "Epistle Dedicatory" and "Conclusion" (1548) by John Bale* (Lincoln: University of Nebraska Press, 1993), 111.

10 See Ann Lake Prescott, "The Pearl of the Valois and Elizabeth I," in *Silent but for the Word: Tudor Women as Patrons, Translators, and Writers of Religious Works*, ed. Margaret Hannay, et al. (Kent: Kent State University Press, 1985), 72–73.

11 John King, "The Godly Woman in Elizabethan Iconography," *Renaissance Quarterly*, 38 (1985): 57. Since the hairstyle of the figure is more French than English, and since Elizabeth was not yet crowned, as this figure is, I believe it also purposefully conflates Marguerite with Elizabeth. See Ruth Luborsky, *A Guide to English Illustrated Books, 1536-1603*, vol. 1 (Tempe: MRTS, 1998), 567.

12 See *Works*, 413–27. She also wrote a prayer in 1574 after her progress to Bristol, and another ca.1591 for the protection of her army. See *Queen Elizabeth I: Selected Works*, ed. Steven W. May, forthcoming from the Folger Library and Washington Square Press, 2003 (hereafter referred to as May).

13 Elizabeth I, *Works*, 331 ff.; William P. Haugaard, "Elizabeth Tudor's *Book of Devotions*: A Neglected Clue to the Queen's Life and Character," *Sixteenth Century Journal*, 12 (1981): 80, 81. Peter Beal (in conversation) and Leah Marcus and Henry Woudhuysen have queried the authenticity of Elizabeth's hand in this manuscript. See Elizabeth I, *Autograph Compositions and Foreign Language Originals*, ed. Janel Mueller and Leah Marcus (Chicago: University of Chicago Press, 2003), 44, note 1. (I am grateful to Leah Marcus for the preview of this book in proof.)

14 Haugaard, "Elizabeth Tudor," 92, 93.

15 From the First English Prayer quoted in Elizabeth I, *Works*, 312–13.

16 *Works*, 314, 315.

17 *Works*, 317, 318.

18 Haugaard writes, "It is hardly surprising that the image of God as king should be prominent in Elizabeth's devotions since she, after all, judged that good order in English society depended on her own subjects' obedience to her own royal authority" ("Elizabeth Tudor," 84).

19 *Works*, 188. This passage is not in the versions of the speech quoted in May.

The holie Bible
The "Bishops' Bible"
[London: Richard Iugge, 1568]
STC 2099, c.3

William Byrd (1542/43–1623)
Liber primus sacrarum cantionum quinque vocum
[London]: Thomas Est, 1589
STC 4247, c.1

Richard Day (b.1552)
A booke of Christian prayers
London: Iohn Daye, 1578
STC 6429

Marguerite de Navarre (1492–1549)
A godly medytacyon of the christen sowle.
Trans. Princess Elizabeth
[Wesel: Dirik van der Straten, 1548]
STC 17320

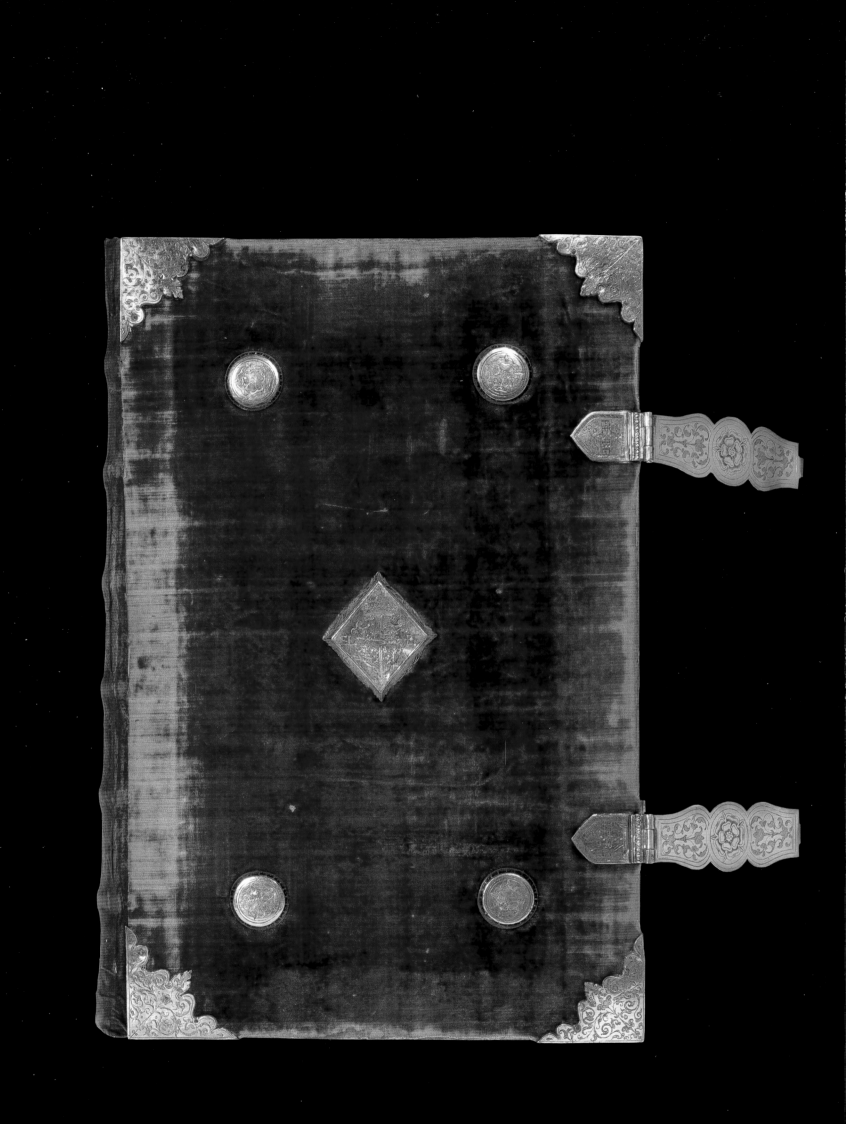

The "Bishops' Bible"

Peter W. M. Blayney

In 1560 the English Protestant exiles in Geneva at last finished and published their new translation of the Bible, which they dedicated to Elizabeth. But although the translation itself was widely praised, many English churchmen considered its annotations to be dangerously radical. Matthew Parker, archbishop of Canterbury, therefore did what he could to prevent the Geneva version from being printed in England. During the 1560s he also commissioned a group of scholars to revise the older translation known as the "Great Bible," which had been the English version authorized for use in churches since 1539.

Because most of the translators were bishops, Parker's new version would become known as the "Bishops' Bible." It was printed in 1568 by Richard Jugge, one of the Queen's Printers. Each translator's group of books was supposed to be marked at either the beginning or end with his initials, although a few omissions and inconsistencies made it difficult for a reader to be sure who had translated each individual book or epistle. The main exceptions were the two gospels and twelve epistles translated by Parker himself, most of which were separately initialed. Parker's role in the project was also celebrated by the use of his coat of arms and initials in two woodcut display capitals in the introductory material; the patronage and assistance of Sir William Cecil (later Lord Burghley) and the earl of Leicester were acknowledged by the inclusion of an engraved portrait of each man.

On October 5, 1568, the archbishop sent a specially-bound copy of the first edition to Cecil, with a covering letter asking him to present it to the queen. That copy, displayed here, is richly bound in red velvet with decorated silver gilt corners and clasps. Inside the book, Parker's initials have been hand-stamped on one gospel and one epistle that the printer forgot to mark. (His initials were also wrongly stamped on a gospel translated by the bishop of Peterborough, so a patch with the correct initials has been pasted over them.) In addition, each of the engraved portraits has been expertly painted by hand—the coloring of Elizabeth's favorite, Leicester, being particularly fine.

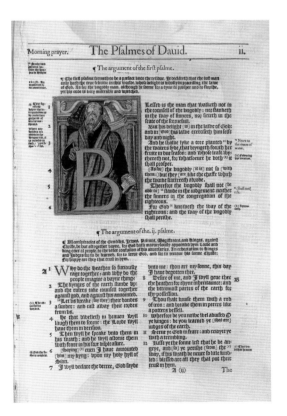

Left: The holie Bible. (London, 1568). STC 2099 c.3, binding.

Right above: Franz Hogenberg. Engraved portrait of Robert Dudley, earl of Leicester, in *The holie Bible* (London, 1568). STC 2099 c.3, Second part, sig. A(i)r.

Right below: Franz Hogenberg. Engraved portrait of William Cecil, Lord Burghley, in *The holie Bible* (London, 1568). STC 2099 c.3, Third part, sig. A(ii)r.

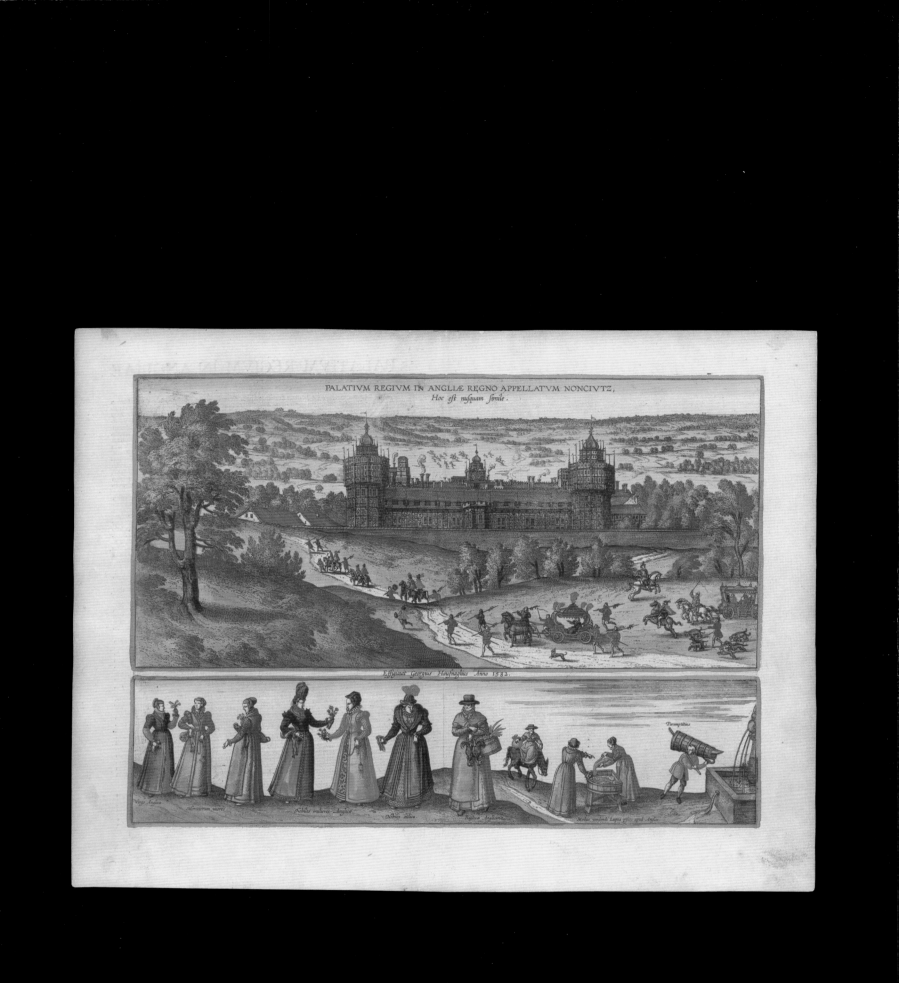

Elizabeth's Progresses

ELIZABETH REIGNED FOR MORE THAN FORTY YEARS, and during that time she traveled frequently from the court in London. Sometimes these were short trips to stay at her other palaces or homes of nearby courtiers. Twenty-three of these, however, were longer trips, usually undertaken during the summer months, when she traveled farther afield. Her itineraries have been mapped out with some detail by Mary Hill Cole, who notes that the twenty-five of the fifty-two counties visited by Elizabeth were mainly in the south and midlands. She did not venture north into Yorkshire or Northumberland, or west into Cornwall and Wales, but she did travel as far west as Bristol, east to Norwich in East Anglia, and southeast to Canterbury and Dover.[1] In a time when there were no newspapers, magazines, or television, these progresses enabled Elizabeth to see and be seen by all levels of her subjects, from kitchen servants and stable boys to prosperous merchant families, scholars at Oxford and Cambridge, the gentry, and the nobility—not all of whose families could attend her in London.

Moving the royal household with hundreds of courtiers and servants was a major undertaking, requiring "a baggage train of between four hundred to six hundred carts."[2] "A few days before the Queen was due to arrive, a team of eight to ten men would come to make arrangements for the Queen's accommodation."[3] Though civic or private hosts would spend thousands of pounds to fix up their houses, or clean the city, and purchase food and gifts for the queen, some of the expense was born by the queen herself. A crowd as enormous as her retinue would leave any place in a shambles. While accommodations were provided for the closest members of the queen's household, many others were left to shift with less-pleasant arrangements, and between the people and horses, sanitary conditions deteriorated rapidly. Though some of Elizabeth's advisors and noblemen complained from time to time about the expense to the queen and to themselves, and about her absence during times of international crisis, nevertheless, the queen persisted in her progresses over the years, recognizing their potential in establishing good public relations.[4]

When the queen visited a city, almost everyone took part in the preparations. Before she

Joris Hoefnagel. *Palatium regium in Angliae regno appellatum Nonciutz*, 1582. Engraved by Franz Hogenberg (ca.1598). Art Box H716 no.1.

arrived in Sandwich in 1573, orders went out that the streets were to be paved, "all dung and filth to be removed," "no persons to keep hogs but in certain appointed places," and all brewers "to brew good beer." Accordingly, when she passed through the town at sundown, the streets were "strewed with rushes [and] herbs, . . . every howse having a nombre of grene bowes [boughs] standing against the dores and walls, every howse paynted whyte and black."[5] The wives of the mayor and judges prepared a huge banquet of 140 dishes which were served on a long table in the school-house garden. The queen "was very merrye" and indicated her appreciation by eating without having her food tasted, and asking for certain dishes to be carried back to her lodgings.[6]

Some of the queen's visits were further celebrated and memorialized by written accounts of the events that were printed and circulated more widely. The Folger Library has some half dozen or so of these, recording her visits to Oxford, Cambridge, Norwich, Suffolk and Norfolk, Saffron Weldon, Kenilworth, and Woodstock, as well as an important manuscript record of her visit to Harefield. Looking at three of these in more detail will give us a vivid picture of what it was like to entertain the queen.

The most spectacular entertainment was provided by the queen's favorite, Robert Dudley, at his Warwickshire castle, Kenilworth, from July 9–27, 1575. This was Elizabeth's third visit to Kenilworth—a castle that the queen herself had given to Dudley in 1563 when she made him earl of Leicester. For all of his attractiveness, Leicester was conceited and hot-headed, and he used this occasion once again to push his own agenda of marrying the queen and reporting to the Netherlands to serve in the Protestant cause against Spain. Both ploys failed, but fortunately we are left with two printed books that give somewhat divergent accounts of the occasion, allowing modern scholars to recognize in it a power play between Leicester and the queen. One of these texts, by the poet George Gascoigne, is entitled *The Princely Pleasures at the Courte at Kenelwoorth*; the other—*A Letter: Whearin, part of the entertainment, vntoo the Queenz Maiesty, at Killingwoorth Castl . . .*—also known as *Laneham's Letter*—purported to be a letter from a Mr. Laneham at court to "hiz frænd a Citizen, and Merchaunt of London." David Scott has now established that this second book was really written by William Patten, who worked for Burghley, "apparently as an elaborate joke on a court officeholder, Robert Langham."[7] As Susan Frye has shown, *Laneham's Letter* nicely undercuts the rosier view presented by Gascoigne's *Princely Pleasures* by its comments on the court or on things that go wrong during the queen's stay, or on remarks that she makes.[8] Only by taking the two pieces together do we get a more complete picture of the festivities.

Kenilworth Castle is colorfully described in *Laneham's Letter*: "euery room so spacioous, so well belighted, and so hy roofed within: . . . a day time on euerye side so glittering by glasse; a nights, by continuall brightnesse of candel, fyre & torchlight transparent . . . ."[9] It is possible here to give only a sketch of the activities laid on for the queen. These included music, dancing, hunting, bear-baiting, banqueting, entertainment by the countryfolk, and several nights of spectacular fireworks— which, according to Gascoigne's account, "shewed vpon the water . . . as sometimes passing vnder the water a long space, when all men had thought they had bene quenched, they would rise and mount out of the water againe, and burne very furiously vntill they were vtterlie consumed."[10] The theme of the dramatic entertainments was Arthurian, recalling Henry VIII's claims of Arthurian ancestry as a way of legitimizing his kingship, but here used by Leicester to create a more noble ancestry for himself.[11] Leicester's versions of the theme did not entirely meet with Elizabeth's approval, however. When she arrived at Kenilworth, she was greeted by the Lady of the Lake:

I am the Lady of this pleasant Lake,
who since the time of great king Arthures reigne
That here with royal Court aboade did make, . . .
Til now that this your third arriuall here,
doth cause me come abroad, and boldly thus appeare.[12]

Patten gives us the queen's polite but sarcastic reaction: "It pleazed her highnes too thank this Lady, & too ad withall, we had thought indæd the Lake had been oours, and doo you call it yourz noow:Well we will hærin common commune more with yoo heerafter."[13] Kenilworth Castle still belonged to the queen; though she had once bestowed it on Leicester, she was quite capable of taking it back again. One of the entertainments prepared by Leicester never materialized at all and one had to be quickly rewritten. Presumably the queen had her suspicions of Leicester's intent, and foiled his little plans.

We know about the substitution because Gascoigne included both versions in his book and says he had to pen these verses "vpon a very great sudden."[14] He refers to a (rather tedious) dialogue between Echo and a Wild Man of the forest dressed in ivy, which ends by praising the queen and having the Wild Man submit to her. This episode occurred as the queen was returning from hunting; she then began to cross a little bridge, when Tryton appeared "in likenesse of a Mermaide," and appealed to the queen to rescue the Lady of the Lake who had been forced to live in water to escape from the rapist Sir Bruse. According to Merlin's prophecy, "it seemed she coulde neuer bee deliuered but by the presence of a better meide then hir selfe."—enter Queen Elizabeth as her rescuer. The Lady of the Lake, floating with her Nymphs on "heapes of Bulrushes," arrives to thank the queen on behalf of herself, and "Nymphs and sisters all, Of this large Lake."[15] The original version of this masque, written by three men, would have featured a battle between a Captain (Leicester) and Sir Bruse, in which the rapist would have been put to flight. The Captain would then have called up to the queen in the castle, asking her to save the Lady of the Lake. As Susan Frye has skillfully shown, "the allegorized threat of Sir Bruse represents a male force seeking to control, through rape, the virtue of female chastity. . . . the resolution of his threat can be counter-acted only by still another strong male presence: the rescuer." (82) In Elizabeth's version, the queen maintains autonomy and authority; it is she alone who frees the Lady of the Lake.[16]

Gascoigne attributes the suppression of his own masque about Diana, Iris and Juno to "lack of opportunitie and seasonable weather" (sig. Ciiv), but it also contained politically "hot" subject matter. In the masque, Elizabeth's imprisonment as a young woman is recalled with the suggestion that she was saved by Juno, goddess of marriage, rather than by Diana, goddess of chastity. Such a view totally undercut the line taken by Elizabeth and by many of her Protestant supporters since her succession, that when imprisoned at Woodstock and in the Tower by her sister, Mary Tudor, she was saved by God as a reward for her virtue, rather than by her sister Mary's plots to wed her off.[17] Elizabeth ultimately took control of the Kenilworth festivities, then, by the suppression of this masque, the revision of the Lady of the Lake masque, and the last-minute inclusion of two ceremonies of her own: creating five knights from outside the Protestant (and therefore Leicester) faction, and engaging in the laying-on-of-hands, an ancient practice of healing by royal touch.

One of the queen's longest progresses took place from July 11 until September 25, 1578, when she traveled slowly via Cambridge to Norwich in East Anglia, stopping at a number of private houses along the way. The events have been documented in the printed texts by Bernard Garter, *The Ioyfvll Receyuing of the Queenes most excellent Maiestie into hir Highnesse Citie of Norwich* (1578), and Thomas Churchyard, *A Discovrse of The Queenes Maiesties entertainement in Suffolk and Norffolk* (1578), and in various local and family records. At Cambridge she was welcomed with a Latin oration and received a Greek New Testament "bound in red velvet and decorated with gold and enamel, and a pair of perfumed and embroidered gloves."[18] She passed a few days at Audley End, home of the Howards, during which time her Council met, then traveled on into Suffolk, where she was welcomed by "two hundred yong Gentlemen, cladde all in white velvet" and three hundred more in black.[19] In Suffolk she stayed for a time at Melford Hall, home of Sir

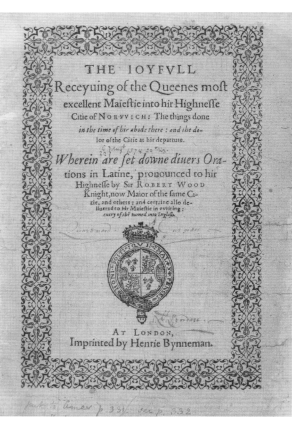

William Cordell, Master of the Rolls. While here, she kept informed on foreign affairs, meeting with the French and Scottish ambassadors. Elizabeth moved on to Bury St. Edmunds, then crossed into Norfolk to stay at Kenninghall Palace, originally the home of the wealthy dukes of Norfolk. Finally, on the afternoon of August 16, Elizabeth arrived in Norwich, the second largest city in England at that time, with a population of 16,000, a number of whom were Protestant refugees from the Continent come to practice the worsted weaving trade.[20]

The printed reports by Garter and Churchyard provide a full account of her entertainments in Norwich, but only the highlights can be touched on here. After being greeted by the Mayor in Latin and receiving a sword of the city and gilt cup filled with money, the queen entered the city by St. Stephen's gate, decorated on the outside with the queen's arms and the arms of St. George and the city, and on the inside with red and white roses, symbolizing the union of the houses of Lancaster and York. The first street pageant showcased the city's weaving industry by presenting eight girls spinning worsted yarn and eight knitting worsted hose, along with several looms producing the kinds of fabric for which the city was known. Garter reports that "This shewe pleased hir Maiestie so greatlye, as she particularlye viewed the knitting and spinning of the children, perused the Loombes, and noted the seuerall . . . commodities which were made."[21] The second pageant presented "five personages apparelled like women," representing the City of Norwich, the biblical heroines Deborah, Judith and Esther to whom Elizabeth was sometimes compared, and Martia, ancient queen of England.

Thomas Churchyard had gone on ahead to Norwich to prepare several entertainments. On the Monday he devised a coach all decorated with birds "and naked Sprites hanging by the heeles in the aire and cloudes, cunningly painted" (sig. Ciir), which drove very fast to the place where the queen was staying, then halted so that Mercury could jump out and greet her. On Tuesday, as

---

B[ernard] G[arter]. *The ioyfull receyuing of the Queenes most excellent Maiestie into hir Highnesse citie of Norvvich.* (London, [1578]). STC 11627 c.1, title page.

the queen rode out "to hunt in Lady Jerningham's 1,000 acre deer park,"[22] Churchyard presented a masque of Chastity where Chastity and Modesty win out over Cupid, and at Chastity's request, Modesty comes to Elizabeth looking for "a worthy noble Queene" whose court she can inhabit—much more pleasing to Elizabeth than Leicester's proposed masque of marriage. On Thursday, Churchyard ran into bad luck. He had prepared a wonderful device of twelve nymphs in a cave with music for the queen to see as she rode by, but a thunderstorm prevented the ride and soaked the performers so that they looked "like drowned Rattes."[23]

The queen left Norwich on August 22, and spent another leisurely month traveling back to her palace of Richmond near London. On the way, she stayed at a number of other houses, including Kirtling Tower in Cambridgeshire, the home of Roger, Lord North. This visit is documented in detailed expense accounts kept by Lord North that provide us with a firsthand opportunity to see what it took to entertain her majesty. He paid over 32 pounds for a banqueting house, new kitchens, and redecorating of other rooms. Half that amount, 16 pounds—a great deal of money —was spent on sugar! Other food included: 74 hogs heads of beer; 6 hogs heads of claret and one of white wine; enormous amounts of mutton, veal, lamb, pigs, geese, turkeys, and all kinds of wild birds; "a cartload & 2 horseloads" of oysters; one barrel of anchovies; as well as much eggs and butter, 6 Holland cheeses, and 10 marchepanes. Two hundred nine pounds went towards gifts for the queen and various noblemen and servants, including 120 pounds for the queen's jewel. All in all, Lord North recokened he had spent 762 pounds, 4 shillings, 2 pence for the visit. Not, perhaps, as much as the earl of Leicester, but still a goodly sum.[24]

Elizabeth's last progress in the summer of 1602 when she was 68 years old took her to Harefield in Middlesex, the home of Sir Thomas Egerton, Lord Keeper, and his wife Alice.[25] She stayed there for a long weekend from July 31 until August 4. The household accounts for this visitation indicate that wealthy neighbors chipped in to provide quantities of food for the occasion.[26] Unfortunately, it seems to have been another rainy weekend at the end of an unusually rainy summer, a fact noted in parts of the entertainment. No one source recording the entire entertainment has survived, but seven events may be reconstructed from various manuscript sources and a 1608 printed edition of three of them.[27] They were as follows: "(i) a dialogue between a Bailiff and a Dairymaid, delivered as the Queen entered the grounds, . . . (ii) a dialogue between Time and Place, delivered on the steps of the house . . . (iii) a complaint of Five

The device to entertain Her Majesty at Harefield the house of Sir Thomas Egerton (1602). Folger MS X.d.172, leaf 5r.

Satyrs against the Nymphs; (iv) a song by a Sailor who brought a Lottery-box; and (v) a list of the lottery-prizes, the verses which accompanied them, and their recipients; (vi) a poem which accompanied the presentation of 'a robe of rainbows' to the Queen; and (vii) a speech by Place in mourning robes made as the Queen departed."[28]

One of the most important records of several of these devices occurs in a manuscript now at the Folger Library, originally part of the Conway family papers. It includes the poem, "Beawtyes rose and vertues booke," recited on the queen's departure as she received a rainbow robe; the Mariner's song, "Cynthia queene of seas and landes"; and the Lottery verses with names of recipients.[29] Written in two period hands, it appears to be a scribal copy of an original manuscript by the poet Sir John Davies, now recognized as author of these devices.[30] The device of the Mariner and Lottery may have occurred in the Hall on Sunday. The Mariner is "supposed to come from the Carrick," perhaps a reference to a Portuguese treasure ship captured by the English in June of 1602.[31] He sings that the sea nymphs brought Cynthia (i.e., Elizabeth) "Many a Jewell, many a Jemme," then he opens his box and invites the ladies to take their chances at the verses and gifts therein. These were obviously carefully calibrated ahead of time, as the first "winner" is the queen, who receives Fortune's wheels—probably in the form of a jewel. The accompanying verse reads: "Fortune must now noe more in tryumphe ride;/ The wheeles ar yours thatt did hir chariott guide." Most of the other women who participated seem to have been Elizabeth's maids of honor or friends of the Egertons', and the gifts were appropriately designated. Lady Anne Clifford, for example, received a piece of lace with the words "Give hir the lace thatt loves to be straite laced;/ Soe fortunes little gifte is aptly placed." Apparently she was known to be "straite laced" in manner.[32]

On the Monday morning of her departure, the queen received "The Humble Petition of a Guiltless Lady"—a poem about St. Swithin[33] and Iris, the goddess of the rainbow. Iris is described, "In hir moiste roabe of collors gaye,/ And when she comes she ever stayes/ For the full space of fortye dayes,/ And more or lesse Raines every daye." Swithin takes the robe from Iris and gives it to the queen: "Tis fitt itt shoulde with you remayne,/ For you know better how to raigne," he says, with a neat pun. This little device enabled the queen's hosts to give her another present, one recalling a favorite image associated with her. Just two years earlier, Robert Cecil her Secretary of State, had commissioned her portrait holding a rainbow, the allegorical program for which was likely designed by John Davies, who then worked on the Harefield entertainment.[34] Above her hand on the portrait is painted the motto: "Non Sine Sole Iris" – "No rainbow (Iris) without the Sun (Elizabeth)." The Egertons could not have known that the queen's "sun" would set within the year, but they did honor the long years she had already shone over her kingdom.

1 Mary Hill Cole, *The Portable Queen: Elizabeth I and the Politics of Ceremony* (Amherst: University of Massachusetts Press, 1999), 23.

2 Anne Somerset, *Elizabeth I* (New York: St. Martin's Press, 1991), 371.

3 Zillah Dovey, *An Elizabethan Progress: the Queen's Journey into East Anglia, 1578*, foreword David Loades (Madison, NJ: Fairleigh Dickinson University Press, 1996), 4.

4 Lord Burghley "estimated that it cost Elizabeth up to £2,000 a year to go traveling about the country" (Somerset, *Elizabeth I*, 375).

5 John Nichols, *The Progresses and Public Processions of Queen Elizabeth*, vol. 1 (London: Nichols, 1823), 337.

6 Nichols, *Progresses*, vol. 1, 338–39.

7 Susan Frye, *Elizabeth I: the Competition for Representation* (New York: Oxford University Press, 1993), 63.

8 Frye, *Elizabeth I*, 64–65.

9 William Patten, *A Letter: Whearin, part of the entertainment vntoo the Queenz Maiesty, at Killingwoorth Castl* (London, 1585), 66.

10 George Gascoigne, *The princelie pleasures at Kenelworth Castle* in *The Whole Woorkes* (London, 1587), sig. Aiiiv-Aiiiir.

11 Frye, *Elizabeth I*, 68. The Tudors traced their Arthurian ancestry back through the Welshman, Owen Tewdwr, second husband of Katharine, widowed Queen of Henry V.

12 Gascoigne, sig. Aiiv.

13 Patten, 10–11.

14 Gascoigne, sig. Aviiv.

15 Gascoigne, sig. Aviiv, Aviiiv-Bir.

16 Frye, *Elizabeth I*, 86.

17 See Frye, *Elizabeth I*, 72.

18 Dovey, *Elizabethan Progress*, 34.

19 Churchyard, *A Discovrse of The Queenes Maiesties entertainment in Suffolk and Norffolk* (London, 1578), sig. Biiir.

20 Dovey, *Elizabethan Progress*, 63.

21 Bernard Garter, *The Ioyfvll Receyuing of the Queenes most excellent Maiestie into hir Highnesse Citie of Norwich* (London, 1578), sig. Bivv.

22 Dovey, *Elizabethan Progress*, 76.

23 Churchyard, *Entertainement*, sig. Eiiv, Eivv.

24 Nichols, *Progresses*, vol. 2, 237–38.

25 As daughter of Sir John Spencer of Althorp, Lady Alice was a distant ancestor of Princess Di.

26 Jean Wilson, "The Harefield Entertainment and the Cult of Elizabeth." *The Antiquaries Journal*, 66 (1986): 319.

27 See Wilson, *Harefield*, 318. Francis Davison, *A Poetical Rhapsody* (London, 1608). Nineteen sources for the entertainments are listed in *Research Opportunities in Renaissance Drama*, 24 (1981): 147–51.

28 Wilson, *Harefield*, 318. I have changed the order of her list to conform to the final order of events that she outlines on p. 327.

29 Folger MS X.d.172.

30 See *The Poems of Sir John Davies*, ed. Robert Krueger (Oxford: Clarendon Press, 1975).

31 Identified by Grossart; see Davies, *Poems*, 411.

32 Davies, *Poems*, 208, 211, 411.

33 The feast day of Swithin, an early English saint, was celebrated on July 15. The weather on that day supposedly determined the weather for the next forty days, rather like Ground Hog Day in the United States.

34 Davies, *Poems*, 215, 216; Roy Strong, *Gloriana: the Portraits of Queen Elizabeth I* (London: Thames & Hudson, 1987), 157.

Thomas Churchyard
(1520?–1604)
A discourse of the Queenes Maiesties entertainement in Suffolk and Norffolk
London: Henrie Bynneman, 1578
STC 5226

B[ernard] G[arter]
The ioyfull receyuing of the Queenes most excellent Maiestie into hir Highnesse citie of Norvvich
London: Henrie Bynneman, [1578]
STC 11627, c.1

George Gascoigne (1542?–1577)
The pleasauntest workes . . . [with] *the pleasure at Kenelworth Castle*
London: Abell Ieffes [for R. Smith], 1587
STC 11639

The device to entertain Her Majesty at Harefield the house of Sir Thomas Egerton
1602
Folger MS X.d.172

Anonymous.
Court costumes of the time of James I
Watercolor, ca.1607
ART Vol c91

Georg Hoefnagel (1542–1600)
Palatium regium in Angliae regno appellatum Nonciutz
1582
Engraved by Franz Hogenberg
ca.1598
ART Box H716 no.1

George Gower (ca.1540–1596)
The Plimpton "Sieve" Portrait of Queen Elizabeth I
Oil on panel, 1579
ART 246171

Jodocus Hondius (1563–1612)
The Kingdome of England
Engraved map based on design by Christopher Saxton, augmented by John Speed
London, 1610
STC 23041.2

Procerum   Cācellarius   Thesaurarius   A primogenitu?

R Scotiæ   P Walliæ

Cancellarij sessio

Foreign Relations

DURING THE EARLY YEARS OF ELIZABETH'S REIGN, there were an unusual number of women holding seats of power in other parts of Europe. Margaret of Parma served as regent in the Netherlands from 1559 to 1567. She had been placed there by her half-brother, Philip II of Spain, who held the Netherlands under Hapsburg rule. But she was also following in the footsteps of her great-aunt, Margaret of Austria, and her aunt, Mary of Hungary, both of whom preceded her as regents in that territory. Farther south, Catherine de Médicis held the French throne as regent for her son, Charles IX, who became king at the age of ten in 1560. Even after he reached maturity, she remained a strong force behind the throne, and when he died in 1574, her third son took the throne as Henri III. Catherine had also helped to raise the girl Mary Stuart, who had married her first son, Francis II. To Elizabeth's north, Mary Stuart's mother, Mary of Guise, served as regent in Scotland from 1554 to 1560. An astute politician, she was interested in fostering the ties between Scotland and France. After her death, her daughter, now a widow, returned to Scotland as Mary, Queen of Scots, and ruled until 1567 when she was forced to abdicate. All of these women, except for Mary Stuart and Elizabeth herself, were regents instead of queens regnant; that is, they were standing in for (usually male) relatives who really held the throne. Nevertheless, they were women to be reckoned with, and Elizabeth had dealings with most of them.

Elizabeth's relations with Scotland will be discussed later in more detail when we consider Mary, Queen of Scots, and James, her son. For now, it is important to note that during Elizabeth's reign, Scotland was fighting off its ties with the French Catholics and turning more strongly towards the Calvinist form of Protestantism. While not wishing to interfere too openly in its rivalries, Elizabeth and her advisers saw the wisdom of supporting this Protestant trend whenever possible, and in 1586 they signed a solid treaty with Mary's son James, now king of Scotland. From the time of her abdication, Mary herself was a troublesome figure, serving as a possible rallying point for the French and for English Catholics, until her execution in 1587.

While England developed friendly relations with its northern neighbor, it never seemed quite to know how to handle the island neighbor to its west, Ireland, considering it a kind of

Renold Elstracke. Queen Elizabeth in Parliament. Engraving in Robert Glover, *Nobilitas politica vel ciuilis* (London, 1608). STC 11922, c.1, sig. M5r.

Third-World country, though a colony technically ruled by England. The English had been present in Ireland since at least the time of the Norman Conquest in the eleventh century. By Elizabeth's time, the Old English families went back for generations and had more or less acclimatized to the country. They settled primarily in and around Dublin in an area known as the "Pale," and had developed terms of coexistence with the Gaelic chieftains. Policy during Elizabeth's reign turned more towards conquest than peaceful coexistence, with "opinion in governing circles increasingly polarized between conciliatory and coercive strategies of conquest."[1] It didn't help that the prevailing view of the native Irish was that expressed by Shakespeare in *Richard II*, where the King calls them "those rough rug-headed kerns,/ Which live like venom" (2.1.156–57). He might have derived his idea from John Derrick's description of the Irish Karnes or Woodkarnes with their "straunge and monstrous" clothing and beastly manners. Derrick wrote his book in 1578, partly as a piece of propaganda in favor of Sir Henry Sidney, then governor of Ireland. Entitled *The Image of Ireland*, the book was printed in 1581, and illustrated with a number of woodcuts that served to "normalize" English atrocities against the "beastly" Irish. The popularity of book and pictures is attested by the fact that few copies survive, and of those, few still retain the illustrations.[2]

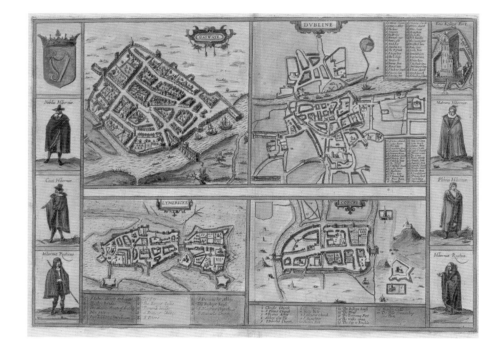

Recent historians have likened the English attitude toward and treatment of Ireland to the often brutal methods of conquest and subjection used by the Spanish and others in conquering the New World during the same period. As Steven Ellis has written, "Certain features of Gaelic society—in particular its highly individual religious practices, transhumance (which was mistaken for nomadism), and the insubstantial dwellings even of chiefs—had long suggested to English officials that Ireland's indigenous peoples were not a civilized society but primitive savages."[3] The process of "colonizing" Ireland had begun under Mary Tudor who "granted uncultivated tracts of territory to English gentlemen and other adventurers to cultivate at their own expense and risk"—in other words, Mary was giving away land which actually belonged to the Irish and was not hers to give.[4]

When Elizabeth came to the throne, the older policy of gradual conquest was already giving way to a desire for quick results, popular "among English adventurers hoping to get rich quick on Irish land."[5] Furthermore, the Elizabethans seemed to have a knack for alienating the Old English as well, by levying heavy military taxes, questioning their loyalty, and generally excluding them "from any real political influence."[6] The English governor in Ireland since 1556 had been Thomas Radcliffe, now earl of Sussex. He was followed by Sir Henry Sidney, Philip Sidney's father, from 1565 to 1571 and 1575 to 1578. Both men were involved in attempts to tame, and eventually crush, Shane O'Neill, the Gaelic Lord from Ulster, who had assumed great power for himself that appeared to threaten English government in Ireland. He also annoyed the English by raiding the

Georg Braun and Franz Hogenberg. Map of Four Irish Cities. Engraving from *Civitates orbis terrarum* (Cologne, 1572–1618). MAP 229985.11.

Pale. Elizabeth tried conciliation. She received O'Neill in London during the Christmas season of 1561–62, but once back in Ireland, he was up to his old tricks. After O'Neill defeated Sussex in 1563, Elizabeth tried to placate him once more by making him ruler of Ulster, but back home again, he became an even greater threat to the English when he asked the French to send 6,000 troops in his aid. Eventually he was defeated and killed by the Mac Donnells, a clan with strong ties to the Catholic Scots Mac Donnells. This event only meant that Elizabeth now faced seven years of trying to deal with the Mac Donnells and *their* leader Sorley Boy.[7] Ireland could quickly prove a monetary sinkhole, and Elizabeth's strategy of diplomacy over open warfare was due in part to her desire to keep the costs down. There were times, however, when her hand was forced, especially with the intervention of other foreign powers in Ireland. These powers were generally France and Spain, the two most important European countries with whom Elizabeth had to deal.[8]

England's ties with France were ancient, going back to the days when the Normans, whose over-lord was France, conquered England in 1066 and became the ruling class. From Edward III in the fourteenth century through Henry V, English kings conquered and ruled over French territories, and after the battle of Agincourt in 1415, Henry V was recognized as heir to the French throne. Beginning with Henry VI, however, the English lost most of their foothold in France. Their last stronghold, the important port city of Calais, was recaptured by the French in 1558 just before Elizabeth came to the throne.[9] This loss did not prevent Elizabeth from including the fleur-de-lis, symbol of France, in her great seal and coat of arms, and for some time she hoped to regain Calais.

During most of Elizabeth's reign, as we saw, France was ruled by a series of sons of Henri II and Catherine de Médicis, with Catherine herself as regent. French political power was compromised during much of this time by religious-dynastic conflicts that pitted the ultra-Catholic Guise family against the Huguenot leaders, "the princes of Condé and Navarre."[10] In 1562, Elizabeth signed the Treaty of Hampton Court, sending soldiers and money to help the Huguenots under Condé, with the real hope that she could get Calais back in exchange for Le Havre and Dieppe. When Condé was defeated, Elizabeth held onto Le Havre as long as possible, but in the end she had to admit defeat as well and the loss of her dream to reclaim Calais.[11]

In 1570, Charles IX signed a peace treaty with the Huguenots, who proposed a marriage between Elizabeth and Charles's brother Henri, duc d'Anjou (later Henri III). On their side, the Huguenots believed that such an alliance would "cement the religious pacification in France" and "construct a league against Spain in the Netherlands." Elizabeth was amenable to the proposal, though she did not want to destroy her relationship with the Spanish, just to make Philip "restore commercial relations," and she hoped to pressure the French to stop sending aid to Mary, Queen of Scots. In the end, the match failed when Henri, a dedicated Catholic, realized he could not practice his religion fully in England. And he was probably not enthusiastic about marrying a woman eighteen years older than himself.[12] The French and English did sign a treaty of mutual defense, however, in April 1572—the Treaty of Blois—which did not jeopardize England's desire to maintain good relations with Spain. By this treaty, France also accepted the English position that James VI was the ruler of Scotland.[13]

In August 1572, however, England's relationship with France was severely shaken by the St. Bartholomew Massacre. On August 18, a large number of Protestants were in Paris for the wedding of Henri de Navarre and Marguerite de Valois, sister of Charles IX. Four days later, an attempt was made on the life of the Huguenot leader, Gaspard de Coligny, by a Guise assassin. The Protestants were angry and spoke of revenge. Believing that they might cause a major uprising against Catholics, Catherine de Médicis and some of her associates "decided to forestall the Huguenots by killing them first, before they could carry out their plan." She persuaded her son Charles IX to let Guise finish off Coligny, knowing "that if the King's guards and Guise's followers began the work, they could rely on the people of Paris to complete it." When it was over, close to 13,000 Protestants had been killed in France.[14] Elizabeth and the English were horrified; nevertheless, Elizabeth did not wish to break diplomatic ties with France. While she gave unofficial help to the Huguenots and took in many refugees, and while she publicly protested the massacre, she felt that "diplomatic intervention might persuade Charles to agree to a new peace, which would grant the Huguenots security and a degree of toleration."[15]

Two years later, Charles IX died at the age of twenty-four and was succeeded by his brother Henri III, a Catholic under the influence of the Guise party. A set of instructions to Lord North, from Elizabeth, signed by herself and her Secretary of State, Sir Francis Walsingham, survives at the Folger Library. Elizabeth sends North on her behalf to greet the new French king, and to bring condolences to the Queen Mother (Catherine de Médicis) and to the twenty-year-old widow, Elizabeth of Austria. He is to tell Henri III "that as they found the late King a good neighbour and ally, the Queen would have great sorrow not to find like affection in him." Furthermore, she hopes "that the crown that has long languished in civil troubles may by his discreet government be restored to its former and ancient quietness," particularly urging that he consider religious toleration.[16]

From 1578 through 1579, Elizabeth pursued a plan of marriage with Henri III's younger brother, Francis, duc d'Alençon, whom she called "Monsieur."[17] Again, there were important political reasons for the match, and in prolonging the negotiations, Elizabeth bought time that she needed to decide what to do about the situation in the Netherlands, where the rebel leader, William of Orange, was asking for help against attacks by the Spanish regent, Don John. They were also asking for help from the French, via Alençon, which Elizabeth did not like, "for fear that the French would be granted influence or territory as a reward for their aid." If she married Alençon, then he would stop dabbling in the Netherlands and perhaps Philip might be frightened into making peace there.[18] Alençon was the only one of Elizabeth's foreign suitors to visit her in England, and she seemed to enjoy his twelve-day visit in August of 1579. There was much resistance, however, on the part of English Protestants to such a match. Notably, the twenty-five-year-old Sir Philip Sidney wrote Elizabeth a strong letter, "dwelling on the treachery of French Catholics (he had been . . . in Paris during the St. Bartholomew Massacre), and the offensiveness of the marriage to English Protestants."[19]

Henri III refused to sign a treaty with Elizabeth unless she would agree to marry his brother, but Elizabeth did not want to undertake open war with France against Spain, and satisfied herself instead with covertly giving loans to Alençon in the Netherlands.[20] After Alençon's death in 1584, Elizabeth began loaning money and men to Henry of Navarre, a Protestant and next in line to the French throne. Navarre was engaged in a desperate struggle against the Catholic League, organized by the Guise faction. His struggle increased when he became king after the assassination of Henri III in 1589 and the Guise attempt to put their own candidate on the French throne. Elizabeth sent him more aid in 1589 and 1591. Finally, however, Navarre felt that in order to stabilize the country, he must convert to Catholicism. He did so in 1593 and was finally crowned as Henri IV in early 1594.[21]

Henri IV was twenty years younger than Elizabeth, and she initially tried to treat him rather like a son, aiding him, advising him, sending him gifts. Her affectionate advice is evident in a letter to him, written in her own hand in French, now at the Folger Library. Dated about 1590, the letter warns him to be valorous but careful of his person: "For the honor of God, consider how much it matters to the whole cause—the preservation of your person!" She does not want him to appear a coward—"For as to my son, if I had had one, I would rather have seen him dead than a coward" —he must take necessary risks, but he needs also to remember that he is not "a private soldier but . . . a great prince." "It may be that you will disdain this advice as coming from the fearful heart of a woman," she writes, but he should remember how many times she has not flinched from attempts on her life. Finally, she asks God "to grant you the grace always to take the best path in all your enterprises, and to preserve you as the darling of His eye."[22] Henri's most important legacy was the establishment of religious toleration in France by the Edict of Nantes in 1598.

During most of Elizabeth's reign, Spain was the strongest European power. It had benefited from the breakup of the Holy Roman Empire in the late 1550s, when Charles V placed "Italy, the Americas, the Netherlands, Franche-Comté and Spain" in the hands of his son, Philip II of Spain.[23] Philip had married Elizabeth's sister Mary, though she was eleven years his senior, but he spent little time in England, and on Mary's death, he considered asking Elizabeth to marry him. Their age difference—he was six years older than Elizabeth—was certainly more suitable, but there was no question that she would marry a Catholic king just when she was trying to re-establish the Protestant church in England. Nevertheless, good relations with Spain were important to Elizabeth, partly to maintain the English wool trade through Antwerp in the Netherlands. On his side, Philip also felt that he needed the security of good relations with the English against any possible aggression by the French. One sore point in their relationship came from Philip's regent in the Netherlands in 1563. Margaret of Parma placed a temporary embargo on English trade with the Netherlands because she was upset with higher tariffs on English cloth, among other concerns. The English simply sent their cloth to another port off the North Sea, just beyond Spanish territory.[24]

In February 1566, Elizabeth had occasion to write a letter to Philip concerning the holding of English ships and sailors who had been caught at Gibraltar two years earlier in a conflict with the French.[25] This letter, in Latin, survives at the Folger Library. Elizabeth insists that "The whole damage, if any proceeded from us, was, as we have credibly learned, called forth by the very base insolence of the French" ["*Gallorum insolentia evocata fuit*"]. Philip has already, by his "mercy and kindness" ["*clementia et bonitas*"] released the sailors involved. She now asks him for the return of the ships and goods, reminding Philip that she would treat any Spanish merchants who happened to be driven into English waters justly and humanely. The letter is firm but cordial, beginning with her address to him as "our very dear brother, kinsman and friend, Greeting, and a very happy increase in all fortunate things."

Nicolas de Larmessin. *Henry. 4e . . . roy de France* (Paris, 1679?). Engraving. ART File H518.4 no.1.

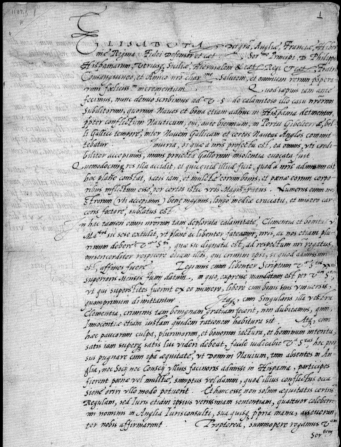

ELISABETA Dei grã Angliæ, Franciæ, Hiberniæ Regina, Fidei Defensor et cet. Serᵐᵒ Principi D. Philippo Hispaniarum, Utriusq. Siciliæ, Hierusalem & cet. Regi et cet. Fratri Consanguineo, et Amico nr̃o chariss.ᵐᵒ Salutem, et omnium rerum prosperarum felicissᵐᵘ incrementum.

Quod sæpius iam ante fecimus, nunc denuo scribimus ad Vᵃᵐ Sᵗᵉᵐ de calamitoso illo casu nr̃orum subditorum, quorum Naues et bona etiam adhuc in Hispania detinentur, propter conflictum Nauticum, qui, ante biennium, in Portu Giboltero, bello Gallico tempore, inter Nauem Gallicam et certos Nautas Anglos committebatur ... iniuria, ut quæ a nr̃is profecta est, ea omnis, uti credibiliter accepimus, minus proiectis Gallorum insolentia euacata ...

Quomodocunq. res illa accidit, et quicquid illud fuit, quod a nr̃is admissum est hoc plane constat, satis iam, et multo ... eorum bonis, et pæne omnium corporibus insumtum esse, per certos istos uros Magᵉˢ præsens. Numerum enim nostrorum (uti accepimus) bene magnus, longo media cruciatu, et misero carceris factore, sublatus est.

In hac tamen enim nr̃orum tam deplorata calamitate, Clementia et bonitas Vᵃ ... sic sese extulit, ut plane ac libenter fateamur, nr̃os, ac nos etiam plurimum debere Vᵃᵉ Sᵗⁱ, quæ sic dignata est, ad respectum nr̃i rogatus misericorditer respicere etiam illos, qui criminis ipsi, si quod admissum est, affines fuere. Legimus enim libenter Scriptum Vᵃᵉ Sᵗⁱˢ xxu superiori mensis Iunii datum, in quo, expresse mandatum est per Vᵃᵐ Sᵗᵉᵐ, ut qui superstites fuerint ex eo numero, libere cum bonis suis uniuersis quamprimum dimittantur. Itaq, cum singularis illa Vᵃᵉ ... Clementia, criminis tam benignam gratiam fecerit, non dubitamus, quin Innocentiæ etiam iustam quidem rationem habitura sit. Atq, cum hæc paucorum culpa, plurimorum, et bonorum iactura, et hominum intentu, satis iam superq. satis sui uideri debeat, facile iudicabit Vᵃ Sᵗᵃˢ hoc prorsus pugnare cum ipsa æquitate, ut Domini Nauium, tum absentes in Anglia, nec Socij nec Conscij ullius facinoris admissi in Hispania, participes fierent pæne vel mulctæ, sumptus vel damni, quod illius conflictus occasione et in ullo modo potuerit. Et hanc esse, non solum æquitatis certis Regulam, sed Iuris etiam ipsius ueriss.mam sententiam, quatuor celeberrimi nominis in Anglia Iurisconsulti, sua quisq. ipse manu, asseueranter nobis affirmarunt. Propterea, summopere rogamus Vᵃᵐ Sᵗᵉᵐ

This cordiality was soon to be strained, however. Later the same year, Protestant radicals revolted in the Netherlands. They were put down, but Philip was disturbed enough to send Spanish troops back into the country under the Duke of Alva, who was to take over from Margaret of Parma. Under the Duke's suppression, many skilled Protestant artisans fled to England and from there sent support to their fellows back home.[26] A more serious rupture with Spain began in 1568 with the English capture of Spanish ships carrying money borrowed from the Genoese "to pay Alva's troops." Bad weather forced the ships into English ports where Cecil had the money unloaded "for safekeeping;" he may also have intended Elizabeth "to take over the loan herself." Alva responded by taking English ships in the Netherlands, upon which the English suspended trade with all countries ruled by Spain.[27]

Such moves and countermoves continued over the next twenty years, becoming gradually more serious. A flareup of civil war in France led England and Spain to seek better relations in 1574. They signed the Treaty of Bristol, restoring "diplomatic and commercial relations"; the English also returned the contested money to the Genoese bankers. But the harm had already been done. The English could not forget that in 1569–70 Philip had intended to encourage Irish Catholics in their support of Mary, Queen of Scots, and he approved the so-called Ridolphi Plot "to put Mary on the English throne."[28] Elizabeth still tried to maintain cordial relations with Philip by helping the Protestants in the Netherlands covertly, rather than overtly, and trying to negotiate a peace there with the removal of Spanish troops, but to no avail. In 1580 Spain conquered Portugal, and Spanish and Italian soldiers were sent to man the garrison of Smerwick in Ireland on behalf of the pope; they were brutally massacred by the English. Shortly thereafter, Spain was implicated in two plots against the life of Elizabeth, the Throckmorton Plot of 1583 and the Parry Plot of 1584.[29]

The Netherlands were always a complicating factor in Elizabeth's relationships with Spain. The Protestant faction there under William of Orange finally managed to join the various provinces together as the States General in 1576, but they were still trying to free themselves from foreign soldiers and heresy laws. Elizabeth signed the Treaty of Nonsuch with the States in 1585, agreeing to supply them with money and men, but refused to take on the sovereignty they offered her, fearing that such a move would lead to outright war with Philip. At the same time, she was unsuccessful in her attempt to forge an international Protestant League with Danish and German states.[30]

While not attacking Philip directly, Elizabeth allowed her sea pirates to prey on his shipping. From 1585 to 1587 Sir Francis Drake raided northern Spain, "then moved on to sack the Canaries and Cape Verde Islands on his way to the Caribbean where he captured Santo Domingo and Cartagena," causing millions of ducats worth of damage.[31] In the process, he managed to delay the sailing of the huge Armada that Philip was preparing against England in retaliation for the latter's maritime predations and intervention in the Netherlands. But in May of 1588, about 150 ships with some 26,000 men finally set sail from Lisbon under the Duke of Medina Sidonia.[32] The plan was to join with foot soldiers from Parma's troops in the Netherlands, but bad weather, lack of good preparation on the part of Parma, and fleeting attacks by the faster, more modern English fleet jeopardized the whole enterprise. As the defeated Spanish attempted to sail northward "around the Shetlands" and then turn west and south back to La Coruña, they were battered by storms along the coast of Ireland. Close to 11,000 men perished.[33]

Top: Elizabeth I. Autograph letter, signed, to King Henri IV of France (ca.1595). Folger MS V.b.131.

Bottom: Elizabeth I. Letter to Philip II of Spain (February 17, 1565/66), in hand of Roger Ascham; signed by the queen. Folger MS X.d.138 (2).

VERA EFFIGIES R.di IN CHRISTO PATRIS GEORGII CARLETON EPISC. CICESTRIEN.

GEORGIUS CARLETONVS ἀγαγγ...
Age, tu solus regni cor.
Orbis cor, Sol est, regni cor, tu (Pater) ut Sol
Orbe micat, regno sic tua scripta micant.
Si Cor principium vitæ est, tota Anglia recte
Per tua jam diei Vivere scripta potest.

A THANKFVLL REMEMBRANCE OF GODS MERCIE. by G. C.

London Printed for Robert Milbourne, and Humphry Robinson.

CHAPTER XII.

The Invincible Armie described. At the first setting out shaken sore with a tempest. The gests of each day related particularly and punctually. They trusted in their strength, we in the name of our God; They are fallen, and we stand upright.

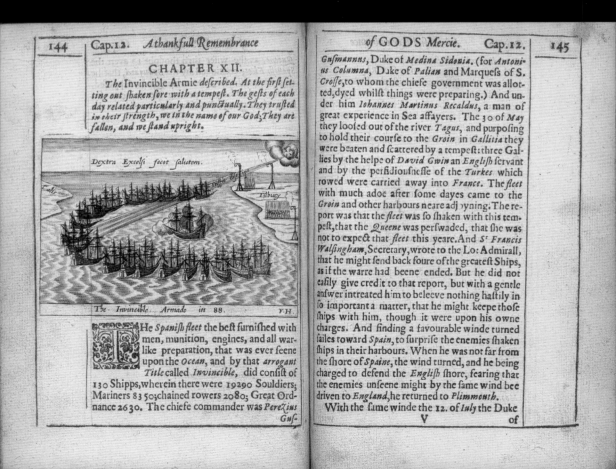

Dextra Excelsi fecit salutem.

Tilbury

The Invincible Armado in 88.   F.H.

He *Spanish fleet* the best furnished with men, munition, engines, and all warlike preparation, that was ever seene upon the *Ocean*, and by that *arrogant Title* called *Invincible*, did consist of 130 Shipps, wherein there were 19290 Souldiers, Mariners 8350; chained rowers 2080; Great Ordnance 2630. The chiefe commander was *Perezius Gus-*

Gusmannus, Duke of *Medina Sidonia*. (for *Antonius Columna*, Duke of *Palian* and Marquesse of S. *Crosse*, to whom the chiefe government was allotted, dyed whilst things were preparing.) And under him *Iohannes Martinus Recaldus*, a man of great experience in Sea affayers. The 30 of *May* they loosed out of the river *Tagus*, and purposing to hold their course to the *Groin* in *Gallisia* they were beaten and scattered by a tempest: three Gallies by the helpe of *David Gwin* an *English* servant and by the perfidiousnesse of the *Turkes* which rowed were carried away into *France*. The *fleet* with much adoe after some dayes came to the *Groin* and other harbours neare adjoyning: The report was that the *fleet* was so shaken with this tempest, that the *Queene* was perswaded, that she was not to expect that *fleet* this yeare. And St *Francis Walsingham*, Secretary, wrote to the Lo: Admirall, that he might send back foure of the greatest Ships, as if the warre had beene ended. But he did not easily give credit to that report, but with a gentle answer intreated him to beleeve nothing hastily in so important a matter, that he might keepe those ships with him, though it were upon his owne charges. And finding a favourable winde turned sailes toward *Spain*, to surprise the enemies shaken ships in their harbours. When he was not far from the shore of *Spaine*, the wind turned, and he being charged to defend the *English* shore, fearing that the enemies unseene might by the same wind bee driven to *England*, he returned to *Plimmouth*.

With the same winde the 12. of *Iuly* the Duke

V   of

The English, of course, were jubilant. They were prepared for a land war, which fortunately never came, but Elizabeth had gone down to the army camp at Tilbury to speak to the troops. The historian William Camden described her visit thus: "the Queene with a manly courage tooke view of her Army and Campe at *Tilbury*, and walking through the rankes of armed men placed on both sides, with a Leaders trunchion in her hand, sometimes with a martiall pace, and sometimes like a woman, incredible it is how much shee strengthened the hearts of her Captaines and Souldiers by her presence and speech."[34] The mixed gendering in Camden's description of the Queen—sometimes "with a manly courage" sometimes "like a woman"—recalls her double role of royal prince and human woman, a role that she herself played up in her speech on the occasion:

Wherefore I am come among you . . . being resolved in the midst and heat of the battle to live and die amongst you all, to lay down for my God and for my kingdom and for my people mine honor and my blood even in the dust. I know I have the body but of a weak and feeble woman, but I have the heart and stomach of a king and of a king of England too—and take foul scorn that Parma or any prince of Europe should dare to invade the borders of my realm.[35]

Needless to say, there was much triumph and rejoicing on the part of the English and their Protestant friends, and much soul-searching on the part of the Spanish. Several portraits of Elizabeth were painted with a background showing the Armada destroyed on the rough cliffs off Ireland.[36] Commemorative medals were struck in England and the Netherlands. The English medal has Elizabeth's portrait on one side; on the reverse is a bay tree struck by lightening but standing firmly on an island. The motto reads: "*Non Ipsa Pericula Tangunt*"—"Not even danger affects it."[37] A copy of the Dutch medal is at the Folger. It shows on one side the Spanish fleet dashed against rocks and on the other, a council of the pope with kings and bishops, all "with bandaged eyes, the floor covered with spikes. This satirizes the unsuccessful confederation of the pope, the emperor, Philip II, the Duke of Guise and other princes against Elizabeth."[38]

All sorts of news pamphlets appeared in the press, some of which are in the Folger's collections. They bear titles such as: *Certaine Advertisements Out of Ireland, Concerning the losses and distresses happened to the Spanish Navie, upon the West coastes of Ireland*; *The Copie of a Letter Sent Out of England to Don Bernardin Mendoza Ambassadour in France for the King of Spaine*; and *A Packe of Spanish Lyes*. *The Copie of a Letter* purported to have been written by a Catholic, Richard Field, but was actually a propaganda piece composed by Burghley, and printed in French, Spanish and Dutch as well as English. The booklet "aimed at countering stories of the Armada's success put out by Mendoza." It was also intended to show that the Catholic cause was ruined in England. *A Packe of Spanish Lyes* was another brilliant piece of English propaganda written to counter rumor and Spanish reports of a victory. It was printed in double columns with the Spanish lies on the left and the English replies to the right, and "was translated into every major language in Europe."[39] To underline the differences, the printer set the Spanish lies in old-fashioned Gothic type, and the English replies in the newer Roman style type. Another pamphlet, *A true Discourse of the Armie which the king of Spaine caused to bee assembled in the Hauen of Lisbon* (London, 1588), provides

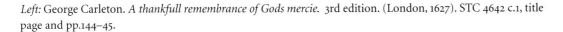

Left: George Carleton. *A thankfull remembrance of Gods mercie.* 3rd edition. (London, 1627). STC 4642 c.1, title page and pp.144–45.

Right: Armada Medal. Silver coin (Netherlands, 1588). ART Inv. 1001. Obverse showing the Armada; reverse showing council of pope, kings, and bishops.

the names of the Armada ships with their weights, and arms, as well as lists of names of the captains and others. The pious author's purpose is evidently to point up the great military strength from which England has been saved through the grace of God: "For when we shal see from what strange crueltie, and forraine power we haue bene deliuered, shall we not alwaies after say, Praysed be the Lord which hath not giuen us as a pray [prey] vnto their teeth"(12–13).

Spain tried again in 1596 and 1597 to send Armadas against England. Although Essex was involved in a successful attack on the Spanish fleet at Cadiz in 1596, the English bungled other aspects of this expedition and did not attack Philip's main fleet in Lisbon that was preparing for the second Armada. Fortunately, bad weather did the work for them, as it did again in 1597. Philip II died in 1598, after signing a peace treaty with Henri IV of France. He was succeeded by his son, Philip III, with whom Elizabeth tried to negotiate a peace, but they disagreed over the Netherlands. Though still under Spanish rule, the United Provinces had been recognized as a sovereign Protestant state under Elizabeth's treaty with them in 1598, a position that Philip III could not accept.[40]

It is at this point that the political fortunes of Spain and Ireland joined forces at the end of Elizabeth's reign. In 1598, the English were soundly defeated by the Irish under Hugh O'Neill, earl of Tyrone. Three years later, Philip III sent about 3,400 troops to aid Tyrone in his uprising. While the Spaniards waited at Kinsale for Tyrone's reinforcements, Lord Mountjoy leading the English troops surrounded them. Though Mountjoy was forced to fight off Gaelic lords who came to relieve Kinsale, he won the battle and in early 1602 the Spanish surrendered.[41] Mountjoy had succeeded Essex who had tried to make a private agreement with Tyrone in 1599. The conditions for peace offered by Tyrone at that time, however, only angered Elizabeth. By 1602 he was living as a fugitive, difficult to capture, but Elizabeth was intent on continuing war against him, instead of accepting his submission in return for a pardon. Finally in early 1603, her council persuaded her to agree. Tyrone made his submission to Mountjoy on March 30, 1603, six days after the Queen's death, a fact known to Mountjoy but not to Tyrone.[42] The Irish wars "had cost England nearly £2,000,000,"[43] but had left a bitter legacy. The brutality of the English measures of massacre, starvation, and religious intolerance created the roots for future unrest.

During her reign Elizabeth gave more careful attention to policy within England and with other European powers than she did to Ireland. Paul Hammer suggests that Elizabeth put Ireland—part of her territory—in a different category from foreign states. The latter involved formal diplomacy while the former meant dealing with those who were (notionally) her subjects but who were unwilling to accept her authority. According to Wallace MacCaffrey, much of her foreign policy consisted of crisis management. This method worked more or less well with the ever-changing intricacies of France and Spain, but measures for the short-run would never solve the problems with Ireland. What was needed was someone with political vision, and that Elizabeth never had.[44]

A Packe of Spa- | 3 |
nish lies.   A Condemnation of the
                    Spanish lies.

From Spaine.   *From England.*

By a letter of Diego Peres, chiefe Postmaster of Logrono, dated the second of September. 1588.

2 The newes of England is confirmed here, by a letter of the Gouernour of Roan. He writeth he hath in his power the chiefe Pilot of captaine Drake, and that hee knoweth that all the English armie remained ouerthrowen, hauing sunke two and twentie shippes, and taken fourtie, (d) and imprisoned Francis Drake, hauing giuen them chase almost as hie as (e) Abspurge, and slaine many by ye sword, and likewise sayeth that there was found in captaine Drakes shippe, a piece of ordinance of fiue and twentie foote long, which discharged a shotte of a hundreth weight at once, made of purpose, with one onely shot to sinke our Spanish Admirall; and it pleased God although shee was somewhat battered,

2 THe Gouernour of *Roan* is accompted a worthy noble man, and therefore he shall do wel to make this report of him to bee knowen for a lie: for so surely he knoweth it to be, that there was neuer either a chiefe Pilote or the value of a boy of Captaine *Drakes* taken and brought to him as a prisoner. The Gouernours of *Bollen* and *Calleis* can informe the Gouernour of *Roan*, how false a report it was, that the English Armie remained ouerthrowen afore *Calleis*: the English armie fought with the Spanish, chased the Spanish as a brace of Greyhounds would a herde of Deere: the *Spaniards* ships were beate, spoyled, burnt, sunke, some in the maine seas afore *Dunkirke*, some afore *Flushing*, and the rest chased away, so as they fledde continually afore the English Nauie in their best order for stregth, without daring to abide any fight: yea, some one of the English shippes fought with 3. of their *Galleasses*, the *Spaniards* neuer attepting to board any English, but as many of them as coulde saile away, fled with all their sailes, & were followed by the English, vntil they were chased out of all the English seas, and forced then to runne a violent course about *Scotland*, and so fo to *Ireland*, where a great
A 3   number

A packe of Spanish lyes, sent abroad in the vvorld (London, 1588). STC 23011 Bd.w. STC 15412 c.2, sig. A3r.

1 Steven G. Ellis, *Ireland in the Age of the Tudors, 1447–1603* (London; New York: Longman, 1998), 283.

2 See David B. Quinn, "Introduction," in *The Image of Ireland* (Belfast: Blackstaff Press, 1985), xvii. The Folger Library has the only recorded copy of Derricke in the United States, unfortunately without woodcuts.

3 Ellis, *Ireland*, 285. "Transhumance" refers to the lifestyle of shepherds or cattlemen who move herds seasonally from one type of grazing ground to another. They are not "nomads" because they have one or two fixed residences.

4 Jasper Ridley, *Elizabeth I* (New York: Viking, 1988), 215.

5 Ellis, *Ireland*, 282.

6 Ellis, *Ireland*, 283.

7 Ridley, *Elizabeth I*, 216–18.

8 Elizabeth also had contact with Russia and Turkey. English merchants had a foothold in Russia via the Muscovy Company. Through them, Elizabeth established relations with the successive czars: Ivan the Terrible, Feodor, and Boris Godunov, who himself sent an ambassador to London in 1600. Elizabeth also sent ambassadors overland to the Sultan of Turkey, Amurath III, hoping for his aid against Spain. The Turks welcomed the friendly overtures, but were more interested in trade. See Ridley, *Elizabeth I*, 314–15.

9 Susan Doran, *Elizabeth I and Foreign Policy 1558–1603* (London; New York: Routledge, 2000), 1–2.

10 Doran, *Foreign Policy*, 21.

11 Doran, *Foreign Policy*, 23.

12 Doran, *Foreign Policy*, 30–31.

13 Doran, *Foreign Policy*, 31; Ridley, *Elizabeth I*, 174.

14 Ridley, *Elizabeth I*, 182; Doran, *Foreign Policy*, 32.

15 Doran, *Foreign Policy*, 32.

16 Folger MS X.d.90, in Latin, summarized in SPD (1574) 560ff. Roger North, second Baron North, was sent as ambassador extraordinary. The English ambassador in residence at this time in France was Dr. Valentine Dale.

17 Francis, duc d'Alençon became duc d'Anjou in 1576.

18 Doran, *Foreign Policy*, 37, 38.

19 Paul Johnson, *Elizabeth I: a Study in Power and Intellect* (London: Futura, 1976), 256.

20 Doran, *Foreign Policy*, 40–41.

21 Doran, *Foreign Policy*, 58.

22 Translation quoted from Elizabeth I, *Works*, 363–64.

23 Doran, *Foreign Policy*, 7.

24 Doran, *Foreign Policy*, 16.

25 Folger MS X.d.138 (2)

26 Wallace T. McCaffrey, *Elizabeth I* (London: Edward Arnold, 1993), 157–58.

27 Doran, *Foreign Policy*, 29.

28 Doran, *Foreign Policy*, 33, 29.

29 Doran, *Foreign Policy*, 39–42.

30 Doran, *Foreign Policy*, 36, 42–43.

31 Doran, *Foreign Policy*, 53.

32 M. J. Rodríguez-Salgado, et al., *Armada* (London; New York: Penguin Books in association with the National Maritime Museum, 1988), 31.

33 *Armada*, 263.

34 William Camden, *The Historie of. . .Princesse Elizabeth* (London: Benjamin Fisher, 1630), sig. Ss3v.

35 Elizabeth I, *Works*, 326. See also Carole Levin, *The Heart and Stomach of a King* (Philadelphia: University of Pennsylvania Press, 1994), 143–145.

36 Roy Strong believes that one of these "could have been commissioned by Sir Francis Drake." (Roy Strong, *Gloriana: the Portraits of Queen Elizabeth I* [London: Thames & Hudson, 1987], 131).

37 Roy Strong identifies the portrait type as by Hilliard. He notes that this medal and another of about the same time were struck in a variety of metals, intended to be worn across the social classes. "It was a Protestant use of the sacred image of the Virgin Queen exactly paralleling the wearing of holy images by Catholics" (Strong, *Gloriana*, 121). See also *The Currency of Fame: Portrait Medals of the Renaissance*, ed. Stephen K. Scher (New York: Abrams, 1994), 358–59 and plates 366, 367.

38 *Armada*, 276.

39 *Armada*, 275.

40 Doran, *Foreign Policy*, 61.

41 Doran, *Foreign Policy*, 61–62.

42 Somerset, *Elizabeth I*, 558–59.

43 Doran, *Foreign Policy*, 62.

44 Paul Hammer, written comment. MacCaffrey, *Elizabeth I*, 432–33. I am grateful to Paul Hammer and to Vincent Carey for their helpful readings of this essay.

John Derricke
The image of Irelande, with a discouerie of vvoodkarne
London: [J. Kingston for] Ihon Daie, 1581
STC 6734

Edmund Spenser (1552?–1599)
The historie of Ireland, collected by three learned authors
[Meredith Hanmer, Edmund Campion, Edmund Spenser]
Dublin: Societie of Stationers; [London: Thomas Harper], 1633
STC 25067a

Thomas Stafford (fl.1633)
Pacata Hibernia, Ireland appeased and reduced: or, an historie of the late vvarrres of Ireland
London: A[ugustine] M[athewes], 1633
STC 23132a

Richard Verstegen (fl.1565–1620)
Theatrum crudelitatum haereticorum nostri temporis
Antwerp: Adrian Hubert, 1592
BR1605 V4 1592 Cage

Georg Braun and Franz Hogenberg.
[Map of Four Irish Cities], from *Civitates orbis terrarum*
Cologne, 1572–1618
ART 229985.11

James Thomson.
Edmund Spenser
Engraving
London: Charles Knight, 18??
ART File S848 no. 1, c.2

George Carleton (1559–1628)
A thankfull remembrance of Gods mercy
3rd edition
London: M. Flesher for Robert Mylbourne and Humphrey Robinson, 1627
STC 4642, c.1

A packe of Spanish lyes, sent abroad in the vvorld
London: Christopher Barker, 1588
STC 23011 Bd.w. STC 15412, c.2

A true discourse of the armie which the King of Spaine caused to bee assembled in the hauen of Lisbon . . . in the yeare 1588
London: Iohn Wolfe, 1588
STC 22999

Great Britain. Sovereigns. Elizabeth
Letter to Philip II of Spain. February 17, 1565/66
Letter in hand of Roger Ascham; signed by the queen
Folger MS X.d.138 (2)

Great Britain. Sovereigns. Elizabeth
Autograph letter, signed, to King Henri IV of France
ca.1595
Folger MS V.b.131

Great Britain. Sovereigns. Elizabeth
Instructions to Lord North, English ambassador to France. October 1574
Signed by the queen and Sir Francis Walsingham
Folger MS X.d.90

Nicolas de Larmessin (ca.1640–1725)
Henry. 4e . . . roy de France
Engraving
[Paris, 1679?]
ART File H518.4 no.1

Armada Medal
Silver coin
Netherlands, 1588
ART Inv. 1001

Elizabeth I (1533–1603)
Second Great Seal
Designed in 1584 by Nicholas Hilliard
Attached here to a "license of alienation," 2 September 1586
Folger MS Z.c.38 (6)

Renold Elstrack (1570–1630?)
Queen Elizabeth in Parliament
Engraving in Robert Glover, *Nobilitas politica vel ciuilis*
London: William Jaggard, 1608
STC 11922, c.1

Illustriss: Robertus
Dudleius, comes
Leicestriæ, baro
Denbigh: &c.
obijt anno. 1588.

The right honourable and noble Lord Robert Dudley Earle of Leicester, Baron of Denbigh, Knight of the
noble Ordres of St George and St Michael. Mr of the horse to Queene ELIZABETH, high Steward of her
Houshold and of her Privy Counsell. Lord Governour and Captaine Generall of the United Provinces
in Netherland etc. He deceassed in September Ano 1588. and lieth Honourably entombed at
Warwick: by the Right noble and vertuous Lady LETICE Countesse of Leicester, unto whom
this Portraicture is humbly consecrated.

Are to be sould by Comp. Holland.
over against the Exchange.

Ro. Vaughan sculp.

Leicester and Essex

ELIZABETH HAD MANY MEN IN HER LIFE, but two of the most colorful, whose reputations have lasted as long as hers, are Robert Dudley, earl of Leicester, and Robert Devereux, earl of Essex. Mention Essex, and most people think of his dashing portrayal on film by Errol Flynn in the 1930s, while the older Leicester was well captured by Robert Hardy in the 1970s *Elizabeth R* series. But who were the real men behind the actors?

As the fifth son of John Dudley, duke of Northumberland, and Jane Guildford, Robert Dudley did not inherit the earldom but had to work on his own for position and prestige. He was born around 1533, making him almost the same age as Elizabeth, and in fact, they had known each other since childhood. Dudley was one of the youthful companions of Elizabeth's brother Edward, whom he served in various capacities at court when Edward became king. After Edward's early death, the earl of Northumberland was executed for upholding the claim of his niece, Lady Jane Grey. On that occasion, Dudley was thrown into the Tower with his brothers and father, but he managed to escape conviction and went off to serve successfully with the English forces in France, before returning to the good graces of the government at home.

Dudley was tall for his time, with a swarthy complexion, and kept himself in shape by horseback riding, hunting, jousting, tennis, and fishing. His fine physique was complemented by intelligence and a sense of humor, all qualities which appealed to Elizabeth. As her biographer Paul Johnson notes, for her Dudley "represented the pleasure-principle as well as the duty-principle; he could switch from affairs of state to the latest entertainment . . . and back again, without changing gear—and Elizabeth always liked to mingle business with pleasure."[1] No sooner had she become queen, than she made him her Master of Horse, an important position in which he supervised the breeding, training, and housing of approximately 275 horses in the queen's stables.[2] This position also enabled him to be close to her and the court. Unfortunately, such proximity led to behavior that, however innocent, caused much comment at home and abroad. Count de Feria, the Spanish ambassador, who was a great gossip, wrote in April 1559: "During the last few days Lord Robert has come so much into favour that he does whatever he likes with affairs and it is

Robert Vaughan. Robert Dudley, Earl of Leicester (ca.1625). Engraving. STC 7758.3 v.3 no.11.

even said that her Majesty visits him in his chamber day and night."[3]

Most of Elizabeth's suitors over the years were foreign royalty or nobility—Philip of Spain, Eric of Sweden, Archduke Charles of Austria, Henry duke of Anjou and Francis duke of Alençon from France, among others—but Dudley was the only serious English candidate. He also was probably the person whom Elizabeth was most drawn to marry, had that been possible. She once said that "she has taken a vow to marry no man whom she has not seen, and will not trust portrait painters...."[4] Dudley, however, was already married to Amy Robsart, and the mysterious circumstances surrounding her death in 1560 did not make it possible for Elizabeth to marry him "on the rebound," as we would say. Furthermore, Dudley was disliked by a lot of people at court, including Cecil, Elizabeth's chief Secretary. Part of this dislike was no doubt jealousy, but part was due to a real strain of deceit on Dudley's part. In 1561–62, however, the desire to have the queen choose *someone* to marry in order to secure the succession led to some support for Dudley. He tried to help his own cause by sponsoring entertainments at Twelfth Night in 1562, ending with a masque of "Beauty and Desire" "in which Lady Beauty (signifying Elizabeth) was successfully courted by Desire (Dudley), and wed in the Temple of Pallas." This conceit was followed by a dance in which Dudley himself as the Christmas Prince asked the queen to dance.[5] When it became known that Dudley had sought Spanish Catholic help in his suit to the queen, however, Elizabeth realized that an alliance with him would compromise her reputation abroad. And furthermore, Dudley's actions had made English Protestants suspicious of him.[6] The match was off. His sponsorship of entertainments, however, points to his lifelong interest in supporting the arts. He was patron to writers and scholars, amassed an important collection of paintings, and supported the first "official" acting company in England—the Earl of Leicester's Men—established in 1574 and headed by Richard Burbage.

Elizabeth had created Robert Dudley "Earl of Leicester" in 1564, partly to make him more attractive as a match for Mary, Queen of Scots. But neither Leicester nor Mary wanted the match, and in the event, she married Lord Darnley. Leicester kept hoping that Elizabeth would have him, but while she bestowed licenses and manors on him and made him high steward of Cambridge University and chancellor of Oxford, she had evidently decided that marriage was one honor she could not accord him. Though Leicester was contracted to Douglas Sheffield in 1573, and married Lettice Knollys in 1578, he and the queen seem to have had an emotional tie which could not be broken, in spite of some stormy disagreements.

In 1584 a virulently libelous pamphlet about Leicester, entitled *Leicester's Commonwealth*, appeared. Printed in France, the book was smuggled into England where it was confiscated and the government authorities tried to track down its source. Scholarship on the book has verified what Elizabeth's Secretary, Francis Walsingham, had surmised, that it was written by a group of disaffected English Catholic ex-courtiers, including Charles Arundell, Lord Paget, Thomas Fitzherbert and others.[7] According to D. C. Peck, who has recently edited the volume, its authors harbored a personal hatred against Leicester, but they also wanted to use him as a scapegoat for rising religious tensions in England caused by anxiety about Mary, Queen of Scots, and her attempt at the English throne. Beginning in the 1570s, Leicester had thrown his support to the staunchly Protestant faction at court, thus exacerbating Catholic dislike of him. Though copies

Top: Leycesters Common-wealth.... (Printed 1641). L968.8, title page.

Bottom: Robert Dudley, Earl of Leicester. Autograph letter, signed, to Queen Elizabeth I. From Tilbury (August 3, 1588). Folger MS Add 1006.

The right Hon.ble Robert Dudley Earle of Leicester, Baron of Denbigh, knight of the noble order of St. George & St. Michall, and late one of her Ma.ties ho.ble privy counsell etc.

W Marshall sculpsit.

LEYCESTERS Common-wealth:

CONCEIVED, SPOKEN, AND

published with most earnest protestation of all dutifull good will and affection towards this Realme;

For whose good onely it is made common to many.

Iob 20.27.

The heavens shall reveale his iniquity, and the earth shall rise up against him.

Printed, 1641.

I am loth my most dere La. to trouble you
w[ith] out some speciall cause, w[hi]ch at this tyme
god be thanked, ther ys none [illegible]
here but all things as well as [illegible] & as
forwardly bent to yo[u]r s[er]vice as any soldyers
or subjects in y[e] world cā be. but yet
I may not forgett to offer my bounde dewty to yo[ur]
[illegible] moost swete self, all humble & dutyfull
thanks for y[e] greate comfort I ever hadd fro
yo[u]r owne swete self. I am sorry that
I cā wryte yo[u] nothing worth, yet most
glad yt I may hold by any hand to god
for y[e] rightfull dealing he hath towards
you, for [illegible] he fighteth
for you & yo[u]r enemyes fall before you.
Lett all good prayse & glory be geven him
therfor, & loose not gracious La. any occasion
[illegible] against [illegible] enemyes & you.
[illegible]
[illegible]
[illegible]
[illegible]
[illegible] I think. [illegible]
[illegible]
[illegible]
[illegible] god evermore preserve
my most dere La. [illegible]
[illegible]
[illegible] from Tylbury this saturday
[illegible]

by yo[u]r most faythfull & most
obedient [illegible]

R. Leycester

were confiscated at the time, the book—as many scandalous pieces do—took on a longer life, and was republished later in the seventeenth century.

It is true that Leicester tended to be vain, impetuous, and bad at following orders. In 1585 Elizabeth made him Lieutenant-General of the forces she was sending to relieve the Netherlands in their fight with Catholic Spain, though she almost reversed herself at the last minute, as she didn't want him to go. He set off in great style and received a warm and festive welcome from the Dutch, who also pressed him to take on the position of Governor of the United Provinces of the Netherlands. This was beyond his stated duty, and Elizabeth was furious when the news reached her. Her counselors, as well as the Dutch, urged her to agree to the position so that the real business of war with Spain could get underway. Elizabeth *did* agree, but Leicester's subsequent attempts in the field were disastrous, and his recall to the Netherlands in 1587 accomplished little.

By this time, however, England itself faced serious threats from Spain where Philip hoped to claim the English throne.[8] Leicester was made "Lieutenant and Captain General of the Queen's armies" and in August of 1588 as he waited at Tilbury with 12,500 English troops for the arrival of the Spanish, he wrote a letter—one of his last—to Elizabeth.[9] This remarkable document is now in the Folger Library; it is remarkable because it combines an official report with an intimate tone. He says that all is "well" and "quyett" with the army, and that he is "sorry that I can wryte your majestie no newes," but he just wants to tell her "all humble & dutyful thankes for your great comfort I receive ever from your own swete self." He speaks of Lord Ormond and Mr. Stanhope who have come to review the troops, and he ends the letter, "god ever more preserve my moost dere Lady that she may to ye comfort of his people & Church end in peace as she hath begoun . . . in some hast from Tylbury this saturday by your most faythfull & most obedient ["Eyes" symbol] R. Leycester." Twice in the text he puts little eye-brows over the o's in "moost" and he draws eyes before his signature at the end, intimate reminders of the Queen's nickname for him, her "Eyes." The letter was written shortly before Elizabeth herself visited Tilbury and delivered her famous speech to the troops. One month later, Leicester died, not fighting the Spanish, but fighting a fever at home in bed. He was fifty-five years old. Elizabeth was grief-stricken, shutting herself away for days to mourn in privacy. At some point she must have realized that the two of them would never have got on as man and wife—they were too much alike in some respects, and the political obstacles would have been great—but over the years they grew with each other, and he came closest to being the husband she might have had.

The young man who stepped in to help fill the void left by Leicester was his stepson, Robert Devereux, Earl of Essex. In 1588 he was twenty-two, handsome, intelligent, impetuous and head-strong—and already a favorite with the queen. People noted that she always had him about her when she went out, and at court the two of them stayed up until all hours playing cards and other games. Essex's mother was Lettice Knollys, who had married the Earl of Leicester in 1578 when Essex was twelve, after the death of her first husband, Walter Devereux, in 1576. Essex's sister Penelope married Lord Rich, but she was admired by Sir Philip Sidney who addressed his sonnet sequence to her. Essex himself was raised in the household of Lord Burghley, Elizabeth's Secretary of State, and then did a degree at Trinity College, Cambridge.

What we see in Essex is a young man who wanted to serve the queen, but who was impatient to be out doing things, rather than hanging around court, and who was quickly jealous of any

School of Nicholas Hilliard. Lettice Knollys, Countess of Leicester (ca. 1590–95). Watercolor on vellum. Art Acc no. 231301.

favors she showed towards others. He was always picking quarrels with Walter Raleigh, and after the queen made Essex stay at court during the Armada episode, he ran off with Drake and Norris on an expedition to Portugal, from which she angrily demanded his return. About a year later in 1590 he again incurred her rage by secretly marrying Frances Walsingham, widow of Sir Philip Sidney. Elizabeth did not take kindly to many of the marriages made by her courtiers, probably feeling jealous that *she* was not the main focus of their attention. In any case, Essex was able to placate her by agreeing that his wife would live with her mother.

Essex was wary of the continuing influence of the Cecils at court, and began to surround himself with others who eventually formed an anti-Cecil faction. Two of his good friends were the Bacon brothers, Francis and Anthony, who introduced him to the world of foreign politics, and Essex supported Francis in his applications for legal offices at court, but to no avail. By the mid-1590s, however, Essex's favor with the queen was high, and she agreed that he could lead an expedition against Spain. She even wrote a prayer on the occasion, asking God "to prosper the work and with best forewinds guide the journey, speed the victory, and make the return the advancement of Thy glory, the triumph of their fame, and surety to the realm, with the least loss of English blood."[10] Essex took Cadiz, but was prevented by his colleagues from intercepting the Spanish treasure fleet, which, as it turned out, he probably could have done. The Cadiz expedition was the most successful of Essex's martial enterprises. His voyage to the Azores in 1597 with a similar goal was a failure, but it was his expedition to Ireland in 1599 that proved the most disastrous to his career.

Essex left for Ireland with many hopes that he would at last be able to deal with these recalcitrant people. At first he had some success, but finally after setbacks and arguments with the queen, Essex took it upon himself to meet personally and agree to a treaty with Tyrone, a powerful Gaelic lord. Learning of the queen's great anger, Essex rushed back from Ireland and entered her chamber early in the morning to try to vindicate himself. But he was too late. Essex was charged by Elizabeth's council and put under house arrest. During that winter of 1599–1600 he became very ill. His sister, Penelope Devereux, Lady Rich, wrote on his behalf to the queen, asking for her leniency, and asking to be allowed to visit him, but she was refused. One of her letters is copied out in a manuscript commonplace book belonging to Francis ap Rice, now at the Folger Library. Lady Rich writes of "those Combining enimyes that labour vpon false ground[es] to build his ruyne [ruin]," and she asks Elizabeth to intercede on his behalf: "yo[u]r maiesties grac[i]ous conclusion in giving hope of the victory is all the Comfort I haue." At the same time, she is realistic about the chances of her brother's full re-instatement at court:

And soe his blemished reputac[i]on must disable him for euer serving againe his sacred goddesse whose ex[c]ellent be[a]utyes and perfecc[i]ons will neuer suffer those faire eyes to tourne so farre from Compassion but that at the least if hee may not retourne to the happines of his former seruice to liue at the feete of his admired mistres yet he may sit downe by a priuate life without his imputac[i]ons of infamye.[11]

This letter was also published in one edition of a little pamphlet, *An Apologie of the Earle of Essex, against those which falsly and maliciously taxe him to be the onely hinderer of the peace, and quiet of his countrey*. The *Apologie* was written by Essex in the form of a letter to Anthony Bacon

The manner of Robert Earle of Essex his execcution.

On wensday next followinge beeinge the xvᵗʰ of ffebruary Anᵒ Dm 1601 Comonly called Ashwensday in the morninge about one of the Clock the Liutenant of the Towre gaue warninge to the Earle of Essex to prepare himselfe for Execution wᶜʰ should be donne on him the same day followinge as it appeared by a warrant signed to that effect he beinge then in bed presently vpon notice hereof arose Doctor Mountford, Doctor Barlow & mr Asheton his Chapline beinge wᵗʰ him and therewithall desired them to ioyne wᵗʰ him in those Exercises that might best befitt him vnto his death so nere approachinge wᵉᵗᵒ vnto they most willingly condescended beeinge

of

of purpose appointed to be wᵗʰ him to prepare and make him steady to taste the more patiently of that his most bitter Cupp The Exercise then vsed was partly prayer penitent Confessions and Comfortable psalmes The latter of wᶜʰ was performed by mr Asheton at the request of the other Deanes And thus was the tyme spent vntill the morninge wen as the wofull howre drue nere for the finishinge of his Course And now the tyme beinge Come and all thinges prepared for the execution to be donne wen the Towre beheld the howre of say of em of the Clocke in the morninge the Earle was brought by the Liutenant of the Towre to the Scaffold wᶜʰ was sett vp in the large Court where he standes

B   standes

and printed first in 1600 with Penelope Rich's letter. Evidence suggests that Essex had not wanted it to be printed – he probably intended for its circulation in manuscript among some friends. In May 1600, Rowland White wrote to Robert Sidney saying that Essex is "much troubled" by the printing "and has sent to the Stationers to suppress them, for it is done without his knowledge." In a second letter that month he adds, "The Queen is offended that this Apology of peace is printed; for of 200 copies only 8 is hard [heard] of. Yt is sayd that my Lady Riches letter to her Majesty is alsoe printed, which is an exceeding wrong donne to the Earle of Essex."[12] Copies of the pamphlet were evidently withdrawn quickly, and a second edition was not published until 1603, after the earl's death, and possibly after Elizabeth's as well.

In June 1600 Essex was tried on three counts: invading Munster when he had been told by the Irish council not to; making a treaty with Tyrone; and abandoning his post to come back to England. He was put under house arrest again, and eventually freed, but his attempts at gaining the queen's good graces failed. It is hard not to feel that at this point something in Essex snapped; he lost all sense of judgment and decided that he could use force to win his way back into court. In January of 1601 he conspired with a band of friends to force their way in to the queen and demand that she dismiss her counselors. When they realized that the government had wind of the plot, they hurriedly grouped to carry it out on Sunday, February 8. The day before, they watched a production of Shakespeare's old play, *King Richard II*, which they had commissioned to be performed, remembering its scene of the deposing of a king.[13] On Sunday they rode through London, expecting to pick up support from the citizens, but though Essex was a popular man, Londoners were too sensible to back such a fool-hardy scheme. The whole group of them was arrested and imprisoned.

A listing of their distribution among several London prisons is given in Francis ap Rice's manuscript, along with a detailed account of the trial and execution of Essex. He had been sentenced to be hanged and quartered, but when the time came to sign his death warrant, Elizabeth wavered.[14] She finally agreed, and "on Wensday. . .beeing the xvth of ffebruary. . .1601 Com[m]only Called Ashwensday in the morning about one of the Clocke The Luietenant of the Towre gaue warning to the Earle of Essex to prepare himselfe for Execuc[i]on w[hi]ch should be donne on him the same day." The original sentence had been commuted to beheading. As Essex came to the scaffold, wearing "a blacke veluet gowne & a suite of blacke Satten. . .he earnestly desired [th]e people to pray for him." In his last words, he admitted that he had been "honorably tryed and iustly Condemned" of "this sinne against my Souereigne." "Yet," he continued, "I protest I neuer meant hurt to my Souereigne her person, or dignity."[15] The queen had now lost the last of her favorites, but as Anne Somerset has pointed out, "if she grieved at having lost him, she never doubted that she had had no option but to proceed with his execution."[16]

In his recent study of Essex, the historian Paul Hammer writes that while "many observers. . . expected Essex to become another Leicester," that would never have happened. For one thing, their styles were completely different. "Whereas his stepfather had used his favour with Elizabeth to build up enormous political influence over a period of three decades, Essex sought to make an impact in a few short years." In contrast to Leicester's courtly skills, Essex affected "a soldierly bluntness which sometimes jarred with the expectations of Elizabeth and his fellow courtiers." Essex had high ideals of virtue which he attempted to pursue through war, but when things did not go well, he had difficulties, for he could not "accept anything short of success."[17]

Francis ap Rice. Collection of writings relating to the trial of the earl of Essex (1601). Folger MS V.a.164, fol. 87.

The spectacular rise and fall of Essex has about it the quality of one of Marlowe's or Shakespeare's flawed heroes. Like Faustus or Tamburlaine he was an "overreacher," and like Richard II or Anthony he lacked the self-discipline to shape and control his behavior. Shakespeare had had great hopes for him at the time of his going into Ireland, referring to Essex in *Henry V*:

Were now the general of our gracious empress,

As in good time he may, from Ireland coming,

Bringing rebellion broachèd on his sword,

How many would the peaceful city quit

To welcome him! (Act 5 Prologue, lines 31–35)[18]

But instead, Ireland was the beginning of his end.

Thomas Cockson. Robert Devereux, 2nd earl of Essex (ca.1599/1600). Engraving. STC 7758.3 v.3 no.13

1   Paul Johnson, *Elizabeth I: a Study in Power and Intellect* (London: Futura, 1976), 125. For the general biographical outline of the lives of Leicester and Essex, I have used the *Dictionary of National Biography* (rpt. 1959–60).

2   Anne Somerset, *Elizabeth I* (New York: St. Martin's, 1991), 115–16, 111.

3   *Calendar of Letters and State Papers. . .preserved principally in the Archives of Simancas*, vol. 1, 1558–1567, ed. Martin A. S. Hume (London: HMSO, 1892), 57. Referred to as *CSPS*.

4   *CSPS*, vol. 1 (1558–1567), 70.

5   Susan Doran, *Monarchy and Matrimony: the Courtships of Elizabeth I* (London; New York: Routledge, 1996), 57.

6   Doran, *Monarchy*, 59.

7   *Leicester's Commonwealth*, ed. D. C. Peck (Athens, OH: Ohio University Press, 1985), 6, 31.

8   Somerset, *Elizabeth I*, 445.

9   Somerset, *Elizabeth I*, 463.

10 Elizabeth I, *Works*, 426.

11 Folger MS V.a.164, fols. 120v, 121v, 121v–122r.

12 Historical Manuscripts Commission, *Report on the Manuscripts of Lord De L'Isle & Dudley*, vol. 2, ed. C. L. Kingsford (London: HMSO, 1934), 459, 461.

13 Scholars have questioned whether the play was Shakespeare's or another based on a book about Henry IV by John Hayward. See Ray Heffner, "Shakespeare, Hayward, and Essex," PMLA 45 (1930): 754–80; and Leeds Barroll, in "A New History for Shakespeare and His Time," *Shakespeare Quarterly*, 39 (1988): 441–64.

14 For the original sentence, see Robert Lacey, *Robert Earl of Essex* (London: Weidenfeld & Nicolson, 1971), 309–10. Essex also meanly laid blame on his sister, Penelope: "'I must accuse one who is most nearest to me, my sister who did continually urge me on with telling how my friends and followers thought me a coward, and that I had lost all my valour'" (quoted in Lacey, 313).

15 V.a.164, fols. 86v, 87v, 88v. The actual year of the execution was 1600 old style.

16 Somerset, *Elizabeth I*, 552.

17 Paul E. J. Hammer, *The Polarisation of Elizabethan Politics: the Political Career of Robert Devereux, 2nd Earl of Essex* (Cambridge: Cambridge Univ. Press, 1999), 401, 404.

18 While generally thought to refer to Essex, the lines may refer to Lord Mountjoy instead. See William Shakespeare, *The Life of Henry V*, ed. Barbara Mowat and Paul Werstine (New York: Washington Square Press, 1995), 242–43.

Robert Devereux, earl of Essex (1566–1601)
An apologie of the Earle of Essex . . . penned by himselfe in anno 1598
London: Richard Bradocke, 1603
STC 6788, c.1

Leycesters common-wealth
Printed 1641
L968.8

Francis ap Rice
Collection of writings relating to the trial of the earl of Essex
1601
Folger MS V.a.164

Robert Dudley, Earl of Leicester (1532?–1588)
Autograph letter, signed, to Queen Elizabeth I
From Tilbury [August 3, 1588]
Folger MS Add 1006

School of Nicholas Hilliard
Lettice Knollys, Countess of Leicester
Watercolor on vellum
ca.1590–95
ART 231301

Robert Vaughan
(ca.1600–ca.1660)
Robert Dudley, earl of Leicester
Engraving
ca.1625
STC 7758.3 v.3 no.11

Thomas Cockson
(fl. ca.1591–1636?)
Robert Devereux, 2nd earl of Essex
Engraving, ca.1599/1600
STC 7758.3 v.3 no.13

Studio of Marcus Gheeraerts, the Younger
Robert Devereux, 2nd Earl of Essex
Oil on wood, 1596/1601
National Gallery of Art
Gift of Mrs. Henry R. Rea
1947.18.1

POSVI DEVM ADIVTOREM MEVM

HONI SOIT QVI MAI Y PENSE

SEMPER EADEM

Aetatis anno
MIserICorDIæ.

Nata Grenewiciæ
anno Christi
MDXXXIII.
6. Id. Sept.

Elizabeth's Wardrobe

ELIZABETH STANDS IN HER PORTRAITS AS AN ENIGMA, her white face showing little expression, but her power and authority are evoked in all the splendid costumes and their surrounding mythic symbolism. These images are familiar to us: the rich black gown with white sleeves and forepart embroidered with suns in the Armada portrait; the jewelled white silk gown of the Ditchley portrait where she dwarfs the land of England at her feet; the orange-tawny cloak of the Rainbow portrait, curiously embroidered with eyes and ears—and pearls, ropes of them hanging down to her waist, dripping from her collars, outlining the sleeves of her gown, and nestling in her auburn hair. Queen Elizabeth's self-fashioning literally involved the use of "fashion." She dressed to be seen; her clothes made a statement about her power as a female ruler and about the stability and strength of her nation. Their impact was not lost, as testified in the reports of various foreign visitors to the English court, such as the German Paul Hentzner, writing in 1598 when Elizabeth was sixty-five. After noting her red wig and rich drop pearls in her ears he says:

Her Bosom was uncovered, as all the English ladies have it, till they marry; and she had on a Necklace of exceeding fine jewels . . . her Stature neither tall nor low; her air was stately, . . . That day she was dressed in white Silk, bordered with pearls the size of beans, and over it a Mantle of black silk, shot with silver threads; her Train was very long, and the end of it born by a Marchioness; instead of a Chain she had an oblong Collar of gold and jewels. As she went along in all this state and magnificence, she spoke very graciously, first to one, then to another, whether foreign Ministers, or those who attended for different reasons, in English, French, and Italian. . . . The Ladies of the Court followed next to her, very handsome and well-shaped, and for the most part dressed in white . . . .[1]

The queen's clothing and jewelry, as well as her manner, her linguistic skills, and the rich appearance of her courtiers combined to create an image of civilized courtly power.

Crispin van de Passe. Queen Elizabeth I (1603–04). Engraving, after painting by Isaac Oliver. STC 7758.3 v.3 no.2.

The creation of the queen's appearance, however, was no simple task. It took hours to construct and involved dozens of people to make and care for the thousands of costume pieces and jewels. If we ask, how many dresses did the queen have, there is no simple answer, for each dress or costume was composed of many interchangeable parts. Two inventories of the queen's wardrobe survive from the year 1600. The larger lists "the contents of the Wardrobe of Robes remaining in the Tower of London" and at Court. The other, now at the Folger Library, lists "items remaining in the Office of the Wardrobe of Robes near Baynard's Castle."[2] Within these, each type of costume piece is listed separately, and taken together, the inventories provide the following numbers: 128 French gowns, 81 round gowns, 127 loose gowns, 149 kirtles, 193 foreparts, and 152 petticoats. These are in addition to the robes, cloaks, mantles, doublets, fans, buttons and jewelry. Janet Arnold reckons that the two inventories combined record "over 1,900 pieces of clothing and jewels."[3]

Before looking at these items and their construction in more detail, it may be helpful to review what some of them were. The language of costume is ever-changing, and an Elizabethan kirtle is no more a 1940s girdle than a petticoat is a slip. "French gown" seems to refer to a basic gown that probably originally came from France but later incorporated designs from other countries. It generally had a back hem trailing on the ground, while "round gowns" had even hems, and both were worn over other garments as a kind of outer dress.[4] "'Loose gown' seems to be a generic term for over-gowns," which "might fall loosely from shoulders to hem" or "might be fitted at the waist."[5] Generally they were worn over "kirtles," which were bodices with skirts attached. Arnold notes that kirtles were "usually worn with an overgown, as the backs were often made with different materials and obviously not intended to be seen."[6] "Forepart" can "refer to the front part of a gown, kirtle or sleeve" but "when used alone . . . usually refers to the detachable portion of the front skirt."[7] "Petticoats" were underskirts, "usually richly decorated and intended to be seen."[8] Women of this period dressed in several layers, beginning with linen drawers, smock, and stockings, along with farthingales—a kind of hoop skirt—when in fashion, over which would be placed some combination of the above petticoats, kirtles, and gowns, along with sleeves, ruffs, and jewelry. The smocks, made of fine linen, were often embroidered around the collar and cuffs, as they frequently showed beneath sleeves and kirtle, doublet or jacket. The various pieces of dress were tied or pinned together.

Elizabeth was interested in keeping up-to-date on European fashions, frequently using her male political agents to send her information or even pieces of clothing. In 1567, Elizabeth tried—via her secretary Cecil and her newly-named ambassador to France, Sir Henry Norris—to import a French tailor. When that didn't work, arrangements were made to send over French gowns which were reworked for her, and finally her tailor sent patterns so that a French tailor could make up a gown to fit.[9] In 1577, Sir Francis Walsingham corresponded with ambassador Amyas Paulet, who sent over a gown for the queen, followed by a farthingale "'such as is now used by the French Queen and the Queen of Navarre.'"[10] Four years later, Walsingham received a letter from Henry Cobham, reporting on the reception at the French court of a portrait of Elizabeth that had been painted by Catherine de Médicis' own painter, sent over to England. "The great princesses did note and weare very muche satisfied to see her Majestie [Elizabeth] appareled and attyred all over alla francoyse."[11] The 1585 New Year's Gift Roll at the Folger shows that Walsingham gave Elizabeth "a ffrench goune of Russett Satten ffloryshed w[i]th Leves of Sylver . . . w[i]th pendante

Sleves Lyned w[i]th Cloth of Sylver." By this time, he must have known what she liked!

Some decorative items came to Elizabeth from her contacts in far-flung countries. In 1587, czar Ivan the Terrible of Russia sent her many rich goods including four bales of black sable skins (40 skins per bale), "six white well grown spotted" lynx, and two "gowns of white ermines."[12] In 1599 there is record of an even more unusual exchange. Elizabeth had sent an ambassador to the kingdom of Turkey. On his return, he brought back gifts from the Sultana Mother of Turkey, as detailed in a letter to Elizabeth written on behalf of the Sultana by a Jewish woman, Esperanza Malchi. She writes that the Sultana is sending "a robe and a girdle, and two kerchiefs wrought in gold, and three wrought in silk, after the fashion of this kingdom, and a necklace of pearls and rubies," also "a wreath of diamonds from the jewels of her Highness" [i.e. the Sultana]. In return, Esperanza asks that Elizabeth send "cloths of silk or wool" and especially, "distilled waters of every description for the face, and odiferous oils for the hands." She adds, "your Majesty would favor me by transmitting some by my hand for this most serene Queen; by my hand, as, being articles for ladies, she does not wish them to pass through other hands."[13] Such cosmetic waters and oils may have been supplied by the queen's own apothecaries, one of whom was a woman. In the 1585 Gift Roll, "Mrs Morgaynne a potty-cary" is listed as presenting the queen with peaches and candied green ginger.

Elizabeth's courtiers tried hard to choose gifts that they thought would especially please her, partly because they wanted recognition for themselves as well. The earl of Leicester—definitely a favorite but not always in her favor—gave Elizabeth in 1585 a tan colored nightgown (meaning a loose gown often worn at home), lined with carnation velvet and decorated with buttons and loops of Venice gold and plaited lace, along with a sable skin, each foot covered with gold and "fournyshed w[i]th Dyamond[es] and Rubyes." That was especially generous. Others may not have spent as much, but they were equally eager to please. The Folger Library has several letters sent by Sir Anthony Wingfield and his wife Elizabeth, concerning what kind of gift Elizabeth, countess of Shrewsbury, should give to the queen for New Year's 1576. Beginning in October 1575, Sir Anthony at court had consulted with the Ladies Cobham and Sussex about the gift. One suggested a gold cup, the other an embroidered cloak. The cloak won out, and in December, Sir Anthony wrote more details to his wife, saying that the cloak should be of a light blue satin, "be caues she [the queen] hathe no garmente off that collore," and the border or "guard" of carnation velvet should be embroidered with pansies of various colors, trimmed with gold, silver, and small pearls, as "[th]e quene lekes byst off that floware." The gift was a great hit. Elizabeth Wingfield wrote to the Countess of Shrewsbury on January 2 to tell her about its reception:

Elizabeth Wingfield. Autograph letter, signed, to Elizabeth, Countess of Shrewsbury (January 2, 1576 or 1577). Folger MS X.d.428 (130).

"furst her ma[jestie] neuer liked any thinge you gaue her so well the color and strange [unusual] triminge of the garments . . . hath caused her to geue out such good speches of my lo[rd] and your la[dyship] as I neuer hard of better[.] she toulde my lo[rd] of Lester and my lo[rd] chamberlen that you had geven her such garments thys yere as she neuer had any so well lyked her and sayd that good nobell copell [couple] the[y] show in al things what loue the[y] bere me . . ."[14]

Elizabeth had a considerable staff to handle her wardrobe, some of whom seem to have worked for her over a number of years. The Great Wardrobe, which dealt with her clothing, as well as "gifts of clothing for her ladies," and liveries for those who were in her service, was a subdepartment of the Wardrobe of Robes. Another sub-department, the Removing Wardrobe of Beds, dealt with the household furnishings such as beds, cushions, rugs, et cetera that moved with the queen from palace to palace. The queen's chief tailor from 1557 to 1582 was Walter Fyshe. There were also a couple of men who specialized in alterations. Fyshe made garments for the queen as well as garments she ordered as gifts for others. Elizabeth was not wasteful. Garments were frequently made over for her, or remade and given to her ladies. She also gave some of her jewels as gifts. Fyshe was succeeded by another tailor, William Jones, who made the rainbow robe given to Elizabeth during her progress to Harefield.[15]

In addition to her tailors, there were embroiderers, hosiers, cappers, hatters, hoodmakers, shoemakers, glovers, skinners, and farthingale makers. There seem to have been three main embroiderers at any one time, all men, with David Smith doing most of the work for Elizabeth's gowns until 1587.[16] They would have used designs such as those that survive in the two books made by Thomas Trevelyon in the early 1600s. One of these books, now at the Folger Library, contains a number of embroidery designs and patterns as well as a variety of other images, and was compiled in 1608 when Trevelyon was sixty. Not much is known about Trevelyon. The family name suggests origins in Devon or Cornwall, but eventually he seems to have settled in London. "He clearly had an intimate knowledge of the London trade, in print as well as textiles," and may have employed weavers, dyers, and embroiderers himself, perhaps rising to office in a guild.[17] There are specific patterns for nightcaps, and also a number of general all-over patterns, similar to those seen on Elizabeth's gowns or foreparts.

In addition to clothing embroidered by her own staff, Elizabeth received a number of gifts of

Above: Diego de Freyle. *Geometria y Traça para el Oficio de los Sastres* (Seville, 1588). TT575 F8 1588 Cage, sig. A2r.

Opposite: Thomas Trevelyon. Embroidery pattern. *Commonplace Book* (1608). Folger MS V.b.232, fol. 254r.

Elizabeth R

By Sr Thomas Bromley knyght Lord Chauncelor of England in gold and Sylver   Cviij oz

By the Lorde Bowrghley Lord Hygh Threasorer of England in gold   xxti

By the Lord Marques of Wynchester in gold   xxti   { delyvred tolfd gold of the prevey chamber

By the Erle of Lecetor Lorde Steward of the Howssholde A Refegonne of Larmy wroughte wellat one the owtt syde the Insyde beyng Carnation vngornyst wellat bonnd A bobbe wth A Byllimentt lace and Buttons and Lowpes of venys gold and plate lace   delyvred gyftz yeoman of the robes

By the said Erle geven morr A Table Clocke the hed and fowre featte of gold fully fornnyshed wth Dyamondz and Rubys of Sundry sortes

By the Erle of Arrundell A Carkynett of gold conteyning seven peces of gold Cvy trulowesye of smanll sparkes of Dyamondz and many perlle of Sundry bygnes and smaell sparkes of Rubys   delyvered Lady Howard

By the Erle of Shrowesbury in gold   xxti

By the Erle of Darby in gold   xxti   { delyvred forsaid gewes Ratfiord

By the Erle of Sussex in gold   xxti

By the Erle of Lyncolne in gold   xxti

By the Erle of Warwyke A Carkynett of gold conteyning Eyghtene peces Engst sett wth thre smanll Rubys A pece and Engst sett wth smanll perlle lyke knotte   delyvred Barrowe geward

By the Erle of Rutland in gold   xxti

By the Erle of Bedford in gold   xxti   { delyvred forsaid Ratfiord

By the Erle of Huntington in gold   xxti

By the Erle of Pembroke A serparte of whyte Satten enbraudered wth Egentyne flowers and other   delyvred forsaid Ranyf Cope

By the Erle of Bathe in gold   xxti

By the Erle of Combberland A Iwell of gold beyng A Orale garnyshed one the brest and Eris wth Opall and Emroddis   delyvered in thandes to Mr Blanche Parye

By the Erle of Hertff A Doblett of pergrolored Satten enbraudered wth Lase of venys gold and whyte   delyvred forsaid Ranyf Cope

By the vecount Mountagu in gold   xti

Earles &
Vicount

By the Inges of Emmersett in gold   Cm vy oz

By the Lady Marques of Northampton A manlle of Carne Sortworke wth Syze and Olenlews wth A ... Satten vnder the forsaid flesh in gold plate of Sundry bygnes bonnd A sherman marked poz   delyvred forsaid Ranyf Cope

Elizabeth R

embroidered garments, some done professionally, others the work of her ladies. Examples may again be found in the 1585 Gift Roll: from the Baroness Hunsdon, "parte of a forparte of A Kertle of Satten of Dyvers Colers embravdered w[i]th the twelve Synnes [signs of the Zodiac] w[i]th golde sylver & Sylke of dyvers Colers vnmade"; from the Dowager Baroness Chandos, two cambric pillowcases "wrought all ouer w[i]th blacke Sylke"; from Lady Catherine Constable, two fine linen smocks, "wrought with Blacke sylke"; and from Lady Sidney, "A wastcoate or Dublett of Laune [lawn] wrought w[i]th dyvers fflowers and Leves of blacke sylke venis golde [silver-gilt thread from Venice][18] and Sylver." The designation "unmade" that appears on various of the gifts indicates that the piece of material was embroidered for sleeves, or in this case a forepart, but had to be cut out and sewn to fit. Since outfits were constructed of many pieces, and the queen had her own tailors, this type of gift made sense.

The continuing popularity of blackwork embroidery may be seen in several of these gifts. This style of embroidering with black thread on white cloth is traditionally thought to have been brought from Spain to England by Henry VIII's first queen, Catharine of Aragon. The elaborate colored designs of the signs of the Zodiac on the forepart were typical of the emblematic quality of much embroidery in the period. Other such designs appearing on Elizabeth's garments include eyes or eyes and ears, the rainbow, and pyramids. These were taken from books such as Ripa's *Iconologia*, Paradin's *Heroicall Devices*, and Whitney's *Emblems*, and would have been recognized as signifying respectively the "Art of Govern-ment," the peacefulness of her reign, and the monarch herself.[19]

Some of the undergarments, such as smocks, were given as gifts by Elizabeth's ladies, as above; others were provided by her staff. Alice and Roger Montague both embroidered smocks for her, while Alice did fine sewing, washing and starching, and Roger "supplied much of the Queen's headwear in the 1580s and 1590s, in the form of cauls, coifs, . . . and wigs."[20] As she aged, Elizabeth wore mostly red wigs to cover her own hair, but loops, curls, and even devices such as pyramids, leaves, and globes were also constructed of hair as decoration.[21] In addition, Alice Montague was known as a "silkwoman," and supposedly gave the queen her first pair of silk stockings in 1561; thereafter she continued to supply those and other stockings.[22] In the 1590s Elizabeth Rogers made and embroidered smocks and wristbands for the queen, and in 1601, Dorothy Speckard made, washed and starched items such as veils, sleeves, and ruffs. "Her first order . . . included 'one fyne sute of Ruffes', 'two chynne ruffes edged with silver', 'a fyne ruffe pynned upon a Frenche wyer with gold net spangled.'" Roger Montague also made fine sleeves and supplied ribbons and lace; mentions are made of white and silver "bone lace," a kind of lace made originally on bone bobbins.[23]

One of the most popular lace books at the time was Frederico di Vinciolo's *Les Singuliers et Nouveaux Pourtraicts*. The copy in the Folger was printed in Lyon in 1599, but the book first appeared in its French version in 1587 and went through many editions, including an English version in 1591. Vinciolo was an Italian who was probably brought to France by Catherine de

Médicis, to whom he dedicated the first edition of his book, and who herself had a large collection of lace.[24] The title page shows two women working on different kinds of lace. The book itself is in two parts: "the first of Point Coupe, or rich geometric patterns, printed in white upon black ground . . .; the second of Lacis, or subjects in squares . . . with counted stitches."[25] Designs for the latter include the seven planets personified, and a peacock, deer, unicorn, and lion. Vinciolo himself made the large starched ruffs called fraises popularized by Catherine de Médicis,[26] and several of the designs in the first part of the book look like the kind of lace found in some of Elizabeth's large collars.

Not only were special designs worked into embroidery and lace, but naturally they formed part of the jeweler's art as well. The 1585 Gift Roll includes a golden owl with opal and emerald eyes; a gold syckle and wheat shaft garnished with rubies and diamonds; and a gold necklace trimmed with rubies and small pearls spelling out the word "Durabo"—"I will endure." When Elizabeth was courting the duc d'Alençon, she called him her "frog," and received several pieces of frog jewelry, including, from him, a little gold flower "with a frogge thereon" and his picture inside. In 1587, Sir Francis Drake gave Elizabeth a fan of red and white feathers, with a diamond and mother-of-pearl moon in the handle.[27] Like Raleigh, another of her sea captains, Drake associated Elizabeth with Cynthia, the moon who guides the tides. Two other important emblems associated with Elizabeth were the phoenix and the pelican. The legendary phoenix was a bird that arose again from the ashes of its own fire. It carried a range of meanings for the queen, suggesting at once "the perpetuity of hereditary kingship," and her uniqueness and chastity. A medal was struck around 1574 showing the queen's profile on one side and a phoenix on the other. The "Phoenix Jewel," from about the same time, had a similar design. The pelican that sheds its own blood to feed its young also appeared in the queen's jewels, figuring her sacrifices for her people, as well as charity. Hilliard painted two portraits of Elizabeth, one showing a pelican jewel at her breast, the other a phoenix jewel.[28]

We are used to reading Elizabeth's portraits iconographically, but it is worth remembering that the queen herself through her elaborate wardrobe was meant to be "read" as well. We say that fashion is a "statement," but this concept was even more true in Elizabethan times, when sumptuary laws dictated what kinds of cloth or furs could be worn by what degrees of persons, and when the queen dressed in colors, embroideries and jewels whose significance could be "read" on various levels. They might make a political/personal statement, as when she dressed in black during the late summer and autumn of 1585 for the deaths of the Prince of Orange and the duc d'Alençon.[29] They might indicate her feelings towards certain donors if she especially liked to wear their gifts. They might signify aspects of her power and relationship with her people: moon, globes, tower, pelican. And finally, they might create a façade of perpetual brilliance, mystery, and youth on the body of an aging woman—the Phoenix/Queen.

1 Quoted in Janet Arnold, *Queen Elizabeth's Wardrobe Unlock'd* (Leeds: Maney, 1988), 10. This section is based almost exclusively on Arnold's exhaustive and detailed study of Elizabeth's wardrobe.

2 Arnold, 246. There are two copies of the larger inventory: MS Stowe 557 in the British Library and LR 2/121 in the Public Records Office. Transcriptions of the Stowe and Folger inventories (Folger MS V.b.72) are included in Arnold's book.

3 Arnold, 247.

4 Arnold, 114.

5 Arnold, 139.

6 Arnold, 366.

7 Arnold, 364.

8 Arnold, 369.

9 Arnold, 115–16.

10 Arnold, 122.

11 Arnold, 122.

12 Arnold, 98.

13 Arnold, 108, n37.

14 Transcribed by Arnold and discussed, 95.

15 Arnold, 163, 177–78, 180, 174, 179.

16 Arnold, 189–90.

17 Thomas Trevelyon, *The Great Book of Thomas Trevilian: a Facsimile of the Manuscript in the Wormsley Library*, intro. Nicolas Barker, vol. 1 (London: Roxburghe Club, 2000), 128.

18 Arnold, 375.

19 Arnold, 81–87.

20 Arnold 224–25.

21 Arnold, 226.

22 Arnold, 208.

23 Arnold, 225, 226.

24 Elisa Ricci, "Editor's Preface" in Frederico di Vinciolo, *Renaissance Patterns for Lace, Embroidery and Needlepoint* (New York: Dover, 1971), vi.

25 Mrs. Bury Palliser, *History of Lace*, rev. M. Jourdain and Alice Dryden (London: Sampson Low, Marston & Co., 1902), 17–18.

26 Ricci in Vinciolo, vi.

27 Arnold 76, 71.

28 Strong, *Gloriana*, 82–83.

29 Reported by the German traveler, Lupold von Wedel. In August and December 1585 he reports seeing the queen in black for these deaths of a Protestant leader and of her former French suitor. Quoted in Arnold, 6.

Diego de Freyle
Geometria y Traça para el Oficio de los Sastres
Seville: Fernando Diaz, 1588
TT575 F8 1588 Cage

Frederico di Vinciolo
(fl.1587–1599)
Les Singuliers et Nouueaux Pourtraicts . . . pour Toutes Sortes d'Ouurages de Lingerie
Lyon: Leonnard Odet, 1592–99
NK9405 V5 1592 Cage

Great Britain. Sovereigns. Elizabeth
New Year's Gift Roll, 1584/85
Folger MS Z.d.16

Thomas Trevelyon (b.ca.1548)
Embroidery pattern
Commonplace Book, 1608
Folger MS V.b.232, fol. 254v

Anthony Wingfield
(ca.1550–ca.1615)
Autograph letter, signed, to Elizabeth Wingfield
December 13, ca.1575
Folger MS X.d.428 (128)

Elizabeth Wingfield
Autograph letter, signed, to Elizabeth, Countess of Shrewsbury, January 2, [1576 or 1577]
Folger MS X.d.428 (130)

Crispin van de Passe
(ca.1565–1637)
Queen Elizabeth I
Engraving, after painting by Isaac Oliver
1603–04
STC 7758.3 v.3 no.2

Costume
Modern replica of Elizabeth's dress in the Armada Portrait, painted by
George Gower, ca.1588
On loan from Angels The Costumiers, London

Clemens et Regni moderatrix iusta Britāni
Hac forma insigni conspicienda nitet.

Ani Dni

Tristia dum gentes circum omnes bella fatigant;
Cæciq; errores toto grassantur in orbe
pace beas longa, Vera et pietate Britannos:
Iusticia moderans miti sapienter habenas:
Chara domi, celebrisq; foris, longeuaq; regnū
Hic teneas, regno tandem fruitura perenni.

1579

Elizabethan Culture

WHO CAN FORGET THE SUDDEN REVELATION OF QUEEN ELIZABETH in the audience at the Globe Theatre during a performance of *Romeo and Juliet*? That was Judi Dench, of course, playing Elizabeth in the film "Shakespeare in Love." The real Elizabeth would never have set foot in the Globe, though at least once she was spotted visiting the private Blackfriar's Theatre in London. That occasion was January 1601, only two years before her death, when the Children of the Chapel were performing.[1] Blackfriar's was not leased to Shakespeare's company until 1608, long after Elizabeth was gone. Shakespeare has been associated with Elizabeth for so long, that we tend to forget that his birth in 1564 occurred five years after she was crowned, and his career did not actually take off until the last decade of her reign, in the 1590s. That raises the question of what sorts of theatrical productions and other entertainments she would have enjoyed during the first thirty years of her reign.

Records of performances at court can be gleaned from the queen's household accounts and from the accounts of her Office of the Revels. One of the duties of that Office was to choose the plays "to be showen before her Maiestie," and most of the performances occurred in the holiday season between Christmas and the beginning of Lent.[2] The companies that performed for the queen were often the Children of Pauls' and Westminster and the Chapel—in other words, boys from those elite schools. These were joined by various companies, some from the Inns of Court and some sponsored by her courtiers, notably the earls of Leicester, Warwick and Sussex, and Lord Rich, and in 1583 by Elizabeth's own company, The Queen's Men. The titles of some of the plays performed indicate that they were part of the morality tradition—*Truth Faithfulness and Mercy, Loyalty and Beauty, The Seven Deadly Sins* —while others were based on classical tales and heroical romance—*Ajax and Ulysses, Perseus and Andromeda, Iphigenia, Philemon and Philecia*—and still others were just plain comedies—*Beauty and Housewifery, Jack and Jill*. What all these plays have in common is that they are now lost, which unfortunately is the case with many from Elizabeth's reign.[3] Those that survive include *Gorboduc*, performed at court in January 1562 by the Inner Temple. Based on early British history, the play raises the issue of succession, a risky topic at a time when Elizabeth was under pressure to marry and produce an heir. A proclamation published in 1559 at the beginning of her reign forbade any plays dealing with

Remegius Hogenberg (?). Queen Elizabeth as Patroness of Geography and Astronomy. Engraved portrait in Christopher Saxton, [*Atlas of the counties of England and Wales*] ([London, 1590?]). STC 21805.5, title page.

"matters of religion or of the governaunce of the estate of the common weale," except before "grave and discreete persons," which presumably included lawyers from the Inns of Court and the court itself.[4] A number of Latin plays were given at Oxford and Cambridge during Elizabeth's time, and some at court. In 1564 she saw a performance of *Miles Gloriosus* by the Roman writer Plautus, performed by the boys of Westminster, and received a copy of his plays, and in 1592 she attended a performance of a homegrown tragi-comedy called *Bellum Grammaticale* at Christ Church College, Oxford.[5]

A group of plays written for the Children of Paul's by John Lyly, probably the best of the early court dramatists, has also survived. Based on mythological and pastoral traditions, they contain subtle references to the queen. One of these, *Midas*, based on the story of the legendary king from Ovid's *Metamorphoses*, was performed at court in January 1590, as advertised on the title page at its publication in 1592: "Plaied Before the Queenes Maiestie Upon Twelfe Day at night." Many of Lyly's plays were topical, including veiled references to events of the time. *Midas*, written after the English defeat of the Spanish Armada in 1588, shows a tyrannical king who wants to turn all to gold, and his daughter, Sophronia, who provides the voice of wisdom in the play. According to a modern critic, "*Midas* unambiguously offers praise to England's Queen as the archetypal opposite of Midas and of Philip; her wisdom, courage, and moderation are embodied by implication in Sophronia and in the wise perspective offered by this woman on the men's world of violence and self-aggrandizement."[6]

But what of Shakespeare? Twice during the Christmas holidays of 1594/95, Shakespeare along with Will Kemp and Richard Burbage from the Lord Chamberlain's Men was summoned to perform "twoe severall comedies or Enterludes" before the queen. They were paid £20.—a good sum, equal to the yearly pay of the Stratford schoolmaster.[7] We know that *Love's Labour's Lost* and *The Merry Wives of Windsor* were both performed before the queen, because that information appears on the title pages of their first printings in 1598 and 1602 respectively. *Love's Labour's Lost*, written around 1594–95, was not performed at court until the Christmas of 1597 or 98. Undoubtedly the courtly audience understood the oblique references to Henri IV and other players in the French religious wars in the characters of the King of Navarre and his friends, Longaville, Biron, and Dumaine. The perjuries of these men in the play have a certain parallel with Henri IV's own rejection of Protestantism for Catholicism in 1593—still news when the play was written.[8] The tradition that Shakespeare wrote *The Merry Wives of Windsor* at Elizabeth's request, because she wanted to see another play with Falstaff, originated in the early eighteenth century and has no foundation. The play does seem to have been written for an occasion, however, specifically for the Feast of the Garter, celebrated at Westminster in 1597. It may have been written at the request of George Carey, second Baron Hunsdon, Lord Chamberlain (and hence patron of Shakespeare's company), who was elected to the Garter on that occasion. Mistress Quickly, disguised as Queen of the Faeries (and thus humorously as the Queen herself) gives directions near the end of the play:[9]

Search Windsor Castle, elves, within and out.

Strew good luck, oafs, on every sacred room,

That it may stand till the perpetual doom

Clockwise from top: John Lyly. *Midas. Plaied Before The Qveenes Maiestie vpon Tvvelfe Day At night.* (London, 1592). STC 17083, title page.

William Shakespeare. *A Most pleasaunt and excellent conceited Comedie, of Syr Iohn Falstaffe, and the merrie Wiues of Windsor* (London, 1602). STC 22299, title page.

William Shakespeare. *A Pleasant Conceited Comedie called, Loues labors lost* (London, 1598). STC 22294 c.1, title page.

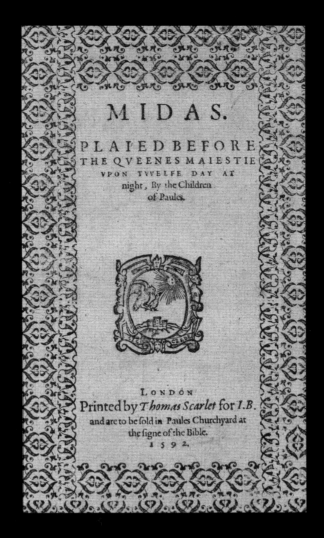

MIDAS.

PLAIED BEFORE
THE QVEENES MAIESTIE
VPON TVVELFE DAY AT
night, By the Children
of Paules.

LONDON
Printed by *Thomas Scarlet* for *I.B.*
and are to be fold in Paules Churchyard at
the figne of the Bible.
1592.

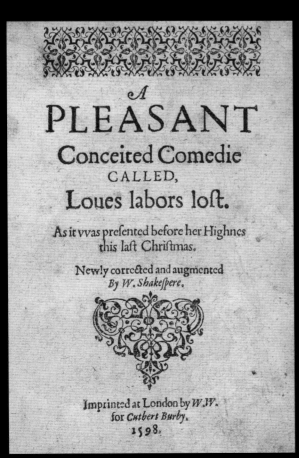

A
PLEASANT
Conceited Comedie
CALLED,
Loues labors loft.

As it vvas prefented before her Highnes
this laft Chriftmas.

Newly corrected and augmented
By *W. Shakefpere.*

Imprinted at London by *W.W.*
for *Cutbert Burby.*
1598.

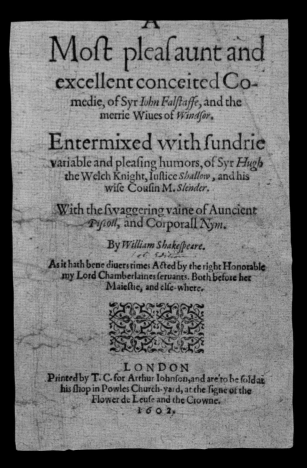

A
Moft pleafaunt and
excellent conceited Co-
medie, of Syr *Iohn Falftaffe*, and the
merrie Wiues of *Windfor.*

Entermixed with fundrie
variable and pleafing humors, of Syr *Hugh*
the Welch Knight, Iuftice *Shallow*, and his
wife Coufin M. *Slender.*

With the fwaggering vaine of Auncient
Piftoll, and Corporall *Nym.*

By *William Shakefpeare.*

As it hath bene diuers times Acted by the right Honorable
my Lord Chamberlaines feruants. Both before her
Maieftie, and elfe-where.

LONDON
Printed by T. C. for Arthur Iohnfon, and are to be fold at
his fhop in Powles Church-yard, at the figne of the
Flower de Leufe and the Crowne.
1602.

In state as wholesome as in state 'tis fit,

Worthy the owner [i.e., Elizabeth], and the owner it. (5.5.49–53)

Another "occasional" play may have been *A Midsummer Night's Dream*, written around 1595–96. Its two epilogues, one by Oberon, the other by Puck, suggest both courtly and popular audiences, and its celebration of three weddings has led scholars to attempt to find a courtly wedding as its occasion. Several have been suggested, but a likely candidate is the wedding of Elizabeth Carey and Sir Thomas Berkeley in 1596.[10] Although Elizabeth is certainly glanced at in the play as "a fair vestal virgin throned by the west" whom Cupid's dart cannot harm (2.2.157–64), and although she did attend several weddings, we do not know if she saw this play at one of them.

In 1574 and 1576, troupes of Italian players are noted at court. On the second occasion they performed a pastoral play at Reading for the queen in July, the records showing that they needed "staves, hooks, and lambskins for shepherds, [and] arrows for nymphs." The Italians also sent

acrobats, leading Thomas Norton to comment on "the unchaste, shamelesse and unnaturall tomblinge of the Italian weomen." What Elizabeth thought, if she saw them, we do not know;[11] she herself favored the dance. In 1565, a foreign visitor at court reported, "I had also seen her dancing in her apartments, some Italian dances, half Pavane and half Galliard."[12] Steps and music for these dances were available in Italian books, such as Cesare Negri's *Nuove inventioni di balli* (1604) with instructions for forty-three dances. Many of these are illustrated with pictures of the steps and include lute tablature; the second section of the book is devoted to the galliard.

The court records indicate that, in addition to plays and acrobatics, the queen saw masques, tourneys, fencing, wrestling, archery, and bull and bear baiting. It is likely that Elizabeth herself participated in archery, and we know that she loved to ride and to hunt. Three woodcuts in George

---

Above: Cesare Negri. *Nuove inventioni di balli* (Milan, 1604). GV1590 N3 Cage, sig. P2v–P3r.

Right: Queen Elizabeth taking assay of the deer. Woodcut in George Gascoigne, *The noble arte of venerie or hunting* (London, [1575]). STC 24328, sig. Fviiir.

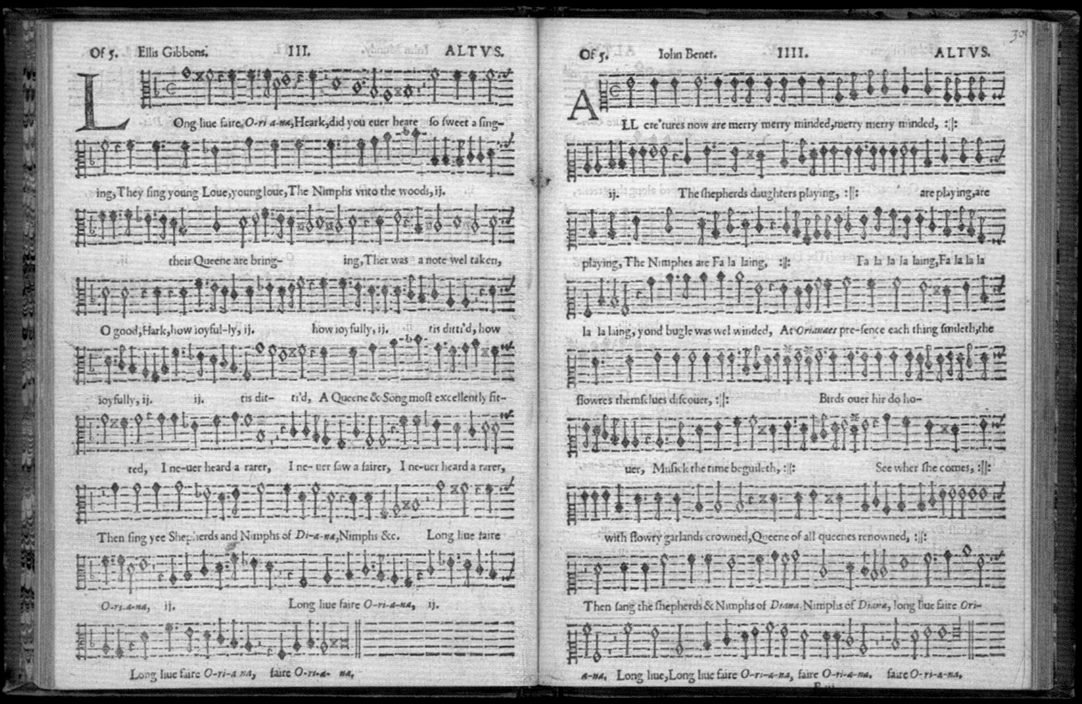
Of 5. Ellis Gibbons. III. ALTVS.
LOng liue faire, O-ri a-na, Heark, did you euer heare so sweet a sing-
ing, They sing young Loue, young loue, The Nimphs vnto the woods, ij.
their Queene are bring- ing, Ther was a note wel taken,
O good, Hark, how ioyful-ly, ij. how ioyfully, ij. tis ditti'd, how
ioyfully, ij. ij. tis dit- ti'd, A Queene & Song most excellently fit-
ted, I ne-uer heard a rarer, I ne- uer saw a fairer, I ne-uer heard a rarer,
Then sing yee Shepherds and Nimphs of Di-a-na, Nimphs &c. Long liue faire
O-ri-a-na, ij. Long liue faire O-ri-a-na, ij.
Long liue faire O-ri-a-na, faire O-ri-a- na,
Of 5. Iohn Benet. IIII. ALTVS.
ALL cre'tures now are merry merry minded, merry merry minded, :||:
ij. The shepherds daughters playing, :||: are playing, are
playing, The Nimphes are Fa la laing, :||: Fa la la la laing, Fa la la la
la la laing, yond bugle was wel winded, At Orianaes pre-sence each thing smileth, the
flowres themselues discouer, :||: Birds ouer hir do ho-
uer, Musick the time beguileth, :||: See wher she comes, :||:
with flowry garlands crowned, Queene of all queenes renowned, :||:
Then sang the shepherds & Nimphs of Diana, Nimphs of Diana, long liue faire Ori-
a-na, Long liue, Long liue faire O-ri-a-na, faire O-ri-a-na, faire O-ri-a-na.

Gascoigne's *The Noble Arte of Venerie or Hunting* (1575) show Elizabeth participating in various aspects of the hunt: sitting with her courtiers "on pleasant gladsome greene,/ Yet vnder shade of stately trees" (91); standing on a platform and being presented by her huntsman with signs of a deer's presence; and after the kill, being offered a knife by her huntsman to make the first cut in the deer. Gascoigne describes the etiquette of this last scene as follows: "The deare being layd vpon his backe, the Prince ... co[m]mes to it: And the chiefe huntsman (kneeling ...) doth holde the Deare by the forefoote, whiles the Prince ... cut a slyt drawn alongst the brysket of the deare, somewhat lower than the brysket towards the belly. This is done to see the goodnesse of the flesh ..." (134).[13]

The image of Elizabeth as virgin huntress gave rise to many references to her in poetry of the period as Diana/Cynthia, goddess of the hunt, the moon and chastity. These include such pieces as Thomas Weelkes's madrigal, "Hark, all ye lovely saints above,/ Diana hath agreed with Love/His fiery weapon to remove," and Walter Raleigh's little lyric: "Prais'd be Diana's fair and harmless light/ ... Prais'd be her power, by which all powers abound/ ...In heaven queen she is among the spheres;/ ... In her is virtue's perfect image cast."[14] The moon which directed the tides was an important image to Raleigh the sailor/explorer. At his death he left fragments of a long poem, *The Ocean to Cynthia*, which he evidently had been writing for some years. In it he attempted to work out some of his own conflicted relationship with his queen; he is the Ocean, she is his Cynthia. We hear in his words the frustration of a courtier voiced as a courtly lover:

When she did well, what did theer else amiss?
When she did ill, what empires would have pleas'd?
No other power effecting woe or bliss,
She gave, she took, she wounded, she appeas'd.

To seek new worlds for golde, for praise, for glory,
To try desire, to try love sever'd far,
When I was gone, she sent her memory,
More stronge than were ten thousand ships of war,

To call me back . . .

Thomas Weelkes's madrigal was one of many such part-songs written during Elizabeth's time, often in her praise. Perhaps the best known is a series of madrigals by various composers gathered by Thomas Morley in 1601 as *The Triumphs of Oriana*. There are twenty-five of them, "linked by the common refrain: 'Then sang the nymphs and shepherds of Diana,/ Long live fair Oriana.'"[15] Oriana was "the chaste and beautiful" love of the hero Amadis, in a French/Spanish chivalric romance, published in the early sixteenth century.[16] This popular tale was probably known to English writers through its French translation; Sidney surely had it in mind when writing his *Arcadia*. The fact that Oriana rhymes nicely with Diana and Gloriana, two of Elizabeth's literary "nicknames," only enhanced its poetic use. The lyrics of "The Triumphs" are pastoral in nature, with a variety of musical settings, ranging from sprightly to melancholy. References to Oriana as "that maiden

---

Top: Thomas Morley. *Madrigales the triumphes of Oriana* (London, [1601]). STC 18130, Altus, sig. Biiv–Biiir.

Bottom: Lute. Workshop of Michielle Harton (Padua, 1598). ART Inv. 1002.

Queen of fairyland," "A crown-graced virgin whom all people honour," and "Queen of all queens renowned," were obvious allusions to Elizabeth. The queen herself was a talented musician, playing the virginals, lyre and lute. "She 'composed ballets and music, and played and danced them.'" She also instituted a series of "free concerts of music to be held at the Royal Exchange [in London], every Sunday and holiday from Lady Day [probably August 15] through Michaelmas [September 25]."[17]

Pastoral themes and direct or veiled references to the queen pervade the works of two of the greatest poets of Elizabeth's time, Sir Philip Sidney and Edmund Spenser. In spite of their connections with the Leicester circle, both men were foiled in their attempts to receive positions at court; Sidney fought on the Protestant side in the Netherlands, where he was fatally wounded at the age of thirty-two, and Spenser became an exile in Ireland after serving there as secretary to the Lord Deputy. Difficulties often encourage creativity, however. When he died, Sidney left a prose treatise, *Apologie for Poetry*, along with a sonnet sequence, *Astrophel and Stella*, and pieces of a long prose romance, the *Arcadia*. All three are major contributions respectively to the history of English literary criticism, to English poetry, and to the development of the English novel. In addition, Sidney scripted tiltyard shows for Elizabeth and wrote an entertainment called *The Lady of May* for her visit to his uncle, the Earl of Leicester, in 1578.

Sidney wrote the first version of the *Arcadia* when he was in his early twenties; he describes its composition to his sister Mary, reminding her that it was "done in loose sheets of paper, most of it in your presence, the rest by sheets sent unto you as fast as they were done."[18] This method of composition suggests that it was read in installments, by herself or by Sidney to her and her ladies when he was present, and we do know that it circulated in a number of manuscripts.[19] The original version is a tightly constructed romance in five books, interspersed with poems. Upon its completion, however, Sidney began to revise and expand it, and it was this incomplete version that was published in 1590, then revised by Mary Sidney, Countess of Pembroke, and printed along with books three to five of the so-called "Old" *Arcadia* in 1593. Known since 1590 as *The Countess of Pembroke's Arcadia*, this semi-complete version remained standard until the printing from manuscript of the "Old" *Arcadia* in 1926.[20]

The intertwined stories in either version are long and involved by modern standards but concern two royal friends, Pyrocles and Mucidorus, who are shipwrecked then find their ways to the household of King Basilius in Arcadia. There various romantic complications occur involving Basilius, his wife Gynecia, and his daughters Philoclea and Pamela, as well as a host of other characters. Sidney's own experience of Elizabethan court life and the queen can be inferred in his depiction of various characters and incidents. As Katherine Duncan-Jones suggests, his description of the Queen of Laconia as "one that seemed born in the confines of beauty's kingdom; for all her lineaments were neither perfect possessions thereof, nor absolute strangers thereto; but

Above: Sir Philip Sidney. *The Covntesse of Pembrokes Arcadia* (London, 1593). STC 22540 c.1, title page.

Opposite top: Edmund Spenser. *The shepheardes calendar* (London, 1579). STC 23089, sig. Ciiiv.

Opposite bottom: Edmund Spenser. *The Faerie Queene, disposed into XII bookes* (London, 1609). STC 23083 c.2, sig. A1v–A2r.

Ægloga Quarta.
ARGVMENT.

THis Æglogue is purposely intended to the honor and prayse of our most
gracious soueraigne, Queene Elizabeth. The speakers herein be Hobbinoll and Thenott, two shepheardes: the which Hobbinoll being before mentioned, greatly to haue loued Colin, is here set forth more largely, complay-
ning him of that boyes great misaduenture in Loue, whereby his mynd was
alienate and withdrawen not onely from him, who moste loued him, but also
from all former delightes and studies, aswell in pleasaunt pyping, as conning
ryming and singing, and other his laudable exercises. Whereby he taketh
occasion, for proofe of his more excellencie and skill in poetrie, to recorde a
songe, which the sayd Colin sometime made in honor of her Maiestie, whom
abruptly he termeth Elysa.

                    Thenot.   Hobbinoll.

TEll me good Hobbinoll, what garres thee greete?
　What? hath some Wolfe thy tender Lambes ytorne?
Or is thy Bagpype broke, that soundes so sweete?
Or art thou of thy loued lasse forlorne?

Or bene thine eyes attempred to the yeare,
　Quenching the gasping furrowes thirst with rayne?

                                                Like

TO THE MOST
HIGH MIGHTY
AND MAGNIFICENT
EMPRESSE, RENOVNED FOR
PIETIE, VERTVE, AND ALL
GRATIOVS GOVERNMENT,
ELIZABETH,
BY THE GRACE OF GOD QVEENE
OF ENGLAND FRAVNCE and IRELAND and
of VIRGINIA, DEFENDOVR of the Faith
&c. Her most humble seruant, *Edmund Spencer*
doth in all humilitie dedicate, present and con-
secrate these his labours, to liue with
the eternitie of her
FAME.

AT LONDON.
Printed by H.L. for Mathew Lownes.

THE FIRST BOOKE
OF THE FAERIE
QVEENE:

CONTAINING
THE LEGENDE OF THE KNIGHT
OF THE RED CROSSE,
OR
Of Holinesse.

LO, I the man, whose Muse whilom did mask,
As time her taught, in lowely Shepheards
weeds,
Am now enforc't a far vnfitter task, (weeds,
For trumpets stern to change mine oaten reeds,
And sing of Knights, & Ladies gentle deeds;
Whose praises hauing slept in silence long,
Mee, all too meane, the sacred Muse areeds
To blazon broad, amongst her learned throng:
Fierce warres, and faithfull loues, shall moralize my song.

2
Helpe then, ô holy Virgin, chiefe of nine,
Thy weaker Novice to performe thy will:
Lay forth out of thine euerlasting scrine
The antique rolles, which there lie hidden still,
Of Faerie Knights, and fairest *Tanaquill,*
Whom that most noble Briton Prince so long
Sought through the world, and suffered so much ill,
That I must rue his vndeserued wrong:
O! help thou my weake wit, and sharpen my dull tongue.

3
And thou most dreaded impe of highest *Ioue,*
Faire *Venus* sonne, that with thy cruell dart
At that good Knight so cunningly didst roue,
That glorious fire it kindled in his hart,
Lay now thy deadly Heben bowe apart,
And with thy mother milde come to mine ayde:
Come both, and with you bring triumphant *Mars,*
In loues and gentle iollities arrayd,
After his murdrous spoiles and bloudy rage allayd.

4
And with them eke, ô Goddesse heauenly bright,
Mirrour of grace and Maiestie divine,
Great Lady of the greatest Isle, whose light
Like *Phœbus* lampe throughout the world doth shine,
Shed thy faire beames into my feeble eyne,
And raise my thoughts, too humble, and too vile,
To thinke of that true glorious type of thine,
The argument of mine afflicted stile:
The which to heare, vouchsafe, ô dearest dread a-while.

she was a queen, and therefore beautiful," may be a young man's "impatience" at the "fiction of the ageing Elizabeth's 'Perfect Beauty.'" Other comments are more serious. The advice that the Delphic oracle gives King Basilius is similar to the advice Sidney himself offered Elizabeth in a letter. The Oracle says, "These thirty years past have you so governed this realm that neither your subjects have wanted justice in you, nor you obedience in them; . . . Let your subjects have you in their eyes, let them see the benefits of your justice daily more and more; and so must they needs rather like of present sureties than uncertain changes."[21]

About the time Sidney was drafting his *Arcadia*, Edmund Spenser wrote a set of twelve eclogues, published as *The Shepheardes Calender* in 1579, and dedicated to his friend Sidney. The identity of the author is hidden behind a mysterious person known only as "E.K." who introduces the book, explaining that part of the author's purpose is to revitalize English as a worthy literary language in its own right without a lot of continental borrowings. Spenser is also beginning his literary career as Virgil did, by writing humble eclogues about country folk before taking on the larger, legendary epic form.[22] And as Virgil's fourth eclogue speaks of Justice returning to earth, "the Golden Age Returns,"[23] so Spenser uses his fourth eclogue for the month of April to praise Elizabeth and her ancestry:

Of fayre *Elisa* be your siluer song,
    that blessed wight:
The flowre of Virgins, may shee florish long,
    In princely plight.
For shee is *Syrinx* daughter without spotte,
Which *Pan* the shepheards God of her begot:
So sprong her grace
Of heauenly race,
No mortall blemishe may her blotte.

Tell me, haue ye seene her angelick face,
    Like *Phoebe* fayre?
Her heauenly haueour [behavior], her princely grace
    can you well compare?
The Redde rose medled with the White yfere,
In either cheeke depeincten [depicting] liuely chere.
    Her modest eye,
    Her Maiestie,
Where haue you seene the like, but there?

E.K. helpfully explains that Pan represents Elizabeth's father, King Henry VIII, and "by the mingling of the Redde rose and the White, is meant the vniting of the two principall houses of Lancaster and of Yorke."[24] The modern scholar Louis Montrose points out that on another level, "the Elisa of *Aprill* is also the idealized personification of the body politic, created by the Queen's poets, artisans, preachers, and councillors to focus the collective energies and emotions of her subjects and to harness and direct their diverse and potentially dangerous personal aspirations."[25]

The little woodcut accompanying *Aprill* shows the queen holding a scepter and a palm branch, surrounded by her ladies, many of whom play musical instruments.[26] They stand in a rural setting with shepherds in the background, while overhead is the zodiac sign of Taurus, which Spenser may be reading here, as elsewhere, as the bull who carried off the virgin Europa in Ovid's *Metamorphoses*. One scholar has read this as a warning to Elizabeth to maintain her virginity and the political status quo, at a time when her negotiations to marry the French Catholic duc d'Alençon seemed quite serious.[27]

Spenser's fascination with Queen Elizabeth pervades his longer and most famous work, *The Faerie Queene*. He had envisioned a full classical epic of twelve books, but he never got beyond the first six and a fragment of a seventh. The first three books were printed in 1589 and again in 1596, along with Books 4–6. Both volumes were dedicated to Elizabeth, and the publication of the whole with the fragments of Book 7 in a folio volume in 1609, still bore the dedication to the queen, though James I had been on the throne for six years. The work itself is a kind of poetic conduct book, for as Spenser writes in an introductory letter to Raleigh, "The generall end therefore of all the booke is to fashion a gentleman or noble person in vertuous and gentle discipline." (Vol. 2: 485).[28] Each book was to have a knight representing one of the virtues, found all together in the idealized figure of Prince Arthur who intercedes at various times to help them. For his chivalric ideal of the noble gentleman, Spenser seems to have had his friend Sidney in mind, who had died in 1586. At the center of the work, however, is the mysterious Faerie Queene herself, figuring Elizabeth, whom Spenser describes thus:

In that Faery Queene I meane glory in my generall intention, but in my particular I conceiue the most excellent and glorious person of our soueraine the Queene, and her kingdome in Faery land. And yet in some places els, I doe otherwise shadow her. For considering she beareth two persons, the one of a most royall Queene or Empresse, the other of a most vertuous and beautifull Lady, this latter part in some places I doe express in Belphoebe, fashioning her name according to your owne [i.e. Raleigh's] excellent conceipt of Cynthia, (Phoebe and Cynthia being both names of Diana)(vol. 2: 486)

Spenser clearly evokes here the concept known as "the king's two bodies"; the idea that a king or queen has both a public, inherited position ordained by God, and a private persona as a man or woman. Spenser seems to adopt the moderate Calvinist view of female sovereignty which asserted that "although government by women is against the laws of God and nature, God sometimes sees fit to raise up notable exceptions to the general rule."[29] In writing of the Amazon queen Radigund in Book V of *The Faerie Queene*, Spenser shows how her tyranny over men is cruel and unnatural, "But vertuous women wisely vnderstand,/ That they were borne to base humilitie,/ Vnlesse the heauens them lift to lawfull soueraintie." (V.v.25). Pamela Benson has suggested that "if Spenser differs from Calvin, it is in his active appreciation of the abilities of women, as long as their talents do not lead them to aspire to a place above their proper one in the social hierarchy."[30] For both Calvin and Spenser, however, Elizabeth is the exception among modern women, not the rule.

Many of the female figures in the poem embody positive or negative characteristics, which the Faerie Queen herself should either adopt or shun. In the introduction to Book III, Spenser asks pardon of Elizabeth, his "dred Soveraine" for not plainly showing her "glorious portrait" but figuring it "in colored shadows." He hopes that she will see herself "in mirrors more than one": "Either *Gloriana* let her chuse,/ Or in *Belphoebe* fashioned to bee:/ In th'one her rule, in th'other her rare chastitee." Gloriana and Belphoebe are, in fact, two aspects of the female knight in Book III, Britomart, who herself is and is not an Elizabeth figure. The critic Sheila Cavanagh describes Britomart's multifaceted character as purposefully created by the narrator to be "as multiply fictive as the Elizabeth he honors. Neither image represents anything close to the reality of a living woman, but the portraits of Britomart and of 'Cynthia, his heavens fairest light'. . . each further other goals. That real women could not emulate Britomart any more than they could model themselves after Elizabeth does not matter in the long run."[31] But while Britomart may be an ambiguous figure of Elizabeth, the insidious Duessa has been recognized as Spenser's portrayal of Mary, Queen of Scots, and her trial in Book V shadows Mary's actual trial and treatment by Elizabeth. In the poem, the queenly figure is Mercilla, another aspect of Elizabeth:

> Thus she did sit in soverayne Maiestie,
> Holding a Scepter in her royall hand,
> The sacred pledge of peace and Clemencie,
> With which high God had blest her happie land (V.ix.30)

Though Duessa is found guilty in Mercilla's court, Mercilla finds it difficult to condemn her, just as Elizabeth waivered before signing Mary's death warrant:

> But she, whose Princely breast was touched nere
> With piteous ruth of her so wretched plight,
> Though plaine she saw by all, that she did heare,
> That she [Duessa] of death was guiltie found by right,
> Yet would not let just vengeance on her light; (V.ix.50)

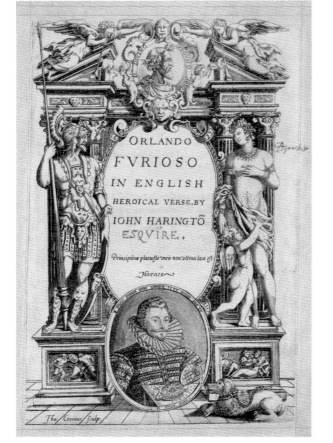

Ultimately, just as all the masculine virtues are joined in Arthur, so the female ones are focused in the figure of the Faery Queene. In Book II, Guyon the knight of Temperance summarizes her, "that great Queene,/ Great and most glorious virgin Queene aliue."

> In her the richesse of all heavenly grace
> In chiefe degree are heaped vp on hye:
> And all that else this worlds enclosure bace
> Hath great or glorious in mortall eye,
> Adornes the person of her Maiestie;
> That men beholding so great excellence,
> And rare perfection in mortalitie,
> Do her adore with sacred reuerence,
> As th'Idole of her makers great magnificence. (II.ii.40, 41)

This figure is indeed the ideal construct of Elizabeth as her courtiers saw her.

Sidney, and especially Spenser, were influenced by the great Italian epic romance of the day, Ariosto's *Orlando Furioso*, published in its finished version in 1532. It was known in England, either through the

Lodovico Ariosto. *Orlando Furioso*. Trans. John Harington (London, 1591). STC 746 c.1, title page.

Italian original or through one of the various editions published in France, until it was translated into English by John Harington, Elizabeth's godson. The story goes that he first translated a racy episode from Book 28 for the ladies at court. When this fact came to the queen's attention, she "sentenced" Harington to stay at home and translate all the rest of the *Orlando*.[32] He did just that, and it was published in a handsome folio volume, beautifully illustrated with engravings copied from the Italian edition.[33] The queen could perfectly well have read the book herself in Italian. As her tutor Roger Ascham noted, "beside her perfit readines, in Latin, Italian, French, & Spanish, she readeth here now at Windsore more Greeke euery day, than some Prebendarie of this Chirch doth read Latin in a whole weeke."[34]

Elizabeth's learning was well-recognized and quite a number of books and manuscripts of many different kinds were dedicated to her.[35] These include a Latin and Greek parallel-text edition of Euripides' play *Phoenissae* published in Strassburg in 1577; a 1559 edition of Seneca's tragedy *Troas* translated into English, where the translator writes to the queen, "none may be a better judge of my doinges herein, then who best understandeth my author"; French works, such as Jacques Bellot's *Le Jardin de Vertu* (1581), and Pierre Boaistuau's *Histoires Tragiques* (1559)— a source for Shakespeare's story of Romeo and Juliet; the English translation of Machi-avelli's *Arte of Warre* (1562) and the Italian edition of Ubaldini's *Militia* (1597); a Spanish book on the Armada (1589); William Turner's *Herbal* (1568); George Putten-ham's *Arte of English Poesie* (1589); the translation of Guillemeau's *The Frenche Chirur-gerye* (1597); John Foxe's popular "Book of Martyrs" (1563); various editions of the Bible, including a translation of the New Testament into Welsh (1567); and John Norden's *Chorographical Description of . . . Middlesex, Essex, Surrey [etc.]* (1595), a manuscript account of the histories of English counties.

E nuy in vaine thou warreſt with our Queene,
L ight of the Weſt, which through the world is ſeene,
I oue in his ſtrength with her full armed goes.
Z eale is ſword wherewith ſhe woundes her foes.
A bundance, peace, power, and happy raigne
B laze foorth her fame : the world can not contayne
E leſt to be, the meruaile of this time.
T o ſtoupe his pride, that ore Emprors did clime,
H elp and refuge to forraigne Realmes in thrall,
A t home, abroade, each where her foes do fall.

R enowne our Queene her diademe doth giue,
E lizabeth alone in peace doth liue :
G lory of God, moſt bleſſed Prince aliue.
I mage of grace, in whome all vertues thriue.
N o death vpon her memorie may feede,
A Phenix right, but one, yet neuer dead.

Under Elizabeth's patronage, one of the greatest works to that time in British geography was carried out, through the efforts of the surveyor Christopher Saxton, working for Thomas Seckford, who provided him with a kind of internal passport, "to be assisted in all places where he shall come for the view of meet places to describe certain counties in cartes [maps]."[36] The result was a general map of Britain and thirty-four county maps of England and Wales, published together in 1579. The maps were printed on single folio-sized sheets, folded in half, and some copies, like the one at the Folger, were hand-colored. There is no "title" on the title page, but none is needed. The elaborate engraving showing Elizabeth enthroned, with figures of Cosmography and Geography next to her, and a mapmaker and astronomer at the bottom, proclaims her "sovereignty over the kingdom as a whole and over each of its provinces."[37] It is a masterful evocation of the ancient ties between the sovereign and the land.

The rich cultural flowering of Elizabeth's reign had many causes, not the least of which were her own intelligence and the remarkable gathering of so many bright, intelligent, and imaginative sub-jects. The fact that her reign was relatively peaceful and that she maintained order through law, allowed philosophy and the arts and sciences to flourish. Francis Bacon recognized this fact when he dedicated to Elizabeth his *Collection . . . of the Common Lawes of England*. He wrote that "Eliza-beth is the 'life of our lawes' and the 'life of our peace, without which lawes are put to silence.' Her reign 'hath beene as a goodly seasonable spring-weather to the aduancing of all excellent arts of peace.'"[38]

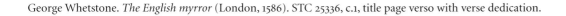

George Whetstone. *The English myrror* (London, 1586). STC 25336, c.1, title page verso with verse dedication.

1 E. K. Chambers, *The Elizabethan Stage*, vol. 4 (Oxford: Clarendon Press, 1923), 114.

2 See the list in Chambers, *Elizabethan*, vol. 4, Appendices A and B; Chambers, vol. 4, 157.

3 See the listing in Alfred Harbage, *Annals of English Drama*, rev. ed. (Philadelphia: University of Pennsylvania Press, 1964).

4 Chambers, *Elizabethan*, vol. 4, 263; see also Richard Dutton, "Licensing and Censorship," in *A Companion to Shakespeare*, ed. David Scott Kastan (Oxford: Blackwell, 2000), 381.

5 *A Literary History of England*, ed. Albert C. Baugh (New York: Appleton-Century-Crofts, 1967), 447; Chambers, *Elizabethan*, vol. 4, 374. The Folger Library has a manuscript copy of a Latin play put on by the boys of Westminster (V.a.212); see Mueller's essay in this catalogue.

6 David Bevington in John Lyly, *Midas*, ed. Bevington (Manchester: Manchester University Press, 2000), 133.

7 Chambers, *Elizabethan*, vol. 4, 164; Scott McMillan, "Professional Playwrighting," in *Companion to Shakespeare*, 235.

8 See G. R. Hibbard in his edition of *Love's Labour's Lost* (Oxford: Clarendon Press, 1990), 42, 49, 51.

9 David Crane in his edition of *The Merry Wives of Windsor* (Cambridge: Cambridge University Press, 1997), 1.

10 See William Shakespeare, *A Midsummer Night's Dream*, ed. Peter Holland (Oxford: Clarendon Press, 1994), 112.

11 Chambers, *Elizabethan*, vol. 2, 262. See the description of an Italian tumbler at Kenilworth (Patten, *A Letter*, 24-25).

12 Adam Zwetkovich to the Emperor Maximilian, quoted in Elkin Calhoun Wilson, *England's Eliza* (New York: Octagon Books, 1966), 260.

13 Roy Strong suggests that these woodcuts may be based on designs by Elizabeth's court artist, Levina Teerlinc (*Gloriana: the Portraits of Queen Elizabeth I* [London: Thames & Hudson, 1987], 56).

14 Raleigh's poems are quoted from Sir Walter Raleigh, *The Poems, with other verse From the Court of Elizabeth I*, ed. Martin Dodsworth (London: Everyman, Dent, 1999), 65, 19. Dodsworth puts "Prais'd be Diana" with the poems sometimes attributed to Raleigh.

15 For lyrics see, *The Triumphs of Oriana (1601)*, vol. 32 of *The English Madrigalists*, ed. Edmund H. Fellowes, rev. Thurston Dart (London: Stainer & Bell, 1962), xi–xvii.

16 Roy Strong, "Queen Elizabeth I as Oriana," *Studies in the Renaissance*, 6 (1959): 252, 253.

17 Paul Johnson, *Elizabeth I: a Study in Power and Intellect* (London: Futura, 1976), 205, 206.

18 Sir Philip Sidney, *The Countess of Pembroke's Arcadia (The Old Arcadia)*, ed. Katherine Duncan-Jones (Oxford; New York: Oxford University Press, 1985), 3.

19 Duncan-Jones in *Old Arcadia*, xiii.

20 See the account of its publication history by Katherine Duncan-Jones in *Old Arcadia*, vii–x.

21 Katherine Duncan-Jones, *Sir Philip Sidney: Courtier Poet* (New Haven: Yale University Press, 1991), 17, 178.

22 See Richard A. McCabe in his edition of Edmund Spenser, *The Shorter Poems* (Harmondsworth: Penguin Books, 1999), 515.

23 Virgil's exact word here is "Virgo" not "Justice" which Spenser would have known, and which makes his parallel with Elizabeth even more evocative. Virgil, *The Eclogues and Georgics*, In the original Latin with a verse translation by C. Day Lewis (Garden City: Anchor Books, 1964), 30, 31.

24 Spenser, *Shorter Poems*, 62, 63, 68.

25 Louis Adrian Montrose, "'Eliza, Queene of shepheardes,' and the Pastoral of Power," *English Literary Renaissance*, 10 (1980): 167.

26 For a discussion of this cut and the calendrical tradition, see Ruth Samson Luborsky, "The Illustrations to *The Shepheardes Calender*," *Spenser Studies*, 2 (1981): 3–53.

27 McCabe in Spenser, *Shorter Poems*, 530.

28 Vol. 2, 485. All quotations are from Edmund Spenser, *Faerie Queene*, ed. J. C. Smith, 2 vols. (Oxford: Clarendon Press, 1909; rpt. 1968).

29 James E. Phillips, "The Woman Ruler in Spenser's *Faerie Queene*," *Huntington Library Quarterly*, 5 (1942), 215.

30 Pamela Benson, "Rule Virginia: Protestant Theories of Female Regiment in *The Faerie Queene*," *English Literary Renaissance*, 15 (1985): 280. Benson extends Spenser's Calvinist view of women to cover what is usually thought to be his more positive feminist stance in Book III (see Benson 281 ff.).

31 Sheila Cavanagh, *Wanton Eyes and Chaste Desires: Female Sexuality in the Faerie Queene* (Bloomington: Indiana University Press, 1994), 152.

32 See the account of this episode by Robert McNulty, Introduction in his edition of *Ludovico Ariosto's Orlando Furioso*, trans. John Harington (Oxford: Clarendon Press, 1972), xxv.

33 See Ruth Luborsky and Elizabeth Ingram, *A Guide to English Illustrated Books, 1536–1603* (Tempe, AZ: MRTS, 1998), vol. 1, 30.

34 Roger Ascham, *The Scholemaster* (London, 1570; facsim. rpt. Amsterdam: Theatrum Orbis Terrarum, 1968), sig. Hi.

35 Lists of books dedicated to Elizabeth may be found in Elkins Calhoun Wilson, *England's Eliza* (Cambridge: Harvard University Press, 1939; rpt. New York: Octagon, 1966) and in Franklin B. Williams, *Index of Dedications and Commendatory Verses* (London: Bibliographical Society, 1962).

36 Quoted in Richard Helgerson, *Forms of Nationhood: the Elizabethan Writing of England* (Chicago: University of Chicago Press, 1992), 109.

37 Helgerson, *Forms*, 112.

38 Quoted in Wilson, *Eliza*, 416.

Lodovico Ariosto (1474–1533)
Orlando Furioso
Trans. John Harington
London: Richard Field, 1591
STC 746, c.1

George Gascoigne (1542?–1577)
The noble arte of venerie or hunting
[London]: Henry Bynneman for Christopher Barker [1575]
STC 24328

John Lyly (1554?–1606)
Midas. Plaied Before The Qveenes Maiestie vpon Tvvelfe Day At night
London: Thomas Scarlet for I[ohn] B[roome], 1592
STC 17083

Thomas Morley (1557–1603?)
Madrigales the triumphes of Oriana
London: Thomas Este, 1601
STC 18130

Cesare Negri (ca.1535–ca.1604)
Nuove inventioni di balli
Milan: Girolamo Bordone, 1604
GV1590 N3 Cage

Christopher Saxton (b. 1542?)
[*Atlas of the counties of England and Wales*]
[London: 1590?]
STC 21805.5

William Shakespeare (1564–1616)
A Pleasant Conceited Comedie called, Loues labors lost. As it was presented before her Highnes
London: W[illiam] W[hite] for Cuthbert Burby, 1598
STC 22294, c.1

William Shakespeare (1564–1616)
A Most pleasaunt and excellent conceited Comedie, of Syr Iohn Falstaffe, and the merrie Wiues of Windsor
London: T[homas] C[reede] for Arthur Iohnson, 1602
STC 22299

Sir Philip Sidney (1554–1586)
The Covntesse of Pembrokes Arcadia
London: [John Windet] for William Ponsonbie, 1593
STC 22540, c.1

Edmund Spenser (1552?–1599)
*The Faerie Queene, disposed
into XII bookes*
London: H[umphrey]
L[ownes] for Mathew Lownes,
1609
STC 23083, c.2

Edmund Spenser (1552?–1599)
The shepheardes calendar
London: Hugh Singleton, 1579
STC 23089

Thomas Trevelyon (b.ca.1548)
Thalia
Commonplace Book, 1608.
Folger MS V.b.232, fol. 147v

Lute
Workshop of Michielle Harton
Padua, 1598.
ART Inv. 1002

marie queene of scotes

marie succeeded to his father James the fift in the yeare of the world·5513·
in the yeare of christ·1543·a princese verteouslye inclined, shee maried
first frances·2·dolphin, and after kyng of france, then after his death
returning home to scotland, shee maried henrye stewarde duke of al=
banye, and lord darly sonne to mathew Earle of lennox, a comelye prince
pronevnoy to henrye the·7·kyng of England, to whome shee bere James
the·6·shee was put to death in england the·8·of februari·1586· after ⟨⟩
18 yeares captiuitie oooooooooooooooooooooooooooooooooooo

Mary, Queen of Scots

THE STORY OF MARY, QUEEN OF SCOTS, READS MORE LIKE ROMANCE FICTION than that of her cousin Elizabeth. Imprisonment, disguise, escape, secret letters, rape, murder—all the ingredients of a soap opera are there in Mary's story. Mary was beautiful and feminine; Elizabeth was handsome and regal. Mary had three husbands, one of whom she supposedly helped to murder, and two pregnancies; Elizabeth never married and was a virgin. Both were educated in languages and music, but Mary never *could* apply her education to politics, while Elizabeth played the political game quite well. Their differences may be summed up in a similar reference made by each, but with totally opposite effects. After the death of her second husband, Lord Darnley, in suspicious circumstances, Mary was abducted and raped by the earl of Bothwell, whom she then married, having declared that "she would follow Bothwell to the end of the world in her petticoat."[1] Elizabeth's reference to that piece of her undergarments was quite different. Forced to reply yet again to Parliament's demands that she should marry or name a successor, Elizabeth remarked: "I am your anointed queen. I will never be by violence constrained to do anything. I thank God I am indeed endued with such qualities that if I were turned out of the realm in my petticoat, I were able to live in any place of Christendom."[2] Two very different women, indeed!

Mary was born in 1542, the daughter of James V of Scotland and Mary of Guise. Shortly thereafter her father died, and she was crowned queen at the age of nine months. When she was six, she moved to France to be educated with the other royal children, including her future husband, Francis, heir to the French throne. In 1558, at the age of sixteen, she married Francis, but two years later she found herself widowed and orphaned, having lost her mother as well. Mary of Guise had been regent of Scotland during her daughter's absence and was a more astute politician than Mary would ever be. As a Catholic Frenchwoman, however, Mary of Guise's hopes were tied to Scotland's alliance with France and to support of Catholicism in a country with a strong conservative Protestant faction. In 1559 Elizabeth had secretly sent financial aid to the breakaway Scottish lords, but against the wishes of her council, she was loath to enter into a more formal alliance of war against Mary of Guise and the French. In February 1560, however, the English and

Thomas Trevelyon. *Marie Queene of Scotes*, from *Commonplace Book* (1608). Folger MS V.b.232, fol. 125r.

Scots signed the Treaty of Berwick in which England agreed to support the Scots against French aggression. Nevertheless, Elizabeth kept communications with the French open, and in July, England and France signed the Treaty of Edinburgh, wherein the French agreed "that henceforward Mary Stuart would renounce all claim to Elizabeth's throne."[3]

Mary wanted Elizabeth's throne very much—she had already been going around voicing her intentions in France. Her claim was that her grandmother, Margaret Tudor, was sister to Henry VIII and thus aunt to Elizabeth. When Mary returned to Scotland in August 1561 to take up her

throne, she agreed to support the Scottish Protestants led by her half-brother James, Earl of Moray, with the idea that they would support *her* as Elizabeth's heir. The English themselves, however, were hardly enthusiastic about her claim, not even when Elizabeth was at death's door with smallpox in 1562.[4] Mary had great hopes for herself in the European marriage market, not realizing perhaps that as queen of a wealthier and more stable country, her cousin Elizabeth was

Trial and execution of Mary Queen of Scots. Engraving, possibly by Hieronymus Wierix. STC 7758.3 v. 3 no.10.

considered a more attractive match. On her side, Elizabeth's great concern was keeping Mary from marrying a strong Catholic prince. In 1564 she therefore made a surprising move to all concerned and offered Robert Dudley to Mary as a possible husband. Neither Mary nor Dudley was amused, and in the end, Mary married Henry, lord Darnley in 1565. Born in England to the exiled earl of Lennox, Darnley also traced his ancestry back to Margaret Tudor. Even before they were married, and without approval of her Parliament, Mary went ahead and named him king of Scotland. The political scene then shifted, with Mary gathering more power around her, against her half-brother, the earl of Moray. All was not well, however.

It soon became evident that Darnley had no strong religious ties, either Catholic or Protestant, that he cared little about governing, and that he in fact was a drunkard. Mary drew away from him more and more and placed her confidence in David Rizzio, one of her musicians whom she now made Secretary for French affairs. This favoritism rankled the Scottish lords, especially those Protestant ones who "had been ousted from power after the Darnley marriage."[5] They made a bond with Darnley which substantially agreed to the murder of Rizzio, and the violent act was carried out in March 1566 in Mary's private apartments at Holyrood palace. Two months later, Mary gave birth to Darnley's child, James, who was baptised in the presence of the earl of Bedford, standing in for Elizabeth as godmother. Elizabeth assured Mary "that provided she undertook not to press her claim to the English throne during the lifetime of Elizabeth or any of her lawful issue, Elizabeth would see to it that no laws were passed in England that were in any way prejudicial to Mary's title."[6] There was still Darnley himself to consider, however, and enough people wanted him out of the way.

Mary had made her peace with the Protestant lords after Rizzio's murder, and now she discussed with her councilors how to get rid of Darnley. In the meantime, she had also become involved with the Earl of Bothwell, who seems to have been behind the explosion that killed Darnley in February 1567. Elizabeth sent off a letter, both supportive and critical, with advice that Mary did not follow. It is worth quoting a passage to show the mixed personal and political style, from one queen to another—a thirty-three-year-old astute politician, to her hairbrained twenty-four-year-old cousin:

Madame:

My ears have been so deafened and my understanding so grieved . . . to hear the dreadful news of the abominable murder of your mad husband and my killed cousin that I scarcely yet have the wits to write about it. . . . I am more sorrowful for you than for him. . . . However, I will not at all dissemble what most people are talking about: which is . . . that you do not take measures that touch those who have done as you wished, as if the thing had been entrusted in a way that the murderers felt assurance in doing it. . . . I beseech you to want no such thought to stick at this point.[7]

It is a masterful piece, expressing Elizabeth's personal feelings of horror but also her honesty in saying she is more sorry for Mary than for Darnley. She then turns to the political fallout, saying that Mary must disassociate herself from any hint that she may have been involved in the murder. Mary might have learned much from Elizabeth, but she went her own way. Instead of punishing the suspects, she rewarded them. Then in April, Bothwell carried her off, and she married him in May. Elizabeth wrote again: "How could a worse choice be made for your honor than in such haste to marry such a subject, who besides other and notorious lacks, public fame hath charged with the murder of your late husband, beside the touching of yourself also in some part, though we trust that in that behalf falsely."[8] In the last sentence, Elizabeth hopes that reports of a rape are false, but they were not. Mary had acted in a manner totally opposite to Elizabeth. Elizabeth had known that she could not marry Leicester after the suspicious death of his first wife, in spite of a public inquiry into that death, but Mary let her passions run away with her. As her biographer Jenny Wormald has pointed out, "one reason why Mary as a political figure was never successful was that personal and political considerations were always too much intertwined in her mind."[9]

A strong anti-Bothwell faction of Scottish lords now rose against Mary. They imprisoned her at Lochleven, Bothwell departed, and Mary was forced to abdicate in the summer of 1567, when the Earl of Moray was named as regent for her tiny son James. She was twenty-five years old, and except for a brief period of two weeks when she managed to escape from Lochleven and raise some forces against the Earl of Moray, she was never free again until her execution in 1587.[10] After her defeat by Moray, Mary fled into England where she stayed in Carlisle while Elizabeth and her council decided what to do. She definitely was a liability: if she remained at large in England, she could easily become the center of revolt by Catholics to establish her on the English throne. Elizabeth was caught in the untenable position of not wanting to accept the abdication of a fellow queen, although suspecting her guilt in Darnley's murder, but of also wanting to support Protestant control of Scotland. In the end, hearings were called at York and Westminster to inquire into Mary's guilt. When Moray publicized the Casket Letters—a secret cache of love letters between Mary and Bothwell that also declared her "abhorring of her husband that was murdered"[11]—Mary's crimes became evident. Elizabeth gave her two chances to clear her name, but Mary refused because Elizabeth would not see her in person. Though Elizabeth declared in January 1569 "that she was unable to pronounce for or against the Queen of Scots," she was sure of Mary's guilt. "Only by allowing the evidence against Mary to be ventilated had it been possible for Elizabeth to justify her refusal to restore her" to the Scottish throne.[12]

Mary was sent to Tutbury, a castle in Staffordshire, under the guardianship of George Talbot, earl of Shrewsbury. In a letter of December 15, 1568, now at the Folger Library, the earl wrote home to his wife Elizabeth that it was now certain that the Queen of Scots would come to Tutbury to his charge.[13] He added this vital information as a postscript to the fairly mundane news in the rest of the letter. Mary was to remain as a permanent "guest" of the Shrewsburys until 1584. She spent her time embroidering, and hatching plots through letters secreted out to those she thought might help her. Susan Frye, drawing on the work of Margaret Swain, has recently written about the bonding that initially occurred between Elizabeth Talbot and Mary through their mutual interest and skill in needlework. Some of the designs that Mary embroidered had definite political implications, such as the picture of "a hand clipping off a barren vine so that the fruitful vine may flourish," topped by Mary's motto: "Virtue flourishes by wounding." Mary had given this cushion cover to the duke of Norfolk who had secret plans to wed her, and it was used as evidence of treason in his later trial, because of the suggestion that Elizabeth was the barren vine they wished to clip.[14] Elizabeth was actually lenient with Norfolk, letting him go when he plotted to wed Mary, when he supported the northern earls in their attempted rebellion of 1569, and when he aided Mary in the Ridolfi plot of 1571 for an invasion of England supported by Spain. On this latter occasion, Elizabeth finally agreed to his execution only to avoid executing Mary instead. Mary was another monarch, and because Elizabeth held the state of inherited monarchy as sacred, she was loath to execute Mary, though she did know that Mary was "bad and utterly unscrupulous" in her plotting.[15]

In 1583 Elizabeth's secret service uncovered another of Mary's plots, this time with the Duke of Guise and the Spanish to bring troops to England, free her, and put her on Elizabeth's throne. Fortunately this plot, known as the Throckmorton Plot, was foiled. Shortly thereafter, James VI in Scotland let it be known that he had no intention of sharing the crown with his mother. This decision meant that Mary would have to stay in England, and Elizabeth put her under greater vigilance, transferring her care to Sir Amyas Paulet in 1585. Fortunately, Walsingham, who had charge of the secret service, continued to monitor her correspondence, and in 1586 Mary was implicated in a plot devised by Anthony Babington and other Catholics to murder Elizabeth,

again with Spanish help, and to free Mary. Babington and accomplices were executed, and Mary was brought to trial. Though Mary's guilt was fully established, and though Parliament demanded her execution, Elizabeth waivered, not wanting it to be known in Catholic countries "that for the safety of her life, a maiden Queen could be content to spill the blood even of her own kinswoman."[16] Even after she signed the warrant for Mary's execution, Elizabeth still hoped that Mary could be done away with more quietly. That was not to be, however, and Mary went to her death at Fotheringay on February 8, 1587.

A contemporary commonplace book (Folger MS E.a.1) gives a detailed account of the execution, including Mary's physical appearance, her last words, and a list of those present. "ffirst she was of stature hieghe, bigge made and s[o]mewhat rownde shouldred, hir faice full, & fatt, doble chynned, and hazell eyed, hir borowed hayre, aburne [i.e., an auburn wig], having on hir heade a

Account of Death of Mary, Queen of Scots, in *Commonplace Book* (1550–1590). Folger MS E.a.1, fol. 21v–22r.

Post varias clades miserorum, & cædis aceruos
Insontum, comes exornat spectacula mater
Supplicio, & regum soror & fidißima coniunx.
Illa Caledonijs diademate claruit oris,
Sed micat in cœlo fulgentior, inde corona
Sanguinis, infandaꝗ manet vindicta securis.

L 3   NOMI-

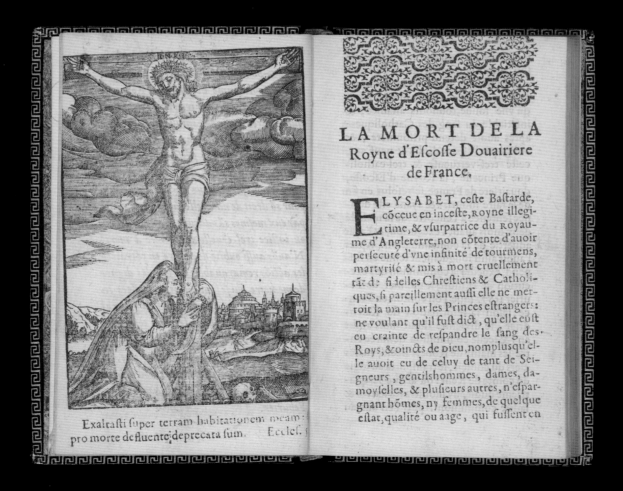

Exaltasti super terram habitationem meam:
pro morte defluentej deprecata sum.   Ecclef.

LA MORT DE LA
Royne d'Escosse Douairiere
de France,

ELYSABET, ceste Bastarde,
cōceue en inceste, royne illegi-
time, & vsurpatrice du royau-
me d'Angleterre, non cōtente d'auoir
persecuté d'vne infinité de tourmens,
martyrisé & mis à mort cruellement
tāt de fideles Chrestiens & Catholiques, si pareillement aussi elle ne met-
toit la main sur les Princes estrangers:
ne voulant qu'il fust dict, qu'elle eust
eu crainte de respandre le sang des
Roys, &coincts de Dieu, nomplusqu'elle auoit eu de celuy de tant de Sei-
gneurs, gentilshommes, dames, da-
moyselles, & plusieurs autres, n'espar-
gnant hōmes, ny femmes, de quelque
estat, qualité ou aage, qui fussent en

dressing of lawne edged w[i]th . . . lace." Mary had been known for her good looks, but she had obviously put on weight during her confinement. She wore "a gowne of blacke satten prynted w[i]th long sleeves . . . sett w[i]th Acorne buttons of Jett trymmed w[i]th pearle" with petticoat and skirts of red. She asked that her servants be allowed to witness her execution, "that they may reporte when they com into theire Countries howe I died A true woman to my religion. . . . I hope yo[u]r m[ist]r[e]s [i.e., Elizabeth] being a Q. [Queen] in regarde of womanhode will suffere me to haue some of myne owne people about me at my death."[17] She also asked that her servants be paid and given safe passage to their homes.

Mary's execution let loose a flood of literature printed on the continent, explaining her death from a Catholic perspective. Some of it was written by "exiled English and Scottish Catholics then living in France."[18] A broadside printed in Antwerp in 1587 has an engraved portrait of Mary with scenes before and after the execution. In the second image, her head is held up for all to see. Beneath are Latin verses by George Crichton, an ardent member of the pro-Catholic League party in France supported by the Guise family. These verses appear as well in a poetic miscellany from the time, also in the Folger Library, *De Jezebalis . . . Poemata*, probably published in Paris or Brussels in 1588.[19] Several of these collections, containing memorials to Mary as well as "invectives against Elizabeth," who was depicted as an English Jezebel for murdering Mary, were published on the continent, apparently with the backing of Crichton's father-in-law, Adam Blackwood. A "poet, lawyer, and Catholic apologist," Blackwood lived in France and had been supported by Mary for many years.[20] In return, he became an ardent spokesman on her behalf. Not only was he behind the poetic miscellanies, but in 1587 he published a "martyrology," *Martyre de la Royne d'Escosse*, followed in 1588 by an account of her death, *La Mort de La Royne d'Escosse*. This book was published anonymously, without a place, but it was probably printed in Paris. It went through four editions in 1588 and 1589 and influenced other publications in "Germany, Italy, and the Netherlands."[21]

The English countered with their own propaganda. Until the Babington Plot and the proclamation of Mary's death sentence in December, 1586, Elizabeth had forbidden all public attacks against Mary. Now, however, the gloves were off. A collection of items, including Parliamentary petitions for Mary's execution and Elizabeth's replies were published as *The Copie of a Letter to . . . the Earle of Leycester*, which was distributed "abroad in Latin, German, Dutch, and French translations."[22] Elizabeth tried to institute a kind of "gag rule" against all followers or supporters of Mary immediately after her death, so that they would not send abroad their version of the execution as Mary's martyrdom. Instead, the English came out with their own account, shortly after the execution, a little pamphlet entitled *A Defence of the Honorable sentence and execution of the Queene of Scots*. It attempts to justify the killing of a monarch through historical, judicial, and ecclesiastical precedents. "Although the persons of Princes are most sacred, and the maiestie of an absolute king very reuerende, as beeing the Lordes annoynted," there are at least two cases in which one prince may justifiably take the life of another. The first is where one prince's life is threatened by another prince, while the second is where "the disturbance of the publicke weale, the subuersion of the state is intended" (sig. I2v, I3r). Correspondence from the Babington Plot is

---

Opposite top: Execution of Mary, Queen of Scots, in Richard Verstegen, *Theatrum crudelitatum haereticorum nostri temporis* (Antwerp, 1592). BR1605 V4 1592 Cage, sig. L3r.

Opposite bottom: Adam Blackwood, supposed author. *La mort de la Royne d'Escosse, Douairiere de France* ([Paris?], 1588). DA787 A1 B55 1588 Cage, sig. aiiiv–aivr.

included for good measure at the end.

Mary was buried at Peterborough with a Protestant ceremony, attended by some Catholics. In 1612, her son James, now king of England as well as Scotland, had her remains removed to Westminster Abbey where they reside today, beneath a lovely marble effigy. Mary was like Elizabeth in that her life did not end with her death. Both queens continued to fascinate the public and produced a rich afterlife of music, art, and literature. In 1627, the Spanish writer Lope de Vega, best known for his many plays, published a five-part poem, *Corona Tragica*—"Tragic Crown: Life and Death of the Most Serene Queen of Scots Mary Stuart." In the Prologue he says it is loosely based on the 1624 Latin life of Mary written by the Scotsman and Catholic prelate George Conn. Lope says that Mary's execution, followed by what he has heard was great rejoicing at the English court, is called by Catholic writers "Teatro de crueldad" – a "theater of cruelty."

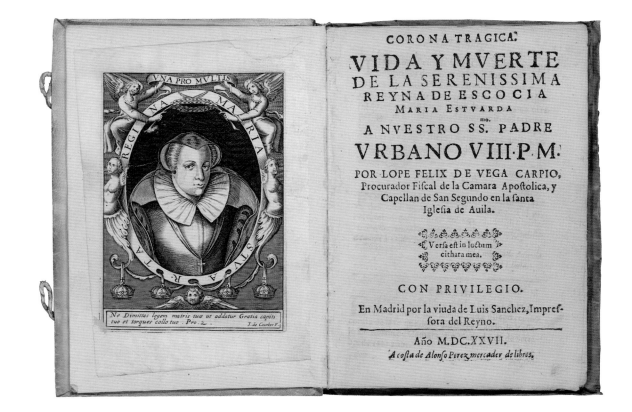

It seems more appropriate, however, to end this brief tale of Mary with a few lines from a poem she wrote early on to Elizabeth, when she hoped to see her cousin.

I've seen a ship blown wildly from her course,

In sight of port, but ere she came to land,

Driven again into the raging sea.

Likewise I fear to come to grief perforce;

O, do not think I fear it at your hand!

But Fate can mar the fairest destiny.[23]

Lope de Vega. *Corona tragica* (Madrid,1627). DA787 A1 V3 Cage, title page.

1   From account by Kirkcaldy of Grange, quoted in Jenny Wormald, *Mary Queen of Scots* (London: Tauris, 2000), 182. This essay is much indebted to Wormald's excellent study.

2   Elizabeth I, *Works*, 97.

3   Somerset, *Elizabeth I*, 127.

4   Wormald, *Mary*, 109, 136.

5   Wormald, *Mary*, 161.

6   Somerset, *Elizabeth I*, 177.

7   *Works*, 116.

8   *Works*, 118.

9   Wormald, *Mary*, 177.

10 Wormald, *Mary*, 170.

11 Earl of Norfolk quoted in Anne Somerset, *Elizabeth I* (New York: St. Martin's, 1991), 210.

12 Somerset, *Elizabeth I*, 212.

13 Folger MS X.d.428 (87).

14 Susan Frye, "Sewing Connections," in *Maids and Mistresses*, ed. Frye and Karen Robertson (New York: Oxford University Press, 1999), 120. See also Margaret H. Swain, *The Needlework of Mary Queen of Scots* (New York: Van Nostrand Reinhold, 1973).

15 Somerset, *Elizabeth I*, 260.

16 Quoted in Somerset, *Elizabeth I*, 433.

17 Folger MS E.a.1, fols. 15v–16v.

18 James E. Phillips, *Images of a Queen: Mary Stuart in Sixteenth-Century Literature* (Berkeley: University of California Press, 1964), 146.

19 Phillips, *Images*, 289 n. 38.

20 Phillips, *Images*, 107.

21 Phillips, *Images*, 177.

22 Phillips, *Images*, 119.

23 Translation from the French by Caroline Bingham in *The Poems of Mary, Queen of Scots*, (Illford, Essex: Royal Stuart Society, 1976), 7.

Adam Blackwood (1539–1613), supposed author
La mort de la Royne d'Escosse, Douairiere de France
[Paris?], 1588
DA787 A1 B55 1588 Cage

A defence of the honorable sentence and execution of the Queene of Scots
London: John Windet, 1587
STC 15098 (STC II 17566.3)

Lope de Vega (1562–1635)
Corona tragica. Vida y muerte de la serenissima reyna de Escocia Maria Estuarda
Madrid: Luis Sanchez, 1627
DA787 A1 V3 Cage

Mary, Queen of Scots (1542–1587)
Trial and execution
Engraving, possibly by Hieronymus Wierix after Thomas de Leu and Antoine Caron
Latin inscription by George Crichton (Scottish, 1555?–1611)
STC 7758.3 v. 3 no.10

George Talbot, earl of Shrewsbury (1528?–1590)
Autograph letter, signed, to his wife, Elizabeth, countess of Shrewsbury, from court
December 13, [1568]
Folger MS X.d.428 (87)

Commonplace Book.
Probably kept by members of a family in Ledbury, Herefordshire [1550–1590]
Folger MS E.a.1

Thomas Trevelyon (b.ca.1548)
Mary, Queen of Scots
Commonplace Book, 1608
Folger MS V.b.232, fol. 125r

Thomas Trevelyon (b.ca.1548)
Queen Elizabeth I
Commonplace Book, 1608
Folger MS V.b.232, fol. 119r

ELISABETH DEL GR· AN GL· FRAN· HIBER· ET VIRGINIA REGINA AVSPICATISSIMA·

POSVI DEVM ADIV-
TORE MEVM

Tantæ si vires, virtus mihi quanta Marina est,
Littora iam pelagi dudum iuga nostra subissent:
Vnde et iam Oceani credor lectissima Nympha.
Quòd si non animo fixum immotumique sederet
Ne cui me vinclo vellem sociare iugali,
Me sibi vel Nereus properasset iungere sponsam.

Cris. de. Pas. scul. et ex.

Religious Settlement

WHEN ELIZABETH SUCCEEDED TO THE THRONE IN 1558, she inherited a country that had already changed religion three times during the last twenty-five years: first, when her father, King Henry VIII, separated from the church in Rome and had himself declared Supreme Head of the Church in England (1533); second, during the reforming of the English Church undertaken by Archbishop Cranmer and others during the reign of her brother, Edward VI; and third, when her sister Mary came to the throne and reinstated Roman Catholicism as the official religion (1553). As Elizabeth peevishly reminded her Parliament in 1566, "It is said I am no divine. Indeed, I studied nothing but divinity till I came to the crown."[1] Her own legitimacy rested on her father's separation from the Catholic Church, thus allowing him legally to divorce Catharine of Aragon and marry Elizabeth's mother, Anne Boleyn. And her very survival during the reign of her sister, Mary, involved a certain amount of religious subterfuge, when Elizabeth was imprisoned and about 300 Protestants were martyred.

Having survived such turmoil, Elizabeth evidently learned that harsh pressure and violence are not the best measures for encouraging religious conformity and keeping the peace. She therefore led England's reinstatement of Protestantism with a moderate tolerance that did not always meet the expectations of her clergy, but which had the long-term effect of gradually moving most of the population over again to the Church of England. As she said thirty years after taking the throne:

> When I first came to the scepter and crown of this realm I did think more of God who gave it me than of the title. And therefore my first care was to set in order those things which did concern the Church of God and this religion in which I was born, in which I was bred, and in which I trust to die, not being ignorant how dangerous a thing it was to work in a kingdom a sudden alteration of religion . . . .[2]

Crispin van de Passe. *Regiae Anglicae maiestatis pictura* (Cologne, 1604). DA391 P33 1604 Cage, fol. 2.

Some of the first acts of Parliament in 1559 involved the establishment of this English Church. The Act of Supremacy made Elizabeth supreme governor, rather than head, of the Church. There were at least two objections to the title "head," which her father had held. First, only Christ could actually be head of the church, and second, no woman could be head of it. Elizabeth agreed to the change, but whether "head" or "governor" her powers were the same. Also under the Act of Supremacy, communion in both kinds (bread and wine) was permitted, and the laws allowing religious persecution under Mary were repealed. The 1559 Act of Uniformity made church attendance compulsory on Sundays and Holy Days, and provided for a new Book of Common Prayer, based on the 1552 Prayer Book of Edward VI but with some changes. The most important of these added to the communion service words taken from the earlier 1549 Prayer Book: "The Body of our Lord Jesus Christ, which was given for thee, preserve thy body and soul unto everlasting life," thus suggesting that the Body of Christ could be symbolically present. This change made it easier for Catholics to attend the service and placated the Lutheran wing of Protestants. Less popular

among Protestants was the order for use of vestments by the clergy and crosses and candlesticks in the churches, but Elizabeth liked such remnants of ceremony.[3]

The Royal Injunctions of 1559, which set out details for the regulation of the Church, managed to combine Catholic and Protestant tendencies. For example, images in churches were protected (unlike the iconoclasm under Henry VIII and Edward VI), while clergy were permitted to marry, a Protestant provision disliked but tolerated by the queen.[4] Provisions were made for monthly sermons such as those in a 1559 book entitled, *Certayne sermons appoynted by the Quenes Maiestie*. Every parish was to have an English bible and no one was to be discouraged from reading it. The Great Bible of 1539 edited by Coverdale was the one issued. It was substantially replaced by the Bishops' Bible of 1568, an edition prepared under the auspices of Elizabeth's Archbishop of Canterbury, Matthew Parker, but including the loved Psalter from the Great Bible. A third bible,

I. B. *A booke of certeine devoute and godlie Praires.* Calligraphic manuscript (1564). Folger MS V.a.482, fols. 24v–25r.

particularly popular in households, was the Geneva Bible. First conceived in Calvinist Geneva by John Knox and other Protestant exiles in 1560, it was finally printed in England in 1576.[5]

It has been said that there is no fanatic like a convert, and that saying applies to no one better than John Knox. Originally a Catholic priest in Scotland, Knox was converted by a fellow-Scot, George Wishart, who had learned his brand of Protestantism in Germany. After Wishart was martyred, Knox went on to become a fiery polemicist in the strict Calvinist tradition. With Mary of Guise regent in Scotland and Mary Tudor on the throne in England, Knox published in 1558 his vehement tirade against women rulers, *First Blast of the Trumpet Against the Monstruous Regiment of Women*. Both women were Catholics, so Knox felt justified in berating them on two heads, that of their religion and their gender, but his timing could not have been worse. Within a few months, Protestant Elizabeth had ascended the throne in England, and she was not amused. How could she like a man who thought of women as "weake, fraile, impatie[n]t, . . . vnconstant, variable, cruele, [and] lacking the spirit of counsel and regime[n]t"; and who wrote that "to pro-mote a woman to beare rule, superioritie, dominion or empire aboue any realme, nation, or citie, is repugna[n]t to nature, co[n]tumelie to God, a thing most contrarious to his reueled [revealed] will and approued ordina[n]ce, and finallie it is the subuersion of good order, of all equitie and iustice"?[6] In addition, Knox had the affrontery to suggest that in certain circumstances, the deposition of an ungodly prince could be justified. Elizabeth's Secretary Cecil knew, "Of all others, Knox's name . . . is most odious here."[7] As Christopher Haigh has written, Knox eventually tempered his argument, "writing that, although female rule was unnatural, God had made an exception so that Elizabeth could restore the Gospel. . . . John Calvin had a similar view: some-times God gave a woman special qualities above her sex to serve his divine plan. This was an argument that Elizabeth herself was to use,"[8] though rather than pressing religious reform personally, she allowed her bishops to carry it out.

During the early years of Elizabeth's reign, Catholics lived in relative peace, and undoubtedly many of them slid over into the Church of England, which was exactly what Elizabeth had hoped would happen. When Elizabeth came to the throne, Catholicism was strong, but by the end of her reign, only one to two percent of the population were Catholic.[9] Catholics did not go out peacefully, however. In addition to recusant priests who remained quietly active, teaching or serving the sacraments, reinforcements began to arrive from the continent, first from the English college at Douai around 1574, then Jesuits from the English College in Rome, beginning in 1580. By this time, political events led to a more determined crackdown against Catholics. In 1561, Mary Stuart had returned to Scotland from France to rule her country in person. She thus became a flash-point for Catholic hopes of her conversion of Scotland and ultimate seat on the English throne. In 1569, the Northern Earls had revolted, with the intent of re-establishing the Catholic church in England. Elizabeth had never traveled north on her progresses and probably did not realize the extent to which Catholicism was still entrenched there. The rebellion collapsed for lack of funds and the elusiveness of Mary Stuart, who was kept from their grasp, but about 500 rebels were executed, including the earl of Northumberland.[10] In 1570, Pope Pius V issued a Bull excommu-nicating Elizabeth, which had the effect of winnowing out the hard-line Catholics who were now willing to stand treasonously with Rome against Elizabeth.[11]

Growing difficulties with Spain and the St. Bartholomew Massacre of Huguenots in France in

1572 led to fear of an international Catholic plot, resulting in more stringent enforcement of the Act of Uniformity and the creation of a special prison for Catholics. In 1581, Parliament passed an Act making it treasonous to attempt to convert anyone to Catholicism and "withdraw allegiance from Elizabeth."[12] Another Act followed in 1585, making it "a felony punishable by death to give a priest aid, refuge or comfort," though this act "was applied only erratically," and in the same year, "a group of Catholic nobles and gentry . . . presented Elizabeth with a petition stating that Catholics owed obedience to her, their lawful monarch, and denying that the Pope had power to authorize . . . regicide."[13] It is probably safe to say that the majority of Catholics remained loyal to Elizabeth, even during the Spanish Armada crisis in 1588.

Two brilliant men who returned to England to support the Catholic cause were Robert Parsons and Robert Southwell. Parsons, a graduate of Oxford and a tutor at Balliol College, resigned under duress in 1574 and traveled first to Louvain, where he was influenced by William Good, an English Jesuit, and then to Rome, where he became a Jesuit priest in 1578. He returned to England in 1580–81 as part of the Jesuit mission, preaching, writing, and organizing others. Parsons had a vision of a reorganized Catholic English society which he wrote down in a manuscript that circulated at the time, but was too dangerous to publish until many years later in 1690. It was called *Memorial of the Reformation of England.*[14] During his lifetime, some of his works were printed on a secret press at a house known as Greenstreet in East Ham, Essex. The press was operated with the aid of Stephen Brinkley and some of his men. It was forced to move from place to place, but one of the earliest books printed at this press was Parsons' tract, *Why Catholiques refuse to go to Church* (1580). Both the author and imprint given on the title page are false. A "learned gentleman" and I. H. or John Howlet both refer to Parsons, and Doway is East Ham, while John Lyon is Greenstreet House Press.[15]

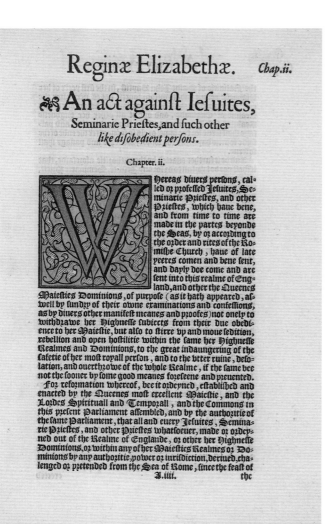

Robert Southwell came from a wealthy family near Norwich. He attended the Jesuit college in Douai, then the Roman College, becoming tutor at the English College in Rome. In 1586 he came to England, where he found the London Catholic community in disarray because of the Babington Plot, in which English Catholics were co-conspirators with the Spanish to kill Elizabeth and replace her with Mary, Queen of Scots. Elizabeth's agent Walsingham had infiltrated the plot, and the conspirators were brutally executed, but as a result of this incident, some of the "safe houses" in London were gone, priests were imprisoned or fled, and the morale of Catholics was low.[16] In some cases, women were aiding the cause; Southwell wrote, "The work of God is being pressed forward—sometimes by delicate

Above: Great Britain. Parliament. *An act against Iesuites, Seminarie Priestes, and such other like disobedient persons* (London, 1585). STC 9485.2, sig. Aiiiir.

Opposite: Elizabethan Conceit (March 8, 1603). Folger MS V.b.319.

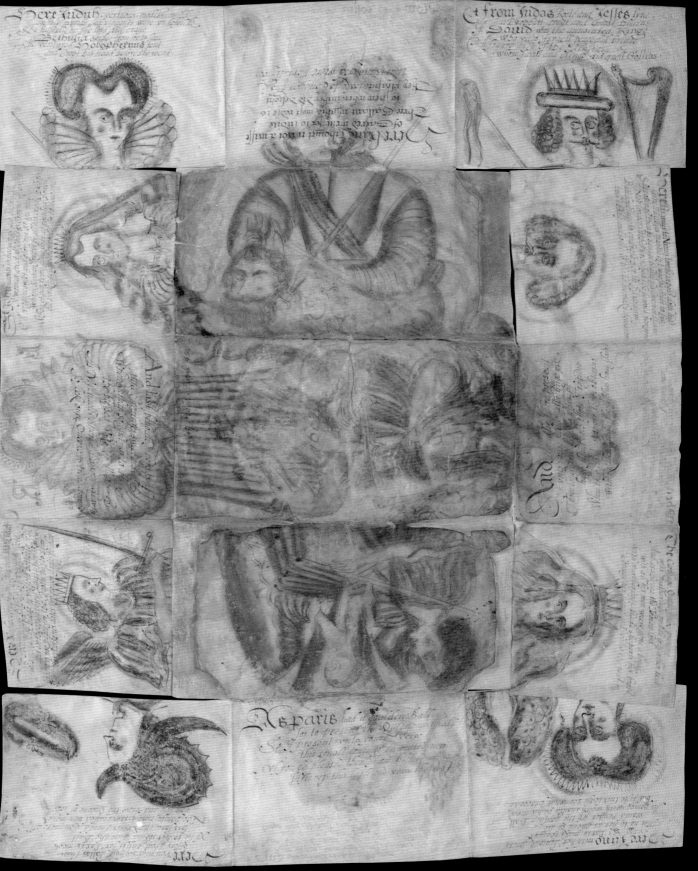

women who have taken on the courage of men." He himself was aided by the Countess of Arundel who provided him with a small house and a secret printing press on which he had published his *Epistle of Comfort* (1587).[17] This work is one of the masterpieces of English devotional literature, showing the command of language that also marked Southwell a poet: "For as to the wayfaring pilgrim, wandering in the darke and mistye night, euery light, though neuer so litle, is comfortable . . . so peraduenture in this foggye night of heresie, . . . this dime [dim] light, which I shall set forth before you, and these my Catholicke, though broken speaches, which I shall vse vnto you will not be altogether vnpleasant" (sig. A4v). Unlike Parsons, who returned to the continent and eventually became rector of the English College in Rome, Southwell was arrested in England, tortured, and died a martyr's death.

Throughout her reign, Elizabeth was also faced with rumblings from the stricter members of her own group, the Protestants. At the extreme end were the Puritans, recently defined by scholars as "Protestants, both lay and clerical, whose religious enthusiasm and zeal marked them off from their more lukewarm contemporaries. They were . . . totally committed to purging the Established Church of its popish 'superstitions' and bringing a biblical morality to English society."[18] During Elizabeth's reign, however, they were merely a subculture of Protestantism. Another group within the Protestant community were those with Presbyterian leanings, a more hard-line fringe of Puritanism. They joined with Puritans in objecting to the re-inforcement of the Prayer Book and Thirty-Nine Articles in 1571 and wanted more reform of the structure of the church itself, moving away from an episcopal structure of bishops to "a preaching ministry in each parish."[19] Politically, these hard-line Protestants were influenced by the possible succession of Catholic Mary, Queen of Scots, should Elizabeth die childless, and by their discontent with Elizabeth's refusal to let the English Church move in a Calvinist direction.[20] Their attempts at reform through Parliament failed, and their cause was also hurt by the publication of the Marprelate Tracts in 1588/89. Even Puritans were shocked at the forthright scurrilous attack against bishops printed in these pamphlets, realizing that it would hurt their cause. They were right. In the process of tracking down the perpetrators, Archbishop Whitgift discovered "the existence of the underground Puritan network," and had it destroyed.[21]

By the end of her reign, the church Elizabeth had established in 1559 was still solidly intact. As she told the French ambassador, "There was only one Jesus Christ, and one faith, and all the rest they disputed about but trifles."[22] Whether Elizabeth really believed this is questionable; after all, she *was* speaking to the ambassador from a newly-converted Catholic king whom she wanted to persuade not to make peace with Spain. Certainly many of her Catholic and Protestant subjects would have objected that to them, "all the rest" was of great importance, but nevertheless, the Church of England took firm root and flourished.

1 Elizabeth I, *Works*, 96.

2 Reply to Parliament, November 24, 1586. Elizabeth I, *Works*, 197.

3 Susan Doran, *Elizabeth I and Religion* (London: Routledge, 1994), 14–15. During Edward's reign, churches had been stripped down with "decoration" now in the form of scriptural quotations painted on the walls. Plain tables were moved in for the service of communion, alms boxes were added, and the pulpit was used only for preaching. The display of the royal coat of arms indicated that this was a reformation from above; "those who ruled the realm… [decided] the form in which the European Reformation would be presented to the people of England" (Diarmaid MacCulloch, *Boy King: Edward VI and the Protestant Reformation* [New York: Palgrave, 2001], 159–160, 163).

4 For a discussion of the 1559 Acts, see Doran, *Religion*, 14–17.

5 See S. L. Greenslade, "English Versions of the Bible, 1525–1611," in *The Cambridge History of the Bible*, vol. 3, ed. Greenslade, 141ff. (Cambridge: the University Press, 1963).

6 John Knox, *The First Blast of the Trumpet Against the Monstrvovs regiment of women* (Geneva, 1558), sig. B2r, B1r.

7 Somerset, *Elizabeth I*, 122.

8 Christopher Haigh, *Elizabeth I*, 2nd ed. (London: Longman, 1998), 13.

9 Doran, *Religion*, 48.

10 Somerset, *Elizabeth I*, 235–37.

11 Michael A. Mullett, *Catholics in Britain and Ireland, 1558-1829* (New York: St. Martin's Press, 1999), 14.

12 Somerset, *Elizabeth I*, 389.

13 Doran, *Religion*, 56, 57.

14 Biographical information from the article by J.H. Pollen in *The Catholic Encyclopedia*, vol. 11 (New York: Appleton, 1911), 729–31; and Michael L. Carrafiello, *Robert Parsons and English Catholicism, 1580-1610* (Selinsgrove: Susquehanna University Press, 1998), 16, 18.

15 For a brief account of this press, see the article by J. Vincent Crowne on "Stephen Brinkley" in *The Catholic Encyclopedia*, vol. 2 (New York: Appleton, 1907), 788.

16 Christopher Devlin, *The Life of Robert Southwell, Poet and Martyr* (New York: Farrar, 1956), 139.

17 Devlin, *Southwell*, 141, 142–44.

18 Doran, *Religion*, 24.

19 Doran, *Religion*, 34.

20 Written comment from Paul Hammer; I am indebted to his helpful reading of this essay.

21 Somerset, *Elizabeth I*, 497.

22 Somerset, *Elizabeth I*, 75.

CATALOGUE

Church of England
Certayne sermons appoynted by the Quenes Maiestie, to be declared and read, by all persones, vycars, and curates, euery Sonday and holy daye
London: Richard Iugge and Iohn Cawood, prynters to the Quenes Maiestie, 1559
STC 13648

Great Britain. Laws
An act against Iesuites, Seminarie Priestes, and such other like disobedient persons in *Anno xxvii. Reginae Elizabethae. At the Parliament begunne and holden at Westminster*
London: Christopher Barker, 1585
STC 9485.2

John Knox (1505–1572)
The first blast of the trumpet against the monstruous regiment of women
Geneva: J. Poullain and A. Rebul, 1558
STC 15070

Robert Parsons (1546–1610)
A brief discours contayning cer-tayne reasons why Catholiques refuse to goe to church
Doway [East Ham]: Iohn Lyon [Greenstreet House Press], 1580
STC 19394

Robert Southwell (1561?–1595)
An epistle of comfort, to the reuerend priestes, & to the honorable, worshipful, & other of the laye sort restrayned in durance for the Catholicke fayth
Paris [London]: John Charlewood? in Arundel House, 1587?
STC 22946

Thomas Trevelyon (b.ca.1548)
John Bale and John Knox
Commonplace Book, 1608
Folger MS V.b.232, fol. 200r

Elizabethan Conceit
March 8, 1603
Folger MS V.b.319

The holie Byble
London: Richarde Iugge, printer to the Queenes Maiestie, 1573
STC 2108

I. B.
A booke of certeine devoute and godlie Praires
Calligraphic manuscript, 1564
Folger MS V.a.482

PER TAL VARIAR SON QVI X.

Lo here her Tÿpe, who was of late, the Propp of Belgia, Stay of France:
Spaynes Foyle Faith's Shield, and Queene of STATE: Of Armes, and Learning, FATE, and Chance:
In briefe; of women, nere was scene so greate a Prince; so good a Queene

Jo: Dauies. Here:

Fr: De: Sculptor: **ELIZABETHA REGINA.**

The Death of Elizabeth

"**TO BE A KING AND WEAR A CROWN** is a thing more glorious to them that see it than it is pleasant to them that bear it." In this simple statement from one of her last speeches to members of Parliament, Elizabeth strangely echoed the thoughts that Shakespeare gave to several of his English kings. She continued:

For myself, I was never so much enticed with the glorious name of a king or royal authority of a queen as delighted that God hath made me His instrument to maintain His truth and glory, and to defend this kingdom . . . from peril, dishonor, tyranny, and oppression. There will never queen sit in my seat with more zeal to my country, care to my subjects, and that will sooner with willingness venture her life for your good and safety, than myself. For it is not my desire to live nor reign longer than my life and reign shall be for your good. And though you have had and may have many princes more mighty and wise sitting in this seat, yet you never had or shall have any that will be more careful and loving.[1]

Elizabeth could not have known in November of 1601 that she had only about a year and a half to live, but there is an elegiac quality to her speech which comes from the heart of a woman who has lived long and seen much, now in the forty-fourth year of her reign. She was a true "career-woman" long before the term was ever coined; her job was her life. Without husband or children of her own, she always saw herself as married to her realm with her people as her children. Something of this feeling occurs in her very last Parliamentary speech of December 1601 where she said: "Concerning our affection to our people, it is our happiest felicity and most inward joy that no prince ever governed a more faithful, valiant, and loving people."[2]

A year later, in January of 1603, Elizabeth went into a decline. She "began somewhat to be sensible of defect of health, & strength, w[i]th [th]e indisposition of [th]e Aire towards [th]e end of January, being a filthy windy & rainy day," states an account of her last days written in a contemporary commonplace book, now at the Folger Library.[3] The unknown writer is basically copying

---

Francis Delaram. *Elizabeth Regina*. Engraving after Nicholas Hilliard (ca.1617–1619). STC 7758.3 v.3 no.1.

their Colours should be laid downe;
& ye Ship, Ordnance, & Merchandize
should be safely delivered up to ye English;
& that in ye meane time, there should be
no shooting from ye Castle out, upon,
or against ye English. The same night
all were dismissed out of ye Carack, except ye Master, & some few more, yt were
set a shoare earely in ye morning. And ye
very same day ye English put forth with
ye Carack having a good winde; brought
home a lusty prey, having not lost above
5. of ye Marriners; ye prey being valued
by ye Portugals at 1000000. Crownes.
After yeir returne, Mounson being sent back
againe towards ye coasts of Spaine, continued there abouts, till ye middest of Winter,
to hinder any attempt upon Ireland.
While hee launched out into ye deepe, towards Spaine, Frederick Spinola with
6. Gallies, yt had gotten out safe at the
skirmish, comming along by ye French
shoare,

£50000

shoare, came at last to ye British O-
cean on ye 23th of September, wth intent
to enter at some Haven or other in Flanders.

Anno Dni. 1603. Containing not fully
3. Moneths of ye raigne of Queen Elizabeth.

The Queen, who hitherto, by her abstinence
from Wine, & moderate Diet, wch shee said was
ye chiefest part of Physick, enjoyed pfect health,
now entring into her Climactericall yeare, to
wit, 70. began somewhat to be sensible of defect
of health, & strength, & ye indisposition of
ye Aire towards ye end of January; being a
filthy windy & rainy day, much improved,
when shee removed from Westminster to
Richmond, on purpose to refresh her olde
age wth quietnes, & to give her selfe to god-
lines wholly. Upon which day, as if shee
were about somewhat else, [I knowe not
whether shee thought upon, or pphesied of
her death] shee said to ye Admirall, whom shee
dearely loved, My Throne is a Throne of
Kings, neither ought any but my next
Heire to succeed mee. The Courtiers yt
observed

remembred, that Thursday hath been
a fatall day to King Henry ye 8th, & all
his posterity: for himself died on Thursday ye 28th of January; King Edward
on Thursday ye 6th of July; Queen Mary on Thursday ye 17th of November;
& Queen Elizabeth on Thursday ye
24th of March. Queen Eliz. was
tall of stature, strong in every limbe
& joynt, her fingers small & long, her
voice loude & shrill; shee was of an
admirable ready wit & memory; very
skilfull in all kinde of Needle-work; had
an excellent eare in Musick; played
well upon divers Instruments; shee
spake ye Greek, Latine, Italian, and
French tongues well, & understood
ye Spanish: shee was resolute, & of an
undaunted spirit: &c. Ao. Di. 1600.
Shee at one time entertained one Duke
& 2. Ambassadours; yt voluntarily, came to see
her

her Matie yt is to say, ye Muscovie Ambassadour, ye Barbarian Ambassadour, &
ye Duke of Brachiano a Romane, whom
shee entertained in all state, love, and
kindenes, in whose presence her Royall
Person daunced, being then 68. yeares
of age.

HER EPITAPH.

ELIZA that great Maiden Queen lies here,
Who govern'd England foure & forty yeres;
Our Coynes refinde, wilde Ireland tade Belgiae tested:
Friended France, foyled Spaine, & Pope rejected:
Princes found her powerfull, ye World vertuous,
Her Subjects wise & just, & to God religious;
God hath her Soule, ye World her admiration:
Subjects her good deeds, Princes her imitation.

Qu: Eliz. did aide Henry 4th ye distressed
King of France. To help him first, Ao. Di.
1589. shee sent him 22000.li. of English
Gold,

out an account published in later editions of William Camden's *History of the Most Renowned and Victorious Princess Elizabeth*. The writer continues: "her appetite to meate grew sensibly worse & worse; whereupon shee became exceeding sad, & seemed to be much grieved at some thing or other."[4] From other accounts we know that she sat for hours on the floor, sometimes sucking her finger and refusing to go to bed. At last she was persuaded into bed, and after sleeping for five hours, she died about 3 o'clock in the morning of March 24, 1603.

The various reports of Elizabeth's death display uncertainty about whether she actually named a successor. Another account that has come down in manuscript was written by Elizabeth Southwell, one of her maids of honor. Southwell was about seventeen years old when she attended the queen through her last days. She stresses the fact, several times, that the queen had her wits about her until the end, but a sore throat made it difficult for her to talk.

she desired to wash yt that she might answer more freelie to what the Councell demanded. which was to know whom she would have king. but they seeing her throt troubled her so much desired her to hold up her finger when they named whom liked her whereupon they named the K of france the K of Scotland at which she never stirred, they named my lord Beaucham whereto she said. I will have no raskalls son in my seat but . . . one worthy to be a king: Hereupon ynstantlie she died: Then the Councell went forth and reported she meant the K of Scots.[5]

Camden's version of the story, transcribed in the Folger commonplace book, is tidied up and made more explicit. It reports that when she first removed to Westminster, she told the Lord Admiral "My Throne is a Throne of Kings, neither ought any but my next Heire to succeed mee" (leaf 23r). This version goes on to find a cause for the queen's deep melancholy in the fact that a number of her nobles and courtiers were already beginning to curry favor with King James in Scotland. When the queen was very near death, her councillors again requested her to acknowledge a successor. She replied:

I have said, My Throne is [th]e Throne of Kings; no ordinary man shall succeed mee. The Secretary asking what shee meant by those words. I will, said shee, that a King succeed mee, & what King, but my neerest Kinsman the King of Scots.[6]

It seems more likely that she *did* say she didn't want "a raskalls son" in her seat, but "one worthy to be king," leaving the name itself open, but it was expedient for printed accounts such as Camden's to specify James of Scotland more specifically, in order to give historical weight to the legality of James's succession.

The Folger manuscript account, like Camden's, notes that she died on "the Eve of [th]e Annunciation of [th]e blessed Virgin Mary," as she was "borne on [th]e Eve of the Nativity of [th]e said blessed Virgin."[7] To her people, most of whom no longer worshiped the Virgin Mary, Elizabeth had been their earthly Virgin Queen, memorialized in one epitaph as:

Historical Commonplace Book, with details of the last three months of Elizabeth's life, ca.1625. Folger MS X.d.393, fols. 22v–23r, 27v–28r.

This mayden Queen of never dying memory:

Shee was, Shee is,

[What can there more bee said?]

In Earth the first,

In Heaven the second Maid.[8]

Elizabeth's funeral took place on April 18, not quite a month after her death. A detailed description of the procession was published at the time by Henry Chettle in *Englands Mourning Garment*, a pastoral piece about the death of the queen and the arrival of a new king. Its politically correct dedication on the title page is made "to all that loued the deceased Queene, and honour the liuing King." The procession consisted of the large number of members of the queen's household, from the children of the woodyard, scullery, and pastry, through the grooms of the poultry, laundry, kitchen, etc., the wine porter, bell ringer, and maker of spice bags, servants of nobles and ambassadors, the children and gentlemen of the chapel, the musicians, apothecaries and various clerks, the Aldermen of London, gentlemen of the privy chamber, to the barons, bishops, earls, and marquesses, and finally the coffin containing the body of the queen. On the leaded coffin lay "the liuely picture of her Highnesse whole body, crowned in her Parliament Robes, with her Scepter in her hand" —a royal effigy made out of wood, horsehair, and cloth, the rudiments of which still exist at Westminster Abbey. The coffin itself was "couered with Purple veluet, borne in a chariot, drawne by foure horses trapt [with trappings] in blacke veluet." After the coffin came the queen's women: Countesses, ladies of honor, viscountesses, earls' daughters, baronesses, and "Maids of Honor of the priuie chamber."[9]

A thirteen-year-old girl, Lady Anne Clifford, who was present at the funeral, has left her impressions.

When the Corps of Q.E. had continued at Whitehall as the Council thought fit, it was carried with great solemnity to Westminster, the Lords & Ladies going on foot to attend it. My Mother & my Aunt Warwick being Mourners, but I was not allowed to be one because I was not high enough, which did much trouble me then, but yet I stood in the Church at Westminster to see the Solemnities performed."[10]

John Stowe's *Annals of . . . England*, augmented by Edmund Howes in 1631, gives a vivid description of the crowds at the funeral procession through the city of Westminster: "multitudes of all sorts of people in their streetes, houses, windows, leads, and gutters, that came to see the obsequie." "When they beheld her statue or picture lying vpon the coffin set foorth in Royall Robes . . . there was such a generall sighing, groning, and weeping, as the like hath not beene seene or knowne in the memory of man, neither doeth any history mention any people, time, or state, to make like lamentation for the death of their soueraigne."[11]

Elizabeth was first buried in the tomb of her grandparents, King Henry VII and Elizabeth of York, at Westminster Abbey. Their joint tomb symbolised the union of the houses of Lancaster and York in the Tudor line ending with Elizabeth. King James, however, had his own dynastic agenda. In 1606 he had Elizabeth's body moved to a side chapel and buried in a tomb with her sister Mary Tudor. Not perhaps the happiest arrangement, but though the tomb contains both bodies, the monument itself features only the marble effigy of Elizabeth. Julia Walker has shown that as James moved to succeed Elizabeth, he made a point of "stressing his own descent from Henry VII," and ultimately had himself buried in Elizabeth's place in the Henry VII tomb. Walker convincingly argues that "even as he builds a tomb honoring the Virgin Queen, James reminds the public of this historical reality: virgins do not found or further the greatness of dynasties." He thus marginalizes Elizabeth and Mary in a joint tomb to the side, while the subsequent tombs of the Stuarts "lie in the south aisle, continuing the line from Margaret Beaufort which was interrupted by those two barren . . . Tudor queens."[12]

We know exactly what James paid for Elizabeth's tomb from a manuscript, now at the Folger Library, that was part of an Exchequer account book. The magnificent funeral itself cost an

enormous sum: 17,301 pounds, 5 shillings, 6 pence. In addition, James paid 965 pounds for the monument, including 95 pounds to "Patrick the blacksmith" and 100 pounds to "John de Crites y^E painter." A near-contemporary picture of the monument appears in Henry Holland's *Heroologia* (1620), a book of brief biographies and eulogies for famous Englishmen and Elizabeth, accompanied by their portraits.[13]

The difficulty of mourning a loved queen while welcoming a new king is evident in the titles of some of the commemorative pamphlets that poured from the presses in 1603: *Sorrowes Joy*; *Weepe with Joy*; *Elizaes Loss and King James his Welcome*. Some of the titles are almost as long as

Order of procession for Queen Elizabeth's funeral, in Philip Holland, attrib., Herald's book of precedence (ca.1605). Folger MS V.a.213, pp. 6–7.

432

Debts due at the death of the late Q. Elizabeth, & paid by King James.

~~There was owing at her death~~

To Sr John Fortescue for the funerall charges of the late Queen — [illegible] £17301. 5. 6

2.

Debts due at the death of the late Queen Elizabeth and paid since by King James.

Charges of the tomb for the late Queene	Maximilian Powtran [illegible] £570		£765
	Patrick the blacksmith [illegible] £95		besides stone to the amount of 200 £
	John de Critz the painter [illegible] £100		all — 965. 0. 0

Payments made by his Matie to the severall officers and particular persons hereafter named, which were due at the tyme of the decease of the late Queen. Viz.

To the Cofferer remaining unpayd upon the determination of his accompt ended the last of September 1602.	[illegible] £5237. 9. 11¾	[illegible] £16751. 2. 1
More due by tallies levied att Easter 1603.	[illegible] £11513. 12. 1¼	
Band of pentioners for the quarter ended att Midsomer 1603.		[illegible] £1041. 7. 1
Tresorer of the Chamber for the quarter then also ended.		[illegible] £2000
Erle of Salisbury for intelligences due att the said feast		[illegible] £200
Mr of the Postes for the quarter then also ended		[illegible] £920. 7. 4
Officers of the workes for Febr. & Marche 1602 and 1603.		[illegible] £700. 2. 3

Tresorer of the navy	Ordinary	Harborow for Jan. Febr. 1602. & Marche 1603.	[illegible] £3142. 2. 9	[illegible] £21573. 16. —
		Narrow Seas for 7 monethes ended the last of Marche 1603.	[illegible] £3683. 2. 10	
	Extraordinary	For repayre of shipps & for mastes.	[illegible] £5000	
		For cordage & remain of 4435-13-9.	[illegible] £2000	
		For discharge of 1500 men sent under the conduct of Sr Richard Leveson.	[illegible] £3400	
Survr of the marine victualls for victualling of shippes att		Harborow for Jan. Feb. & Marche 1602. 1603.	[illegible] £3032. 5	
		Narrow Seas untill the last of Marche 1603.	[illegible] £1314. 5. 5	

2.

Sorrovves Ioy.

OR,

A LAMENTATION for our late deceased Soveraigne ELIZABETH, with a triumph for the prosperous succession of our gratious King, IAMES, &c.

HINC LVCEM ET POCVLA SACRA
ALMA MATER CANTABRIGIA

Park

Printed by IOHN LEGAT, Printer to the Vniversitie of CAMBRIDGE. 1603.

their contents. A twenty-four-page book by James Fenton is advertised as: *King James His Welcome to London. With Elizaes Tombe and Epitaph, And our Kings triumph and epitimie. Lamenting the ones decease, And reioycing at the others accesse*; and a single-sheet popular song is called *A mournefull dittie entituled Elizabeths losse, together with a welcome for King James. To a pleasant new tune.* The ambiguity of the event is perhaps nowhere better revealed than in a poem by Thomas Bradburie, in the volume *Sorrowes Joy*:

Twixt King and Queene while I deuide my heart,
They, each to other, yeeld their doubtfull part:
So turne I griefe to ioy, or ioy to griefe:
For in a kingdome onely one is chiefe.
The title due to both: and both I like:
And both my heart with ioy and griefe doe strike.
Her losse, my griefe: his gaine, my ioy doth claime....[14]

Sorrowes Joy contains poems by members of the colleges of Cambridge University. Both Oxford and Cambridge produced appropriate memorials, mostly in Latin. A learned woman herself, Elizabeth had visited the universities on various occasions, and they now remembered her in death.

Elizabeth was remembered as "Virgin Mother and Maiden Queen." She was praised for her learning, and as one who had maintained peace at home and supported the true (Protestant) religion. The sentiments surrounding her are concisely summarized by the little epitaph in James Fenton's book:

Shee liu'd [lived] to age a glasse, to youth a mirror;
Vnto her friends a ioy; to foes a terror.
Shee was the Souldiers captaine, the law's life,
The Churches deerest spouse, the Churchmans wife,
Learnings greene Lawrell, vertues chiefe refector:
Peaces maintainer, onely Truths protector.
The Orphants parents, and the ritchmans stay:
The poore mans comfort, and the nights cleere day.
The tradsman[s] favorer, and the merchants gaine;
The seamans night starre, and the lyers staine,
The pride of all her sex, all womens boast:
The worlds wonder, that they wondred most.[15]

Truly, no prince ever did govern "a more faithful, valiant and loving people."

Opposite top: Great Britain. Exchequer. *Debts due at the death of the late Queen Elizabeth & paid since by King James* (Aug. 28, 1607). Folger MS X.d.541.

Opposite bottom: Sorrovves Ioy. Or, A Lamentation for our late deceased Soveraigne Elizabeth (London, 1603). STC 7598, title page.

Following page: Henry Holland. *Heroologia Anglica* (Arnheim, 1620). STC 13582, c. 2, sig. D5r.

1   Elizabeth I, *Works*, 339–40.

2   *Works*, 353.

3   Folger MS X.d. 393, fol. 23r.

4   X.d. 393, fol. 23r.

5   Quoted from Catherine Loomis, "Elizabeth Southwell's Manuscript Account of the Death of Queen Elizabeth [with text]," *ELR* 26 (1996): 484. The manuscript is "preserved at Stonyhurst College, Lancashire, among the papers of the Jesuit Robert Persons" (483).

6   X.d. 393, fol. 23r, 26r.

7   X.d. 393, fol. 26v.

8   X.d. 393, fol. 27r. An almost-identical epitaph appeared in St. Mary Aldermary Church in London. See Julia Walker, "Bones of Contention: Posthumous Images of Elizabeth and Stuart Politics," in *Dissing Elizabeth*, ed. Walker (Durham: Duke University Press, 1998), 262.

9   Henry Chettle, *Englands Mourning Garment* (London, 1603), sig. F2r.

10 Lady Anne Clifford, *The Diaries*, ed. D. J. H. Clifford (Stroud, Glous.; Wolfeboro Falls, NH: Alan Sutton, 1994), 22.

11 John Stowe, *Annales, or a Generall Chronicle of England*, aug. Edmund Howes (London: Richard Meighen, 1631), 815. King James had died in 1625, but Howes' enthusiasm here for the degree of mourning at Elizabeth's death feeds into the general rhetoric of Elizabethan nostalgia in the seventeenth century.

12 Julia M. Walker, "Reading the Tombs of Elizabeth I," *ELR* 26 (1991): 516, 524. Walker, "Tombs," also discusses the implications of the grandness and placement of the monument James had built for his mother, Mary, Queen of Scots, which cost more than Elizabeth's monument. See Walker, 523–24. In addition to Elizabeth's actual monument in Westminster Abbey, thirty-one other churches in London had monuments to the queen, according to Stowe's *Survey of London* (1633) (Walker, "Tombs," 528). For a more detailed discussion of these monuments with their inscriptions, see Walker, "Bones of Contention," 258–63.

13 I am grateful to Susan Cerasano for calling my attention to the Exchequer manuscript and for sharing her transcription of it.

14 *Sorrowes Joy* (London, 1603), 12.

15 James Fenton, *King James His Welcome to London* (London, 1603), sig. B2r-B2v.

Henry Chettle (d. 1607?)
Englands mourning garment
London: [E. Short?] for
Thomas Millington, 1603
STC 5122

Sorrowes ioy. Or, A lamentation for our late deceased soveraigne Elizabeth
London: Iohn Legat, 1603
STC 7598

I. F.
King Iames his welcome to London
London: [R. Read?] for
Thomas Pauier, 1603.
STC 10798

Henry Holland (1583–1650?)
Heroologia Anglica
Arnhem: Jan Jansson for
Henry Holland,
London, 1620
STC 13582, c.2

Order of procession for
Queen Elizabeth's funeral, in
Philip Holland, attrib.,
Herald's book of precendence,
ca.1605
Folger MS V.a.213

Historical Commonplace Book
(with details of the last three
months of Elizabeth's life),
ca.1625
Folger MS X.d.393

Great Britain. Exchequer
Debts due at the death of the late Queen Elizabeth & paid since by King James
Aug. 28, 1607
Folger MS X.d.541

William Camden (1551–1623), supposed artist
The funeral procession of Queen Elizabeth, from a drawing of the time, supposed to be by the hand of William Camden
London: Sumptibus Soc.
Antiquar, 1791
ART Flat a2, c.2

James the first of that name kyng of England, scotland, france and Jreland
the first monarch of the whol Jland or countrey was proclamed at the age
of ·36· yaares the ·24· of march· 1602· being the next inheritor to henrye the
seuenth, and Elyzabeth his queene protracted from lady margarat el=
dest daughter of them both in whose most happy coniunction ended the
civil discention of those two families, lancaster and yorke, blesse his raign
olord with true religion, peace and number of yeares to him and his posteriti
oooooooooooooooooooo for Ever oo oooooooooooooo

James I

IN 1598 APPEARED A LITTLE PAMPHLET PRINTED IN EDINBURGH, entitled *A Pithie Exhortation to Her Maiestie for Establishing Her Successor to the crowne.* It had been written around 1587 by Peter Wentworth, Member of Parliament from Northampton, who had a knack for getting himself into trouble by tackling politically "hot" subjects. His concern this time was the succession. For years, Elizabeth's counselors and Parliament had been after her to name a successor. This was a very touchy issue, however, which Elizabeth did *not* like to have raised. In 1563, Parliament had petitioned her to name a successor, and they were at it again in 1566. On the latter occasion, Elizabeth responded sharply: "Your petition is to deal in the limitation of the succession. At this present, it is not convenient, nor never shall be without some peril unto you and certain danger unto me."[1] Elizabeth was not overstating the peril and danger of naming one successor, when—at least early in her reign—"there were at least ten possible claimants to the throne."[2] To have named one above the others would have been to encourage factionalism and possible civil war.

But the issue did not go away, especially as it became obvious that Elizabeth was not going to marry and have children of her own. Attempts to raise it again in 1575/6 and 1580/1 were squashed, but the issue so agitated Wentworth that he wrote out his thoughts in 1587. During the Parliament of 1593, Wentworth met with some colleagues to discuss the best way to present the topic to Parliament. That was a mistake. Members of Parliament were forbidden to discuss business out-of-house, and the men were rounded up and questioned. Wentworth was imprisoned in the Tower, where he died in 1597.[3] While in the Tower, he replied to another pamphlet on the succession, written by Robert Parsons and others under the pseudonym R. Doleman. This reply was printed posthumously along with *A pithie exhortation.* In it, Wentworth ironically upheld the right of James VI of Scotland to succeed to the English throne, an event which in fact transpired upon Elizabeth's death.[4]

For many years, James had been the strongest—though not publicly declared—candidate for the succession. His claim was through his parents, Mary, Queen of Scots, and Lord Darnley, both of whom were descended from Henry VII. In addition he had two other important qualifications:

Thomas Trevelyon. *James the sixt of Scotland,* from *Commonplace Book* (1608). Folger MS V.b.232, fol. 125v.

he was not a foreigner (or at least, not from the Continent), *and* he was solidly Protestant. Born in 1566, he became king of Scotland at the age of thirteen months, an anomalous situation caused by the murder of his father and the abdication of his mother in 1567. James was raised and trained by the strict but renowned scholar, George Buchanan, one of whose pupils had been Montaigne.[5] As he grew older, James sharpened his kingly abilities by dealing strongly with the fractious parties of Scottish nobles and members of the Scottish Kirk. Elizabeth kept in touch with him over the years, and in 1586 when he was twenty, she settled an annual annuity on him of £5,000 in exchange for an alliance in which the Scots would remain neutral in England's war with Spain. And, James would take advice from England and would engage in "no independent initiatives in foreign policy."[6] The Folger Library has an order signed by Elizabeth to the Exchequer requesting the delivery of £2500—"being the half of such gratuitie, as wee are pleased he shall yearly receaue of vs"—to James by his servant Roger Aston, dated June 28, 1602.[7] The two payments were to be made at the feasts of St. John the Baptist and Christmas.

Maurice Lee, in his biography of James, writes that "the succession to the English crown was the great object of James's life—indeed, an obsession. He would do anything to obtain it, even to the extent of risking the patriotic wrath of his subjects after the execution of his mother."[8] When Mary was tried in 1586, James protested a death sentence against her, but he was unwilling to jeopardize his place in the English succession by, for example, going to war with England after Mary's execution in 1587. He actually wrote to the Earl of Leicester in December 1586, "How fond and inconstant I were if I should prefer my mother to the title let all men judge."[9] Putting his own political position over the welfare of his mother seems heartless to us, until we remember that James had hardly known his mother, and having worked extremely hard to get where he was, he meant to stay there and eventually further his career.

The Folger Library also owns a letter that Elizabeth wrote to James in March of 1595, warning him to deal more forcefully with the group of belligerent Catholic earls in Scotland. These men "had signed blank letters addressed to the King of Spain" with the aim of supporting a Spanish

Elizabeth I. Warrant for payment. To the Treasurer of the Exchequer (Signed, June 28, 1602). Folger MS X.d.99.

Catholic invasion of Scotland. Fortunately the plot had been discovered and foiled, but Elizabeth says that they "long ago . . . ought so have smarted as you need not now examine their treachery." The rest of the letter deals with "Francis Stewart Hepburn, fifth earl of Bothwell and nephew of the Bothwell who had married" James's mother Mary after Darnley's death.[10] Francis Hepburn was a militant Protestant who had crossed into England when things got too hot for him at home. James had accused Elizabeth of aiding him, but she sets him straight, calling Hepburn a "lewd, unadvised, headsick fellow." At the end of the letter, when Elizabeth is running out of paper, she apologizes for her handwriting: "Now do I remember your cumber [difficulty] to read such scribbled lines."[11]

Beginning in 1601 after the execution of the Earl of Essex, whom James had unwisely supported, Elizabeth's Secretary of State, Robert Cecil, entered into a secret correspondence with James with the idea that he would support James's claim to the throne upon the death of the queen. Such correspondence was so sensitive that code numbers were used to designate the parties mentioned; Cecil was 10 and James 30.[12] James "even permitted Cecil to draft any correspondence he had with Elizabeth, so that he could be sure of striking exactly the right note."[13] Elizabeth's biographer, Anne Somerset, postulates that the queen probably knew what was going on, but "she trusted Cecil to see that the transfer of power went smoothly, and to the last she believed that this informal arrangement would suit everyone better than an official acknowledgement that James was her heir."[14] After becoming king of England, James grew so familiar with Cecil as to address him as "My little beagle" in his letters.

Sir Robert Carey arrived in Scotland on March 26 to tell James of the death of Elizabeth, two days after it happened. So many English nobles started the trip north to greet the new king, obviously courting his favor, that James was forced to write a letter requesting that "a sufficient number" of them should remain at home "attending at London with your accustomed care upon our affairs."[15] The coronation was held July 25, 1603, St. James's Day, with perhaps fewer festivities than might have been, because of an outbreak of the plague in London.[16]

Those who had questions about the new king's ideas concerning kingship could read his thoughtful treatise on the subject, *Basilikon Doron*. James first wrote this work in 1598 for his son, Prince Henry, then had a few copies privately printed in 1599. By 1603 the work had been pirated, and such popularity led to the publication of an authorized version the same year. This and others of his works appeared in a handsome collected edition in 1616. Like Elizabeth, James was well-read and scholarly, but his writings, unlike hers, seem to have been done with more of an eye towards public transmission. Perhaps it was the difference in their backgrounds and age. Both were tutored by scholarly men—Ascham and Buchanan—who were themselves published

Elizabeth I. Autograph letter, signed, to James VI of Scotland (ca. March 1595). Folger MS X.d.397, verso.

authors, but Elizabeth may have felt more wary about publishing anything she had written. In any case, most of her writing was in the form of political letters, or prayers and translations done for her own amusement, while James wrote scholarly treatises on topics as varied as witchcraft, tobacco, and religious unity.

England welcomed this Protestant king, who came equipped with wife and children. The transition was a smooth one, and it seemed that there would be no problems with future successions. At the end of his account of Elizabeth's reign, William Camden wrote, "The most sorrowfull misse of her, which she left to the *English*, was asswaged by the great hope conceiued of the vertues of King *Iames* her successor: who after a few houres was proclaymed King with the most ioyful shouts and acclamations of all men." Camden ends by quoting James's own words about Elizabeth: "*As who . . . in wisdome and felicity of gouernment, surpassed*, (without enuy be it spoken) *all the Princes since the dayes of* Augustus."[17]

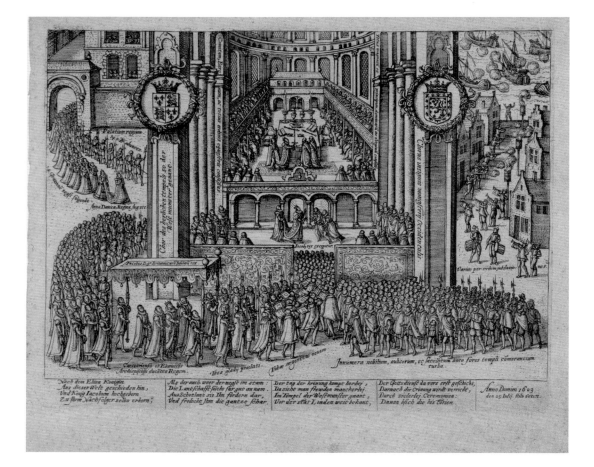

Johann Hogenberg (?). *Krönung Jakobs I. in Westminster* (Cologne, 1603). ART 235612.

1 Elizabeth I, *Works*, 97.

2 Somerset, *Elizabeth* I, 560. She discusses the claimants on pp. 560–61.

3 See Somerset, *Elizabeth I*, 559. Wentworth's wife, Elizabeth, kept him company in the Tower and died there; she was Walsingham's sister (see *DNB*).

4 See J. E. Neale, *Elizabeth I and Her Parliaments, 1584-1601* (London: Jonathan Cape, 1957), 262.

5 Roger Lockyer, *James VI and I* (London; New York: Longman, 1998), 8.

6 Maurice Lee, *Great Britain's Solomon* (Urbana: University of Illinois Press, 1990), 64.

7 Folger MS X.d.99.

8 Lee, 65.

9 Quoted in Lee, 97.

10 Folger MS X.d.397. See the description of this letter by Janel Mueller and Leah S. Marcus in *"The Pen's Excellencie": Treasures from the Manuscript Collection of the Folger Shakespeare Library*, ed. Heather Wolfe (Washington, D.C.: Folger Shakespeare Library, 2002), 54.

11 Letter quoted from Elizabeth I, *Works*, 369.

12 James VI and I, *Letters*, ed. G. P. V. Akrigg (Berkeley: University of California Press, 1984), 178–79.

13 Somerset, *Elizabeth I*, 565.

14 Somerset, 566.

15 James VI and I, *Letters*, 210.

16 Lee, *Solomon*, 108.

17 William Camden, *The Historie of the Most Renowned and Victorious Princesse Elizabeth* (London: Benjamin Fisher, 1630), sig. Eeee4v.

James I, King of England
(1566–1625)
The workes of the most high and mightie prince, Iames. . .King of Great Britaine
London: Robert Barker and Iohn Bill, 1616
STC 14344, c.1

Peter Wentworth
(ca.1530–1596)
A pithie exhortation to her Maiestie for establishing her successor to the crowne
Edinburgh: Robert Waldegrave, 1598
STC 25245

Elizabeth I, Queen of England
(1533–1603)
Autograph letter, signed, to James VI of Scotland
ca. March 1595
Folger MS X.d.397

Elizabeth I, Queen of England
(1533–1603)
Warrant for payment. To the Treasurer of the Exchequer
Signed, June 28, 1602
Folger MS X.d.99

Johann Hogenberg (?)
Krönung Jakobs I. in Westminster
Cologne, 1603
Engraving
ART 235612

Francis Delaram (1589?–1627)
Elizabeth Regina
Engraving after Nicholas Hilliard
ca.1617–19
STC 7758.3 v.3 no.1

Queene Elizabeth

yeare of the queenes raigne vne faynt James day 1555.

Elyzabeth queene of england fecond daughter to kyng henry
the eight to the great comfort of england, was proclamed
queene the 17 day of november, in the yeare of lord 1558: the
15 day of January the queene was crowned at weftmynfter by
doctor oglethorpe byfhop of carlyle, in the theird yeare of the
queenes raigne, one moore profeffed to be chrift our faviour,
and the fame moore was whipped till hee conffeffed chrift to be

Afterwards

Gone is Elizabeth,

whom we haue lou'd so deare,

She our kind Mistris was,

full foure and forty yeare.

THESE LINES FROM A SHORT POEM meant to be sung to the tune of "Phillida flouts me," were published in a little book of popular verse called *The Crowne-Garland of Goulden Roses, Gathered out of Englands royall garden* (London, 1612). They represent the ballad tradition recording stories about Dick Whittington, Jane Seymour, and others, as well as popular songs. Elizabeth, however is remembered in two of the poems. The headnote to the verses quoted above says that they were "made by one of the maides of honor, vpon the death of Queene Elizabeth, which she sowed vppon a sampler in red silke."[1] This unexpected and touching detail personalizes the general grief felt at the old queen's passing. The poem itself is generic, similar to many others commemorating Elizabeth, but the young maid of honor stitched her love and grief into a sampler to make a tangible memory of the queen she had served. The book was republished several times with some changes, but the maid's poem survives in the 1692 edition along with three others about Elizabeth, showing how deeply she was implanted in the common memory of the English people.

The transition in 1603 from Elizabeth to James, while politically smooth, was personally difficult. As Judith Richards has recently shown, after more than forty years on the throne, Elizabeth had come to represent "Englishness" in a way that James never quite understood.[1] People were used to her interactive style—her delight in traveling among her subjects and talking with them. James was uncomfortable with public appearances, as soon became evident when he did not respond as readily as Elizabeth had to the crowds who pressed to greet him when he neared London. It was his consort, Queen Anne, who fell more naturally into the public role of queenship, a fact noted by Arabella Stuart who remarked on the falling off in courtesy, "'for I protest I see little or none of it but in the queen [Anne], who . . . hath spoken to the people as she passeth, and receiveth their prayers

---

Thomas Trevelyon. *Queene Elizabeth*, from *Commonplace Book* (1608). Folger MS V.b.232, fol. 119.

with thanks . . . to the great contentment of native and foreign people.'"[3] David Cressy writes that Elizabeth's continuing popularity in both high and low culture, made her "a rival with whom no living kings could compete. At best they might associate her image with their own; at worst, Elizabeth's memory loomed as a reproach to her less illustrious successors."[4]

The high cultural memory of Elizabeth was kept alive in the writings of historians, preachers, and politicians. The greatest of these was undoubtedly William Camden, learned London school-master, friend of Sir Robert Cotton, co-founder of the Society of Antiquaries, and correspondent with some of the brightest minds of Europe. As early as 1596, Camden's "old patron Lord Burgh-ley suggested to him that he write the history of the reign of Queen Elizabeth," and provided him with access to the state papers.[5] When Burghley died two years later, Camden hoped that some-one else would take on what he obviously felt was a daunting task. But no one came forward, and then around 1605 he suddenly dropped everything and began to work intensely on the history. This time it was under pressure from King James, who wanted to counter the effects of George Buchanan's *History of Scotland* that was making its rounds on the Continent, denigrating James's mother, Mary, Queen of Scots.[6] James wanted Camden to provide a more positive account of that part of Elizabeth's reign to show to the noted French historian, Jacques-Auguste de Thou, who was writing his great history of the period, but when James found his influence did not work with de Thou, he commanded Camden to go ahead and publish his own history, even though it only went up to 1588. Thus in 1615 appeared Camden's *Annales rerum Anglicarum, et Hiberni-carum, regnante Elizabetha.* Camden went on to finish the work, but James was no longer interested in having the rest printed. In order to secure its ultimate appearance, Camden sent the manuscript to his friend Pierre Dupuy, who published it in 1625 in Leiden, after the deaths of both Camden and James.[7] In the same year, an English translation of the earlier part of the *Annales* was published in London. A translation of all four books appeared in 1626, and again in 1630 and 1635.

Camden was really the first great modern English historian. He was writing a new kind of history, based not on "the humanist, merely literary tradition, with its fictitious rhetoric and moral examples," nor on "the ecclesiastical tradition, which embedded history in revelation and prophecy"—the story of the world from Noah to the present. Instead, Camden adopted the new secular history espoused by Jean Bodin, who saw history as "'the study of political conditions and the explanation of human revolutions.'"[8] Camden says in his Introduction that he included ecclesiastical as well as matters of policy and war, for the three cannot really be separated. He also reported speeches as they came to him and did not make them up, as some historians were used to do. Above all, he insists that he has tried to keep a fair mind. Today we recognize that everyone writes from some point of view, but nevertheless it was admirable in Camden to sift out "the judgement of others," rather than too often inserting his own. Camden's last words on Elizabeth were prophetic. "No obliuion shall smother her glory," he wrote, "For her most happy memory liveth, and so shall live in all mens minds to all posterity."[9]

Another early history, more traditional than Camden's, was John Stowe's *Annales, or, A Generall Chronicle of England.* First appearing as *The Chronicles of England, from Brute unto this present yeare 1580,* the popular work "morphed" through various enlargements and abridgements, until it appeared again in the reign of Charles I as the *Annales,* continued by Edmund Howes to the year 1631. At the end of the long chapter on Elizabeth is the following thumb-nail sketch of the queen:

William Camden. *Annales* (London, 1625). STC 4497, c.2, title page.

DIEV ET MON DROIT

Spaine ranfackt by the Erle of Efex and Notingham Ano 1596

St. Iohn of Portorico taken from the Spaniard by the Earle of Cumberland

Semper eadem

ANNALES

The True and Royall History of the famous Empresse

Elizabeth

Queene of ENGLAND FRANCE
and IRELAND &c. True faith's de=
fendresse of Diuine renowne,
and happy Memory
Wherein all such memorable things as happened
during her blessed raigne, with such acts and
treaties as past betwixt hir Ma: and SCOTLAND,
FRANCE, SPAINE, ITALY, GERMANY, POLAND,
SWEDEN, DENMARK, RUSSIA, and the
NETHERLANDS, are exactly described.

LONDON
printed for Beniamin Fisher and are to be sould at
the Talbot in Pater-Noster Rowe
1625

IN THE FIRMITOTS OF GIBRALTAR
WAS

ALBIONS COMFORT, IBERIAS TERROR

Peru
Mare pacifi=
cum
Drake

Carthagena
Panama

Nombre

Engraven by W. Loughen by H. Dantel will. But direction

inuincible Nauie pretended,
prevented and burned

The famous overthrow of the Spanish Nauie the 30th yeare of HER Q. E.

Shee was tall of stature, strong in euery limbe and ioynt, her fingers small and long, her voyce lowd and shrill, shee was of an admirable ready wit and memory, very skilfull in all kind of Needle-worke, had an excellent eare in Musicke, played well vpon divers Instruments, shee spake the Greeke, Latine, Italian, and French tongues well, and vnderstood the Spanish, she was resolute, and of an vndaunted Spirit.[10]

In writing about the ways in which Elizabeth was remembered during the period from the death of James to the Restoration in 1660, John Watkins has outlined how the queen and the politics of her rule were co-opted by both the Royalists and the Parliamentarians. It is the latter and more persistent view that has come down to us, but Watkins indicates that the Royalists under Charles used the Elizabethan precedent for strengthening the prerogative court, and for backing Laudian "high church" reform. "In 1628, Charles reissued the Elizabethan Articles of Religion as a standard for doctrine and discipline throughout the realm," against the inroads of Puritanism.[11] A Royalist broadside poem celebrating important days for the royal family in November includes a verse for Queen Elizabeth's Accession Day on November 17, 1671. It looks back on her reign as a time of order, especially in religion:

That comely Order, which did then adorne
Both Fabricks, now by Facion's [faction] torn;
That Forme, by her allow'd, of *Common Pray'r*
Is styl'd vaine Beating of the Ayre.
How doe they Honour, how forsake Her Crowne!
Her Times are still Cry'd up, but Practis'd Downe.[12]

From the Royalist point of view, "in Elizabeth's day the people were so respectful of monarchy that they would obey a woman. By contrast, the current Parliamentarians' ungentlemanly attacks on royal women indicated their contempt for all civil order."[13]

The continued celebration of Elizabeth's Accession Day by the ringing of church bells and setting of bonfires on November 17, however, was a popular outpouring not a Royalist demonstration. Almanacs made the Accession a red letter day, and beginning in the 1620s, it "became an occasion of popular celebration, with some of the devotion formerly attached to favourite saints." In fact, it quite eclipsed attempts to celebrate the birthdays of Charles I and Queen Henrietta Maria, which unfortunately also occurred in November.[14] The Parliamentarians who opposed the stronger monarchy favored by Charles saw precedence in the times when Elizabeth seemed to be swayed by her Parliament. Twice in the 1640s they reprinted her "Golden Speech," originally delivered in 1601. The version printed at that time was more of a summary and left out the statement reported in many manuscript copies that the queen said, "And though God hath raised me high, yet this I count the glory of my crown—that I have reigned with your loves."[15] This statement was included in the 1642 and 1648 printings to support the Parliamentarians' view of the historic importance of their institution.

The Parliamentarians also tended to represent a more conservative Protestant stance, and as such they popularized the story of Elizabeth as a Deborah and a Judith, the savior of the

Protestant church in England. In 1612, William Leigh published three sermons that he had delivered towards the end of Elizabeth's reign in a book titled *Queene Elizabeth Paraleled in her Princely vertues, with David, Iosua, and Hezekia*. Like these Old Testament figures, she was saved from persecution and protected her church.[16] John Taylor's *Memorial of all the English Monarchs* (1622, 1630) summarized Elizabeth as:

A Deborah, a Judith, a Susanna,

A Virgin, A Virago, a Diana:

Courageous, zealous, learned, wise, and chaste,

With heavenly, earthly gifts, adorn'd and grac'd.

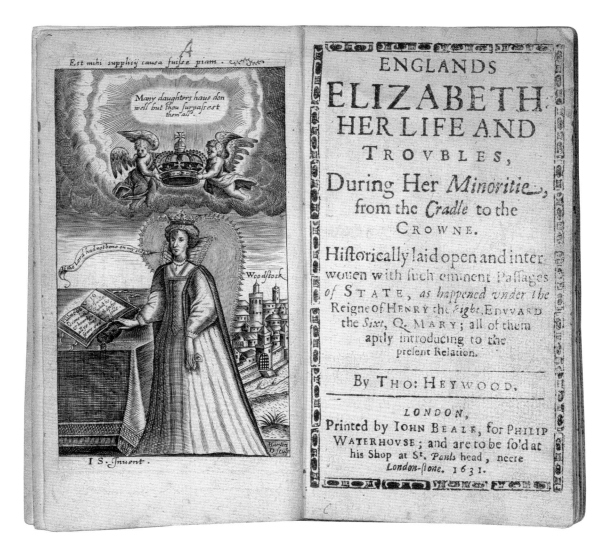

He also referred his readers "'to the great volumes of Hollingshed's story, the reverend learned Camden, Master Speed, and others, who have written more largely of her, though all of them are much short of her unimmestable merits.'"[17] Special emphasis was laid on the story of Elizabeth's deliverance from danger under her Catholic sister Mary. In 1631, Thomas Heywood published *England's Elizabeth: Her Life and Troubles, During Her Minoritie, from the Cradle to the Crowne*. The engraved frontispiece by Martin Droeshout shows Elizabeth standing by a table, touching with her right hand a Bible that is open to Psalm 66, verses 15–17: "O come hither & hear him all ye that feare god & I will tell ye what he hath don for my soule." Coming from her mouth on a streamer are the words, "If the Lord had not bene on my side," while over her head, two angels

Thomas Heywood. *Englands Elizabeth* (London, 1631). STC 13313, c.1, title page.

hold a crown, above which are words in a cloud, "Many daughters haue don well but thou surpassest them all." Behind Elizabeth is Woodstock, where she was under house arrest during part of Mary's reign. This frontispiece ensures that the text which follows will be read in the tradition of John Foxe's account of Elizabeth as a Protestant martyr, albeit one whom God saved for the good of His church.

Heywood's Protestant agenda also determined his presentation of Elizabeth in Part I of his play *If You Know Not Me, You Know Nobody* (1604). The play dramatizes Elizabeth's imprisonment at Woodstock and her receipt of an English Bible from Angels in a dream while she is asleep. "At the end of the play when Elizabeth is Queen, the Mayor of London presents her with a purse and Bible," thus dramatizing episodes from her coronation procession. Heywood believed that the dissemination of the English Bible to the masses was "one of the great services of the Protestant church established by Elizabeth."[18] In a verse account of *The life and death of Queene Elizabeth, From the wombe to the Tombe*, directed to a popular audience and sometimes ascribed to Heywood, the author writes:

And (for her best of workes) she did ordaine
That Gods pure Service might be said and sung
In *England*, in the well-knowne English tongue.[19]

Heywood probably wrote more different pieces about Elizabeth than any other writer at the time. On the one hand, he could turn out scholarly works such as his *Gunaikeion* (1624), a 466-page history of women, while on the other he produced popular works such as the two parts of the plays *If You Know Not Me*; the prose and verse histories of Elizabeth that we have just discussed; another verse history called *Great Britain's Troy* (1609) that includes nineteen stanzas on Elizabeth; and a little work entitled *The Exemplary Lives and Memorable Acts of Nine the Most Worthy Women of the World* (1640). This last work was rather old-fashioned in its time, drawing on the medieval tradition of the "Nine Worthies," lists of (usually) male pagans, Jews, and Christians, as they were termed. Members of this elite group might vary, but they often included Hector, Alexander, Joshua, David, Judas Maccabeus, Arthur, and Charlemagne. Groups of women were more rare, but Heywood put together Deborah, Judith, and Esther from the Old Testament; Bunduca (Boadicea), Penthesilea, and Artimesia from ancient British and classical history; and Elphleda (Aethelflaed), Margaret of Anjou, and Elizabeth for the Christians. Eugene Waith has suggested that Heywood wrote his poems to go with a set of existing engravings by George Glover, *The Nine Women Worthies*, each of which is used to illustrate one of Heywood's women.[20] To us they appear incongruous, as though seventeenth-century ladies had put on fancy dress to impersonate these worthies; only the figure of Elizabeth, being nearer in time, seems based on an actual portrait. To find her in the company of Margaret of Anjou, wife of Henry VI, described by Shakespeare as a "tiger's heart, wrapped in a woman's hide," may seem strange, but Heywood admires Margaret's "brave and Heroick Spirit." Elizabeth herself he presents "as the sum of the heroic excellences of all the most virtuous ladies."[21]

In addition to the works about Elizabeth by Heywood and other male writers of the period, a number of works were also written by women throughout the seventeenth century, drawing

---

Thomas Heywood. *The exemplary lives and memorable acts of nine the most worthy women of the world* (London, 1640). STC 13316, c.1, pp. 182–83.

QVEENE ELIZABETH.

THis Virgin Soveraigne of our Maiden Isle.
On whom blind Fortune did both frowne, and smile
Great Honour, and great Horrour, did indure,
Not safe, being Subject, not being Queene, secure;
Examine both : It is not easily guest,
In which of them she did demeane her best ;
And of those double Fates, 'tis hard to know
In which, she did most dangers undergoe,
Had ʒ more heads then Spanish Gerion, he
Who to one body had no lesse then three,
More hands then great Briareus (to be wondred)
Whose active skill (at once) could moove an hundred,
In every one a pen : As many eyes,
As Iuno's Argus, waking ; to devise,
Of her perfections onely ; Head, Hands, Sight,
(In striving but to patterne her aright)
All, (though in their full vigour) I should finde,
Strucke on the suddaine, Stupid, Dull, and Blinde.
Chaste Virgin, Royall Queene, belov'd and fear'd,
Much on the Earth admir'd, to Heaven indeer'd,
Single, and singular, (without another)
A Nurse to Belgia, and to France; a Mother
Potent by Land, sole Soveraigne of the Maine,
Antagonist to Rome, the scourge of Spaine.

THE

inspiration from Elizabeth. One of the earliest was *A Chaine of Pearle. Or, A Memoriall of the peerles Graces, and Heroick Vertues of Queene Elizabeth, of Glorious Memory* (1630) by Diana Primrose. Not much is known about Primrose, though she may have been the wife of King Charles's chaplain.[22] The work is constructed of eleven poems: an Induction followed by ten "Pearls" each representing a virtue associated with Elizabeth: Religion, Chastity, Prudence, Temperance, Clemency, Justice, Fortitude, Science [learning], Patience, and Bounty. The whole is dedicated "To All Noble Ladies and Gentle-Women." Primrose says that she sends this chain to them,

Which if you please to weare for her sweet sake,
For whom I did this slender Poem make,
You shall erect a Trophie to her Name,
And crowne your selues with neuer-fading Fame.[23]

Pearls were Elizabeth's favorite jewel, but they also represented something of great value, as the biblical "pearl of great price." This metaphorical chain of pearls thus represents the virtues with which good women should attire themselves, modeled on the virtues of their late queen. Like the Arthur of Spenser's *Faerie Queene*, Elizabeth here contains all the princely virtues in her self, but Primrose also sees that they may be emulated by more ordinary women. In her discussion of Chastity, for example, she emphasizes it as Elizabeth's self assertion—"Never would *Shee* condescend/ To *Hymen's* Rihtes [rites]"—the key word being "condescend," but she also broadens the definition of chastity to include virgins, wives (conjugal), and widows (vidual).[24]

Mihoko Suzuki has recently argued "that Elizabeth's 'effect' . . . had a profound influence on the ability of women . . . to imagine political possibilities for themselves in the generations that followed her throughout the seventeenth century."[25] She uses as examples Anne Clifford's attempts to fight for her property rights; Aemilia Lanyer's use of Elizabeth as "the repeatedly invoked historical model of political empowerment and patronage" in her poem *Salve Deus Rex Judaeorum*;[26] Elizabeth Cellier's adoption of Elizabeth's motto, *Semper eadem*, in the account of her treason trial (1680); and Elinor James's defense of Elizabeth in her attack on a pro-Catholic pamphlet (1687). Notably, the list embraces several social classes, including a noblewoman, a musician's daughter, a midwife, and a printer. In addition to these women, the linguist and teacher, Bathsua Makin used Elizabeth as a major example of an educated woman in her *Essay to Revive the Antient Education of Gentlewomen* (1673). Makin extols Elizabeth's learning in religion and languages, as many others had done, but with a twist; she expects women of her own day to make use of such learning, as Elizabeth had done. "Had God intended Women onely as a finer sort of Cattle, he would have not made them reasonable," she remarks.[27] A similar forceful ascerbity may be found in Sarah Jinner's *Almanack or Prognostication for the year of our LORD 1658*, printed near the end of Cromwell's Interregnum:

When, or what Commonwealth was ever better governed than this by the virtuous Q. Elizabeth? I fear I shall never see the like again, most of your Princes now a dayes are like Dunces in comparison of her: either they have not the wit, or the honesty that she had.[28]

Recent scholarship has begun to uncover the more subtle influence of Elizabeth in the writings of Mary Wroth and Margaret Cavendish. In the early seventeenth century, Wroth's ideal queen Pamphilia, in her prose romance *Urania* (1621), struggles with the demands of the "queen's two bodies," her public and her private self. Like Elizabeth, she declares herself wedded to her country; "the consent of so great a people, and so loving to me, must not be neglected." She also represents and defends the virtue of constancy, associated with Elizabeth through her motto *Semper eadem* ("Always the same").[29] Toward the end of the century, Elizabeth posthumously met her match in the wit of Margaret Cavendish. In the Preface to the Reader of *The World's Olio*, after pointing out that in the natural order of things, women are made to be governed by men, Cavendish writes: "And though it seem to be natural, that generally all Women are weaker than Men, both in Body and Understanding, and that the wisest Woman is not so wise as the wisest of Men, wherefore not so fit to Rule; yet some are far wiser than some men." Cavendish goes on to provide little "characters" of some of the English monarchs. Elizabeth she styles as crafty and ruthless:

Queen Elizabeth reigned long and happy; and though she cloathed her self in a Sheeps skin, yet she had a Lions paw, and a Foxes head; she strokes the Cheeks of her Subjects with Flattery, whilst she picks their Purses; and though she seemed loth, yet she never failed to crush to death those that disturbed her waies.[30]

Unlike many of the other women writers, Cavendish keeps her eyes open to the sometimes dubious ways in which Elizabeth exercised power. Though her picture of the queen here seems negative, yet in some of her other writing she figures Elizabeth metaphorically and positively. Claire Jowitt has pointed out that in her poem "A World in an Eare-ring," Cavendish imagines an entire little world that exists independently of the woman who wears it in her ear, much like the armillary sphere that Elizabeth wears in her ear in the Ditchley portrait, where she also stands on a map of England. Jowitt also notes that Cavendish's description of the female ruler, as she is about to go to war in her imaginary "Blazing World," draws on the "Rainbow Portrait" of Elizabeth: "In her left hand she held a buckler to signify the defence of her dominions, which buckler . . . made in the form of an arch, showed like a rainbow." In her fantasy worlds, Cavendish can imagine a woman's power as an absolute monarch, even if this is not yet possible in the masculine world of reason in which she lives.[31]

Perhaps Elizabeth would have been most gratified by a poem written in her memory by a woman in America. After all, it was during Elizabeth's reign that the first English settlement was attempted in the New World near what is now Roanoke Island (1584), providing a name for the whole area—Virginia—in honor of the Virgin Queen. Far to the north, in the colony of Massachusetts, Ann Bradstreet was raising eight children and writing her poetry during the 1640s. Her family had left England in 1630 because of religious persecution, but they were prosperous with a large library, and she was well-read. The first edition of her poems was published by her brother-in-law in London in 1650, a more welcome market for them than Puritanical New England at the time. The collection includes 110 lines "In Honour of that High and Mighty Princess Queen Elizabeth of Happy Memory."[32] Elizabeth would not "disdain t'accept the tribute of a loyal brain," Bradstreet writes confidently, then she opens the poem proper:

No Phoenix pen, nor Spenser's poetry,
No Speed's nor Camden's learned history,
Eliza's works, wars, praise, can e'er compact;
The world's the theatre where she did act.

Having denied the possibility of poetry to "contain" Elizabeth, Bradstreet goes on to review many of the queen's deeds, emphasizing especially her foreign policy and her support of exploration. She also compares her to other great women of history—Semiramus, Dido, Cleopatra, Zenobia—concluding "Yet for our Queen is no fit parallel." For Bradstreet, Elizabeth is larger than history or poetry; her achievements vindicate the rights of women: "She has wiped off th' aspersion of her sex,/ That women wisdom lack to play the rex." Near the end of the poem, Bradstreet asserts the importance of Elizabeth as a model:

Now say, have women worth: or have they none?
Or had they some, but with our Queen is't gone?
Nay masculines, you have thus taxed us long,
But she, though dead, will vindicate our wrong;
Let such as say our sex is void of reason,
Know 'tis a slander now, but once was treason.

Then she draws back, knowing that Elizabeth is dead and those happy days that saw a woman rule are gone. She ends the poem, however, with a millenarian vision of Britain as "the new earth of the righteous" with Elizabeth as Protestant female messiah:[33]

Then wonder not Eliza moves not here. . . .
No more shall rise or set so glorious sun
Until the heaven's great revolution;
If then new things their old forms shall retain,
Eliza shall rule Albion once again.

1 *Crowne-Garland*, sig. C4r–C4v, C4r.

2 Judith M. Richards, "The English Accession of James VI," *English Historical Review*, 67 (2002): 513.

3 Richards, "English Accession," 522–23; 534.

4 David Cressy, *Bonfires and Bells* (Berkeley: University of California Press, 1989), 130.

5 Hugh Trevor-Roper, *Queen Elizabeth's First Historian* (London: Jonathan Cape, 1971), 10.

6 Trevor-Roper, *First Historian*, 10, 9, 11.

7 Trevor-Roper, 17–20.

8 Trevor-Roper, 20–21. Bodin was a French lawyer who had visited England with the duc d'Alençon in 1581, and wrote a treatise proposing new ideas about the writing of history.

9 Camden, *Annales* (London, 1630), sig. Eeee4v.

10 John Stowe, *Annales* (London, 1631), sig. Yyy4r.

11 John Watkins, "'Old Bess in the Ruff': Remembering Elizabeth I, 1625–1660," *English Literary Renaissance*, 30 (2000): 102–4.

12 See Watkins, "Old Bess," 105; poem quoted from William Cartwright, *The Plays and Poems*, ed. G. Blakemore Evans (Madison: University of Wisconsin Press, 1951), 562.

13 Watkins, "Old Bess," 105.

14 Cressy, *Bonfires*, 136, 137

15 Watkins, "Old Bess," 108; and *Works*, 340–44.

16 Cressy, *Bonfires*, 131.

17 Quoted in Cressy, *Bonfires*, 133–34.

18 Georgianna Ziegler, "England's Savior: Elizabeth I in the Writings of Thomas Heywood," *Renaissance Papers* (1980): 33. Other plays dealing with Elizabeth in the period after her death include Chapman's *Bussy d'Ambois* (1604), his *The Conspiracy of Byron* (1608), Dekker's *The Whore of Babylon* (1607), and Massinger's *The Emperor of the East*. See Anne Barton, "Harking Back to Elizabeth: Ben Jonson and Caroline Nostalgia," *English Literary History* 48 (1981): 706–31.

19 *The life and death of Queene Elizabeth* (London, Iohn Okes, 1639), sig. B2r.

20 Eugene M. Waith, "Heywood's Women Worthies," in *Concepts of the Hero in the Middle Ages and the Renaissance*, ed. Norman T. Burns and Christopher J. Reagan (Albany: State University of New York Press, 1975), 232.

21 Waith, "Women Worthies," 229–30. The work is dedicated, through its frontispiece engraving, to Queen Henrietta Maria, hardly a Protestant supporter, but it supports what Waith calls Heywood's "divided allegiance to court and city" (230). Henrietta Maria was also the recipient of a copy of Camden's *Annales* from Oxford University in 1636—were they trying to tell her something? (See Cressy, *Bonfires*, 134.)

22 See Kim Walker, *Women Writers of the English Renaissance* (New York: Twayne, 1996), 219, n. 36.

23 Diana Primrose, *A Chaine of Pearle* (London, 1630), sig. A2r.

24 Primrose, *Chaine*, sig. B2r-B2v. See the discussion by Lisa Gim, "'Faire Eliza's Chaine': Two Female Writers' Literary Links to Queen Elizabeth I," in *Maids and Mistresses, Cousins and Queens*, ed. Susan Frye and Karen Robertson (New York: Oxford University Press, 1999), 192–93.

25 Mihoko Suzuki, "Elizabeth, Gender, and the Political Imaginary of Seventeenth-Century England," in *Debating Gender in Early Modern England, 1500-1700*, ed. Cristina Malcolmson and Mihoko Suzuki (London: Palgrave, 2002), 233.

26 Suzuki, "Elizabeth," 237.

27 Gim, "Faire," 185–86.

28 Quoted in Gim, 194.

29 Quoted in Barbara Lewalski, *Writing Women in Jacobean England* (Cambridge: Harvard University Press, 1993), 271. See also p 273. For a discussion of female sovereignty in Wroth's works, see Naomi Miller, *Changing the Subject: Mary Wroth and Figurations of Gender in Early Modern England* (Lexington: University Press of Kentucky, 1996), chapter 4.

30 Margaret Cavendish, *The World's Olio* (London, 1655), sig. A5v, S2v.

31 Claire Jowitt, "Imperial Dreams? Margaret Cavendish and the Cult of Elizabeth," *Women's Writing*, 4 (1997): 383–84; 391–92, 394–96. In her *Poems and Fancies*, Cavendish noted the number of women rulers their age had produced and "exhorted her women readers, 'let us make the best of our time' in politics and government, in divinity, in philosophy, or poetry, 'or anything that may bring honour to our sex, for they are poor, dejected spirits that are not ambitious of fame.'" See Katie Whitaker, *Mad Madge* (New York: Basic Books, 2002), 153.

32 For biographical information, see Marion Wynne-Davies, *Women Poets of the Renaissance* (New York: Routledge, 1999), 370ff. The poem is quoted from this edition, 260–63.

33 Wynne-Davies, *Women Poets*, 345.

Afterlife: Then

Edmund Bohun (1645–1699)
The character of Queen Elizabeth
London: for Ric. Chiswell, 1693
B3448

Anne Bradstreet (1612?–1672)
The tenth muse lately sprung up in America
London: Stephen Bowtell, 1650
B4167
Lent by the Tracy W. McGregor Library of American History, the Albert and Shirley Small Special Collections Library, University of Virginia

William Camden
Annales the true and royall history of the famous empresse Elizabeth
London: Beniamin Fisher, 1625
STC 4497, c.2

Thomas Heywood (d.1641)
Englands Elizabeth: her life and troubles, during her minoritie, from the cradle to the crowne
London: Iohn Beale for Philip Waterhouse, 1631
STC 13313, c.1

Thomas Heywood (d.1641)
The exemplary lives and memorable acts of nine the most worthy women of the world
London: Tho. Coates for Richard Royston, 1640
STC 13316, c.1

Diana Primrose
A chaine of pearle
London: [John Dawson] for Thomas Paine, 1630
STC 20388
Lent by The Pierpont Morgan Library, New York
Purchased by Pierpont Morgan with Theodore Irwin's library, 1900. PML 6201

Elizabeth I
After John de Critz
Oil on panel, after 1620
FPb66

Afterlife: Now

Alan Axelrod
Elizabeth I, CEO: Strategic Lessons from the Leader Who Built an Empire
New York: Prentice Hall, 2000

Benjamin Britten (1913–1976)
Gloriana: an opera in three acts
London: Boosey & Hawkes, 1953
M1503 B86 G5

Elizabeth
A film written by Michael Hirst, directed by Shekhar Kapur, starring Cate Blanchett, Geoffrey Rush, et al.
New York: PolygramVideo, 1999
VCR 197

Elizabeth R.
A six-part film written by John Hale, et al; directed by Claude Whatham, et al; starring Glenda Jackson
British Broadcasting Corporation, 1971
Distributed by Warner Home Video, Burbank, CA, 2001
DVD 5

Elizabethan Queen
BARBIE© Doll
El Segundo, CA: Mattell, Inc., 1994

Karen Harper
The Tidal Poole: An Elizabethan Mystery
New York: Dell, 2000

Ellen Knill
Queen Elizabeth I Paperdolls to Color
Santa Barbara: Bellerophon Books, 1973

Queen Elizabeth I: the original Collectible Bath Duck
Celebriducks©
San Rafael, CA, 1999
ART 253595

The Queen's Garland: Verses made by her Subjects for Elizabeth I, Queen of England, now collected in Honour of Her Majesty Queen Elizabeth II
Compiled by M. C. Bradbrook
London: Oxford University Press for the Royal Society of Literature, 1953
PR1207 B65

Target Corporation
Advertisement
featuring model as Elizabeth I
U.S. newspapers, 1999

Elizabeth dei gra Anglie Ffrancie & Hibnie Regina fidei defensor &c Omnibus ad quos psentes &c

... Omnibus ... psentes ...

... Habendum ...

... Nolentes ...

... In cuius ...

... Teste me ipa apud Westm ... die Septembr Anno regni ... vicesimo ...

Barrow

Surveying Scholarly Treasures:
Folger Manuscripts by and about Elizabeth I
Janel Mueller

THE FOLGER SHAKESPEARE LIBRARY'S EXHIBITION COMMEMORATING THE LIFE AND REIGN of Elizabeth I in the four hundredth anniversary year of her death offers a prime occasion to pose this question: What does the Folger's manuscript collection offer to scholars in the way of source materials by or about the queen? In addition to thirty-eight documents signed by Elizabeth herself, the Folger has a large number of receipts, political papers, scribally published letters, and historical documents which provide a surprisingly full account of her reign. In this essay I conduct a necessarily partial overview of these rich and extensive holdings, grouping them in categories that trace circuits of influence and interaction radiating out from Elizabeth's royal person and presence. Her most circumscribed ambit, that of the court and its elite members, yields the first set of categories under four headings: coronation; wardrobe and regalia; court festivities and royal progresses; relations with favorites and other courtiers. A second set of four categories encompasses successively widening public circles, including manuscripts on Elizabeth's dealings with Parliament; her royal proclamations; her instruments of command for the army and the navy; and her relations with foreign heads of state. A final category, manuscripts treating her death and funeral, brings this conspectus full circle, to focus on the event whose anniversary prompts this reassessment.

The Court

CORONATION:

Thanks to its acquisition of part of the voluminous Loseley Collection between 1938 and 1954, the Folger Library possesses an almost unimaginably minute and detailed "paper trail" of the provisions and payments made for costumes and headgear in preparation for the revels that attended Elizabeth's coronation in January 1558/9 and the simultaneous New Year's festivities. The Loseley Collection includes the papers of Sir Thomas Cawarden (1551–1593), who was appointed Master of the Tents and Master of the Revels in 1542 and continued to hold the office at the time of Elizabeth's coronation. It also contains an array of official and personal papers from five generations of

Elizabeth I. Second Great Seal. Attached to a "license of alienation" (2 September 1586). Folger MS Z.c.38 (6).

the More family, including those of Cawarden's executor, Sir William More (1520–1600). Cawarden monitored inventories and stood surety for payment of bills submitted for "stuff Recivyd owet of the Revylls" (L.b.109), "Silkes delyured of the store in the Quenes maiesties great warderobe for those of hir Gracis Maskes and Revelles" (L.b.108, 152), the services of tailors in making or altering garments (L.b.34, 146), as well as what we might call "sweating the smaller stuff." Cawarden records payments to Phillip Gunter in late 1558 for pins, needles, thread, sugar candy, bells and other materials for masking apparel (L.b.194); to basket-maker James Sharlow for headpieces and hampers "ageanste the Coronacion and at Candelmas" (L.b.168; paid between January 8 and February 2, 1559); and to Robert Tweselle, for cardinals' hats and other masking headgear for the revels for Christmas and Twelfth Night, and against the coronation (L.b.195). At least 47 separate manuscript items document particulars of the preparations for these seasonal celebrations and the coronation revels.[1]

In the aftermath of these transactions, a narrative emerges from Cawarden's papers. L.b.136 is a memorandum for a warrant to be dated April 1, 1559, and addressed to Sir Richard Sackville, ordering him to pay 188 pounds for the charges of the revels at Elizabeth's coronation; an unusual imitation of the queen's signature is inscribed at the bottom of this small piece of paper. L.b.137–138 are drafts of the actual warrant. L.b.300 is a letter to Cawarden, from Westminster, June 6, 1559, signed by five members of the Privy Council, informing him that the queen desires an account of the expenditures for the revels since her coming to the throne. And L.b.308 is a copy (in Cawarden's hand), of his receipt, dated June 9, 1559, for 188 pounds from Sir Richard Sackville for the charges of the Revels' office during the coronation and the triumph following. As befits a festive narrative, the implicit ending is a happy one: the books balance; all credit has been duly repaid. Nonetheless, Elizabeth's first year of rule would see the death of the conscientious, aging Cawarden.

WARDROBE AND REGALIA:

Among Folger manuscript holdings to be instanced in this category, X.d.265 is a receipt dated June 24, 1565, for petticoats delivered to Mistress Elizabeth Marbery, one of the chamberers to the queen, by Ralph Hope, yeoman of the Robes. Below the six enumerated articles, five of which are marked with an x (presumably "checking off" delivery), Elizabeth Marbery has signed her name. X.d.77 is a charming small receipt dated June 1574 that acknowledges John Bridges's delivery to the Maids of Honor of "Stuff" for their "Remouinge Guarderobe" and of "Twelve pertes of Hangyngis" (probably bed curtains or wall hangings); the text is signed in the older, "secretary" hands of Blanche Parry, Isabel Hobart, and Elizabeth Snow, and in the newer, italic hands of Elizabeth Hastings, Susan Boucher, Mary Howard, Mary Radcliffe, and Abigail Heveningham. X.d.75(6) is an outsized (24 x 25 in.) royal warrant, on paper, bearing at the upper left Elizabeth's sign manual and on the lower left her signet seal; it is dated April 8, 1580, and specifies payment for numerous deliveries of clothing, headgear, and other accessories to named ladies and gentlemen attendant on the queen. X.d.100 is a warrant to the treasurer of the Exchequer, dated June 14, 1602, for payment of 403 pounds, 13 shillings, and 1 pence, to Robert Sharpe, the queen's goldsmith, for making gold and silver spangles to adorn the coats of guards, footmen, and messengers; the close cropping of the top edge of this document and its irregularly cut-away lower edge leave open the possibility that it once bore Elizabeth's sign manual. For its part, V.b.55 presents a lively period touch: the document is a warrant to John Fortescue, Master of the Wardrobe, dated January 29, 1591/2, instructing him to deliver a royal coat of arms to Thomas Knight, Rouge Croix pursuivant. The warrant was signed by Elizabeth and sealed with her seal, to which an Elizabethan sixpence was attached by a thread passed through a hole in its center, obliterating one numeral in its date, "15–2."

Two unusually interesting compendia cap the Folger manuscript holdings related to the queen's wardrobe. Z.d.12–17 comprise a group of six New Year's gift rolls, all signed by Elizabeth, that record gifts given and received by her at dates ranging across her reign, from 1563/4 to 1598/9. The one on display in the current exhibition is Z.d.16, the gift roll for 1585. These rolls are invaluable for understanding the politics of gift-giving in the Elizabethan court, and include the names of relatives, aristocrats and household servants, providing important "snapshots" of the court at various periods. V.b.72 is "A Booke of all suche Robes apparell and garmentes remayninge within thoffice of her highnes warderobe of Robes," dated July 1600; its various categories include "Apparell," "Robes," "Frenche Gow[ns]," "Rounde Gownes," "Loose Gownes," "Kirtells," "Forepartes," "Peticoates," "Lappe Mantles," "Cloakes and Saufegardes," "Dublettes," "Fannes," as well as several suggestive if discrepant headings: "Taken as Fees," "A note of such parcelles as are certefied to bee loste and wantinge" (mostly jeweled buttons), and "Jewells loste and wantinge." Twenty-two items comprise this last category, including "one diamonde from a Jewell of golde like a harte fullye garnished with diamondes, lost by her Ma:^{tie} xiiij.^{to} Februar[y] 1596," "two little pearles and a pendaunt of a diamonde from a Juell of golde like a halfe Moone loste iij.^{cio} Febr[uary] 1599," and "one pendaunt garnished with sparkes of diamondes and Rubies from a Juell of golde like a pellican etc."(fol. 19r-v).[2]

COURT FESTIVITIES AND ROYAL PROGRESSES:

Clustered for the most part in the first and last decades of Elizabeth's reign, Folger manuscript holdings in this dual category cast interesting light on the changes of taste and function that can be traced in texts of entertainments performed for the queen. The 1560s are represented by two significant manuscripts, all in Latin. V.a.212 preserves a copy (ca.1566) of *Sapientia Solomonis: drama comicotragicum*, a Latin play by Sixt Dirck (1500–1554) in five acts, prologue, and epilogue, which the boys of Westminster School acted before Elizabeth at court on January 17, 1565/6. V.a.109 is a copy made ca.1600 of John Bearblock's Latin narrative of the notable events and speeches with which Oxford University welcomed and received the queen in late August and early September 1566, *Commentarij sive ephemorae actionem rerum illustrium Oxonii gestorum in adventu serenissimae principis Elizabethae.*[3]

Comparatively speaking, entertainments and royal progresses in the middle decades of Elizabeth's reign are slenderly represented among the Folger's manuscripts. V.a.189 is a copy, made about 1650 of Robert Langham's piece printed in 1575: "A Letter: Whearin part of the Entertainment untoo the Queens Majesty at Killingworth Castl[e] in Warwik Sheer in this Soomers Pr[o]gress 1575 is signified: from a freend Officer attendant in the Coourt, unto his freend a Citizen & Merchaunt of London," which, as this quotation from the title page shows, retains the bulk of Langham's idiosyncratic spellings.[4] This account of the earl of Leicester's lavish entertainment of Elizabeth at Kenilworth Castle is complemented by a manuscript essay from the pen of the antiquarian James Boaden (1762–1839), on the same subject (Y.d.376 (3)). Also to be noted from the middle decades of Elizabeth's reign is the family "Book of divers necessary remembrances" compiled by three generations of Derings—Richard, Anthony, and Edward—which records Elizabeth's progress into Kent in August 1573, when members of her entourage stayed at Surrenden, the Dering family seat (V.b.296, p. 356).

With the 1590s, however, significant sources of information on royal progresses and entertainments resume. William Smith (1550?–1618) ends his "Alphabet or blazon of arms" (V.b.217) with the order of procession for the queen's progress from Somerset Place to St. Paul's Cathedral in 1598. V.b.213, fols. 1r–13r, is an early copy of Francis Bacon's "A Dialogue. / Betweene A: 1. Melancholly dreaming Hermite. 2. A Mutinous brainesicke Soldier and 3. A Busie, teadious Secretarie," written for the entertainment of Elizabeth by the earl of Essex on the anniversary of her accession, November 17, 1595. By far the most outstanding manuscript holding in this category is X.d.172, long preserved among the Conway Papers before its acquisition by Mr. Folger in 1916. The text and its occasion are described in the essay on the queen's progresses in this catalogue. The manuscript preserves one version of Sir John Davies's "The deuice to entertayne her Ma:^{ty} att Harfielde, the house of Sr Thomas Egerton Lo: keeper and his wife the Countess of Darbye," composed in verse, and written here in a contemporary secretary hand. Another hand of the period has noted as follows in the upper left corner of the first page: "For her Ma:^{ties} progresse. 1602." The manuscript contains some directions for performance—"Sung by 2 mariners presently before the Lottaryes", that is, the drawing of fortunes that supplies the masque's main action— and assigns appropriate two-line verses, each befitting the gifts, to "Hir Ma:^{tye}" and 31 noblewomen and ladies.[5]

RELATIONS WITH FAVORITES AND OTHER COURTIERS:

The queen's enduring relations with her closest favorite, Robert Dudley, whom she created earl of Leicester in 1562, are represented selectively yet suggestively in the manuscript holdings of the Folger Library. Five vellum sheets, each measuring 25.5 by 32 in., comprise Z.c.5, Elizabeth's letters patent to Robert, earl of Leicester, dated April 5, 1574. This huge, compendious writ details in legal Latin the queen's gift of lands and reversions in Bedfordshire, Berkshire, Buckinghamshire, Cornwall, Derbyshire, Devon, Dorset, Gloucestershire, Herefordshire, Hertfordshire, London, Northamptonshire, Oxfordshire, Salop (now Shropshire), Somerset, Suffolk, Surrey, Sussex, Worcestershire, Merionethshire, and Radnorshire (Clero, Poinscastle).[6]

The full collection of early copies of key documents that is V.b.142 opens with a letter from "A.A." at The Hague, January 30, 1585/6, to an unnamed English correspondent describing the development that so infuriated Elizabeth and triggered Leicester's abject submission—his acceptance (soon rescinded) of appointment by the Dutch as Governor General of the United Provinces "with authoryty as full everye way as any governour had in Charles the Vth his tyme" (fol. 1). Last but far from least of the manuscripts relating to Leicester, and a splendid recent gift by Dorothy Rouse-Bottom to the Folger, is MS Add 1006—Leicester's autograph letter to Elizabeth, written "from Tylbury this Saturday," where he was commander-in-chief of the English troops massed to defend against the expected Spanish invasion of July 1588. The letter is described in the Leicester and Essex section of this catalogue.

The exhibition includes one of the Folger's prolific manuscript holdings on Robert Devereux, earl of Essex, Elizabeth's last and uniquely treacherous favorite. A number of historically and politically significant accounts were made detailing the earl's downfall. Among these is one by Francis ap Rice, ornamentally ruled, and beautifully penned in a mixture of secretary and italic hands. It unfolds according to the sections announced on its title page dated "1601": "The manner of the proceedings of Robert Earle of Essex, and Henry Earle of Southampton, with their Arreignement. The Speaches of Ro: Earle of Essex, with his Poem, before his execution. / Letters togither with their answeres, sent vnto the Earle of Essex, by my Lord Keeper, and others. Diuers Speeches against the Earle of Essex and his proceedings in Ireland" (V.a.164, fol. 16r). "A repentant Poem made by Robert Earle of Essex while he was Prisonner in the Towre. 1601" comprises 65 stanzas in sixaines, most of them cleanly enclosed by Rice's ornamental double rules (fols. 134r–144r), but once ominously interrupted by a rubric in italic: "Heere the Earle of Essex paused an howre or twaine, and after some teares, tooke againe his pen & wrott as followeth: Jo: Aggs report" (fol. 138v).[7]

Among many manuscripts related to the earl of Essex, two collections in particular, V.a.321 and V.b.142, preserve contemporary copies of letters and other items on the sensational final phase of the earl of Essex's career. V.a.321 has an initial section of materials possibly compiled, as the penciled note on the flyleaf proposes, in the legible secretary hand of Peter Ferryman, who is the addressee or the referent in a number of the letters. Notable among these is the letter exchange in which Thomas Egerton, Lord Keeper, upbraids Essex for "vnseasonable discontentment" so that "the longer you goe, the further out of the waye" (fol. 1r), and Essex protests that he has been subjected to "violent and vnseasonable stormes come from . . . the passionate indignation of a prince" (fol. 3r).[8] Here, too, are recorded the "Articles wherevpon Therle of Essex was accused in the Starre chamber. 29. November 1599" (fols. 4v–5r), followed by a copy of one of Essex's letters to Elizabeth (1599?), representing his histrionic effusions as "thinges pressed out of a distressed mynde," and, far less obviously, as "offered in all humilitie" (fol. 6r). A copy of a letter from Essex's sister, Penelope Devereux, Lady Rich, appealing to Elizabeth on her brother's behalf, uses the image of the sun hidden by cloud to figure deprivation of the queen's presence (fol. 6v).[9] This group of materials focused on Essex concludes with a transcript of Robert Cecil's speech in Star Chamber, February 1601, and of Dr. Ashton's letter concerning the articles laid against Essex there (fols. 9v–13v).

V.b.142, another collection, contains a number of significant items relating to the heights and depths encompassed by Essex in the late 1590s. From the heights there are two undated letters (ca. 1596?) to the lords of the Privy Council reporting on his military command as "bellum difficile" (fols. 15, 45); a report on the expedition to Cadiz in June 1596, and a list of the regiments commanded by Essex, followed by a copy of the prayer Elizabeth composed for the launching of this action: "Most omnipotent maker and guider of all the worldes masse" (fols. 15r–16r, 17r–20r). The trajectory of descent emerges in a sequence of later documents: "The names of those that have been knighted by the Lord Lieutenant in Ireland [1599]" (fol. 29); a lengthy, tonally extravagant "Apologie of the Erle of Essex against those which falsely & malitiously taxe him to be the only hindrance of the peace & quyetnes of this contrey" (fols. 32r–39v); an equally extravagant but brief appeal by Essex to an unspecified addressee—possibly Elizabeth—from "a hart torne in peeces with care, greife, & travaile" (fol. 41r); and two reports of speeches made about Essex in the court of Star Chamber, November 29, 1599, and February 13, 1600/01 (fols. 49r–52v, 47r). The sinister conclusion of this sequence is the list, "The names of such as be in prison about this late tumult," which records seventy-nine persons, some by last name only, incarcerated in ten prisons, mainly in London (fol. 53).[10]

Public Circles

DEALINGS WITH PARLIAMENT:

The preceding overviews of manuscript materials relating to Leicester and Essex reflect a fact that came frequently to the fore in Elizabeth's reign: the personal and the political were one and the same thing. The prevailing system of personal monarchy partly accounts for this conflation, but it was much more the continuing effect of Elizabeth's resolute self-determination to marry or not, as she chose, and finally as a Virgin Queen who would provide for her successor in her own fashion and in her own good time, as she chose. Elizabeth's earliest Parliaments, from 1558 to 1566, saw stormy dealings between her and both Houses, as she was repeatedly admonished to marry and bear an heir to the throne (or at least to designate one), and she repeatedly admonished Lords and Commons to comport themselves as subjects and not infringe on her royal prerogatives. V.a.143 contains copies (ca.1600) of Elizabeth's April 10, 1563, speech before Parliament as well as several speeches delivered by Sir Nicholas Bacon, Speaker of the Commons, between 1559 and 1580 (the latter the date of his death); by Sir Walter Mildmay; and possibly Sir Christopher Hatton, between 1575 and 1587.[11] V.b.213 also contains early copies of Nicholas Bacon's orations in Elizabeth's first Parliament of 1558–59. A manuscript collection made ca.1625, V.b.151, includes a copy of Sir Thomas Smith's "A Dialogue disputing the conveniencye of Queene Elizabethes Marriage" (fols. 5–50), written in 1560 in the context of the early parliamentary debates. V.a.235, another copy of Smith's work, ca.1610?, was published without its original preface in 1698 as *A Dialogue touching the Queen's marriage* (Wing W6023). From the last decade of the queen's reign, the collection that is V.b.41 contains a copy of a 1592 speech in the Commons by the fiery Peter Wentworth on the succession (pp. 215–42); its text was printed in the same year as *A Pithie exhortation to her Majesty for establishing her successor to the crown* (STC 25245). The cherishing side of Parliament's relations with Elizabeth is well documented in several copies of the Oath or Bond of Association pledging to defend the queen and her sovereign right to rule, which began as a parliamentary Act in 1585 and soon proliferated as a vast write-in campaign by groups of loyal signatories, in response to the Babington Plot and the climactic danger posed by Mary, Queen of Scots, in 1585–6 (see, e.g., V.a.321, fols. 36v–38; V.b.142, fol. 60).

ROYAL PROCLAMATIONS:

Despite Paul L. Hughes's and James F. Larkin's authoritative and convenient assemblage of *Tudor Royal Proclamations* in three hefty volumes (Yale University Press, 1964), a first-hand experience with an outsized, signed and sealed, solemnly official, handwritten Elizabethan proclamation can provide an impressive and informative encounter with the past. Folger manuscript holdings include four of Elizabeth's proclamations, on vellum, all signed by her in the upper left corner with her official signature, her "sign manual." Z.e.29 (1), dated February 12, 1565/6, is one in a series of proclamations against "excesse in Apparell" issued by the queen in the course of her reign, each of which specifies more precisely the offenses, penalties, and ranks and vocations of persons affected in a rhetoric of censure which evidently failed to produce its intended effects. Here, proscribed items include velvet and embroidery or pricking in gold, silver, or silk, and other finery worn by persons of insufficiently high degree. X.d.85, dated March 1, 1568/9, aims at French adherents of the claim of Mary, Queen of Scots, to Elizabeth's throne, who were seeking to stir up support with floods of unauthorized publications. The text of the proclamation, worn to faintness in places and with corrections to two passages, targets owners of "diuers bookes made or translated by certain the Queenes Ma:^tes subiects . . . styrring and nourishing sedition in this Realm . . . ." The queen orders "all maner of persons to forbeare vtterly from the vse or dealing withe any such sedicious bookes made or translated by any persoine conteining mater derogatory to the souuerayn estate of her ma:^te . . . vppon pain of her Ma:^tes greuous Indignation," but instead to bring them to the bishop, who is permitted to keep and read them. X.d. 86 is a proclamation against pirates, August 3, 1569, which also directs "all maner Officers and ministers having rule and charge within any port Towne" to exercise stricter vigilance "for remeady therof." X.d.87, dated June 11, 1573, and signed by Elizabeth in a deep ochre ink, is a proclamation against "som persons of their natures vnquyetly disposed"—the authors of the subsequently named *An Admonition to Parliament* (1572) and their supporters who were agitating for further reforms in the Church of England—to respect and accept the public services conducted in accordance with the Book of Common Prayer "sett fourth and allowed by Parliament." The text concludes by calling in all copies of the *Admonition*, requiring that they be brought to the Bishop of London within 20 days of this proclamation.[12]

INSTRUMENTS OF COMMAND FOR THE ARMY AND THE NAVY:

Although Elizabeth, as a female monarch, could not personally lead English troops into battle on land or sea as her father Henry VIII had done, she nevertheless engaged keenly and directly in military strategy and its accompanying diplomatic negotiations throughout her reign, famously enacting her personal engagement in her appearance before the army at Tilbury in 1588, when a Spanish invasion of the Thames was fully expected. In this connection, Leicester's letter to Elizabeth from Tilbury where he was commander-in-chief (MS Add 1006), merits another mention, as do the several letters from Elizabeth to Essex that variously dictate and castigate his conduct of military operations in Ireland. Among other military documents in the Folger's manuscript holdings are several letters, all signed by Elizabeth: X.d.126, a letter of command to Lord North and the other Commissioners of Muster for Cambridgeshire, July 29, 1565 (this also bears her seal); X.d.127, a letter of command to Sir Henry Sidney, Lord Deputy of Ireland, November 4, 1568; X.d.130, a letter of command to the earl of Nottingham, Lord Lieutenant of Surrey, August 4, 1599, requiring him to assemble thirty-seven men as listed, furnished with horses, arms, and provisions; and X.d.131, a letter of command to the High Sheriff of Warwickshire, July 28, 1602, requiring him to raise forty men and money to equip them, for service in Ireland. L.a.1025 is a "copia vera" (a true copy, compared with the original by the recipient) of her letters patent commissioning George Talbot, earl of Shrewsbury as Lord Lieutenant of Derbyshire and Staffordshire, July 3, 1585—a key move at the height of the anxiety caused by the Babington Plot.[13]

The proposed marriage between Elizabeth and François Hercule de Valois, Duc d'Alençon, the immediate heir to the throne of France, was an active focus of concern between 1579 and 1582. Folger manuscript holdings dealing with the French match include contemporary copies of two letters in French written by Elizabeth, one to "Monsieur," the duc d'Alençon, the other to his mother, Catherine de Médicis of France (V.b.49, fols. 130v–134r). The Folger also has a contemporary copy of the letter written by Thomas Radcliffe, earl of Sussex, to Elizabeth on August 28, 1578, relatively early in the conduct of marriage negotiations, attempting a balanced account of the "commodities" and "discommodities" involved (V.b.303, fols. 158v–166v); and a comparatively late copy (ca.1650) of Sir Philip Sidney's letter to Elizabeth, written about 1580 and advising against marriage with Monsieur (X.d.210).[14]

When Elizabeth came to the throne in 1558, Mary, Queen of Scots, was "a foreign head of state" as queen consort of France, and by 1562 had become queen of Scotland in her own right. After losing this position in 1568, she sought political and personal refuge with Elizabeth, her nearest head of state both by blood ties and by geography. Folger manuscript holdings relating to the 1568/9 royal proclamation against declared defenders of Mary's claim to Elizabeth's throne, to the Babington Plot and the Oath of Association have been signaled in discussion above. Two items contained in the present exhibition deserve to be highlighted in this connection: E.a.1, a commonplace book containing an account of Mary's beheading and funeral; and X.d.428 (87), an autograph letter from George Talbot, earl of Shrewsbury, to his wife Elizabeth, regarding his custody of Mary at Tutbury.[15]

With Mary's son, James VI of Scotland, Elizabeth's relations were no less complex, but they eventually reached a satisfactory conclusion for both parties in his orderly, peaceful, and welcomed succession to her crown. X.d.452 (10) is a letter dated September 18, 1582, signed by nine Scots lords currently residing with the young King James, imploring Elizabeth to send money and other assistance. Eventually, as a facet of Elizabeth's increasingly readable intentions regarding James as her successor, she sent considerable aid north of the border, as a warrant (X.d.99), signed by her and dated June 28, 1602, directs; the treasurer of the Exchequer is to pay 2,500 pounds to Roger Aston, for the King of Scots, as part of an arranged gratuity.

One critical aspect of the mutual understanding and disclosure on which Elizabeth and James built their special relationship was a protracted letter exchange, almost all of it in their own handwriting, conducted between mid-1585 and shortly before Elizabeth's death in 1603. X.d.397 is a splendid exemplar of this correspondence between royals. Using paper watermarked with crowned and intertwined serpents, Elizabeth wrote, signed, and sealed the letter March 16, 1593 (the date at which it is endorsed as having been delivered). This holograph letter apparently refers to the fifth earl of Bothwell's conspiracy against the crown of Scotland, as it bluntly upbraids James for what Elizabeth sees as his laxness and self-deception in leaving proven enemies at large. Her conclusion is a characteristically pithy aphorism—"neuer raigne precario more When you may rule regis regula" (Never reign by means of entreaty when you may rule in the manner of a king). To this she equally characteristically adds a postscript, this one being of especial interest because she acknowledges James's difficulty ("your cumbar") in deciphering her rapid, loosely formed hand ("suche skribled Lines").[16]

An important and characteristic example of Elizabeth's close attentiveness to her relations with other monarchs is found in X.d.90, on display in the present exhibition. Detailing her instructions to Lord North, English ambassador to France in October 1574, regarding the accession of Henri III, this letter is signed by Elizabeth and, at the end, by Sir Francis Walsingham. Widening the ambit of Elizabeth's interactions with other heads of state yet preserving her concerns with political stability and, where applicable, a common Protestant cause, is an assemblage of seven letters, six in Latin, one in English, all signed by Elizabeth (X.d.138 (1–7)).[17] X.d.138 (1) is a brief Latin missive in the beautiful italic hand of Roger Ascham, Elizabeth's former tutor who became her secretary. He signs his own name in the lower right corner under Elizabeth's signature and embellished subscription, "Vestrae Excellentiae Consanguinea" ("Your Excellency's kinswoman"). The letter, dated August 8, 1562, recommends to the good graces of Prince Philip of Hesse the queen's ambassador and relative, Henry Knollys, whom she is presently sending him. X.d.138 (3) dated December 22, 1573, addresses Frederick, Elector Palatine, and proposes that a certain "D. Atheneus" can fitly represent their common interests in religion and Christian tranquility. Elizabeth signs herself "Vostra bona Consanguinea" (Your good kinswoman). In X.d.138 (4, 5) respectively dated July 15, 1590, and November 25, 1590, Elizabeth addresses Prince Christian of Anhalt-Bernburg, soliciting his cooperation in the interests of Protestant unity. She is sending a trusted ambassador, Horatio Pallavicino, a Knight of the Golden Fleece, to treat with Henri IV of France and then to proceed to Germany, as a means of assuring and strengthening their common purposes. In the earlier of this pair of letters, she expresses gratitude for the support of Prince Christian, who eventually declared himself a Calvinist; in the later she implores his support for Pallavicino's diplomacy and hails Prince Christian for his ardor in true religion ("in veram religionem"), which she elsewhere specifies as "vndique per Europam sunt reformatis Ecclesijs vtilissima," ("things most useful to reformed Churches wherever they are in Europe"). This second letter retains Elizabeth's signet seal intact.

X.d.138 (2) is a letter of considerable historical interest: addressed to Philip II of Spain, written in Ascham's hand in Latin, and dated February 17, 1565/6 from Greenwich, it appeals to Philip's sense of justice and to his kind favor, authority, and express command to release certain English subjects who, with their ships and goods, had been held in Spain since 1563 as the result of a conflict between a French ship and some English sailors in the port of Gibraltar.[18] Before signing in her already characteristically elaborate signature, Elizabeth pens and embellishes this subscription: "Serenitatis Vestre bona Soror Consanguineae"—here evoking, perhaps, through the memory of Mary I a measure of extra resonance in the conventional terms "sister" and "kinswoman."

From the end of the reign, X.d.138 (7), a vigorously indignant and lengthy Latin letter of December 20, 1597, addressed to Emperor Rudolf II, protests his unilateral actions and failure to stay in communication with Elizabeth through exchanges of letters. Without inquiring into the truth of accusations of piracy and unfair trade practices brought by the cities of the Hanseatic League against the Merchant Adventurers of London, Rudolf had issued an edict of expulsion that was not only most injurious to English commercial interests but showed him to be under the undue influence of factious persons ("*factiosorum hominum*") and slaves ("*serui*") of the Pope of Rome and the King of Spain, living at his court ("*in Aula vestra elegentes*"). The queen's sole conciliatory notes are her invocation of God's blessing on Rudolf and her signing of herself as

"Your sister" at the close of the letter. The same *cause célèbre* is pursued in a similar but more restrained text, V.b.181, a six-page Latin letter addressed the previous day, December 19, 1597, to Prince John George of Anhalt-Bernburg, Prince Christian's successor, on the injustice and injury of the Edict expelling the Merchant Adventurers from German cities. A particular interest of this lengthy letter is its evocation of a Mediterranean trading network that had flourished despite Europe's religious differences and with the active approval of the Turkish Emperor at Constantinople.[19] Now this amity stands in jeopardy because of the enmity and strife among Christians. Elizabeth appeals to John George to serve as an ally in promoting and assuring trade. She signs this letter and subscribes it "V. Amantiss: Consanguinea" (Your most loving kinswoman).[20] The letter retains Elizabeth's signet seal intact.

In this sequence of letters from late in her reign, actively concerned with defending the Protestant cause in Europe, the most expressive item is Elizabeth's urgent letter in French from about 1595, written, signed, and sealed by her own hand (V.b.131). She exhorts Henri IV to realize how immediately the cause is linked with the safety of his own person, and urges him to be more wary and circumspect in his conduct.[21]

To round out this category of Elizabeth's dealings with foreign heads of state, surely the most publicly celebrated episode was the impromptu Latin reproof she delivered to the young, insubordinate ambassador Paul de Jaline, representing the interests of King Sigismund of Poland to her at court in 1597. V.a.321, fols. 35v–36r, preserves a good early copy of the Latin text and an English translation.[22]

Death and Funeral:

A slim, elegant miscellany (ca.1625), written in a neat italic hand in brown ink with capital letters, numbers, proper nouns (and a few other words) in red ink, contains as one of its entries a retrospective account of Elizabeth's last three months of life (X.d.393, fols. 23r–29r).[23] While the narrative lurches under the rehearsal of her changeful thoughts and moods and the fickle imaginings of unidentified courtiers, the aged queen is always at its full center: refusing to take physic, having her ring cut off and out of the flesh of her finger, praying at length with the archbishop of Canterbury until her voice failed her, and uttering her oracular refrain in red ink, "My Throne is a Throne of Kings, neither ought any but my next Heire to succeed mee" (fol. 23r). This she is asked to explain by Secretary of State Robert Cecil, to which her answer is inscribed in red ink: "'I will,' said shee, 'that a King succeed mee, & what King, but my neerest Kinsman the King of Scots?'" (fol. 26r).

In V.b.142, a late Elizabethan gathering of copies of important documents already noted in conjunction with Essex and James, appears the following notice. "This was set in the Chamber where the Queenes Corps lyeth, ouer the hearse."

Vita quid es? Moritur Regina, & Regia Virtus
Vita quid es? Moritur Princeps, morismur & omnes
Vita quid es? Clamauus Viuat Rex, morietur.
Elizabetha potesne mori? Dic Vita quid es? Mors.[24]

There immediately follows a copy of a letter from the Privy Council to the sheriff and justices of Suffolk, March 25, 1603, announcing the death of Elizabeth, "our late dearest Soueraigne Queene," and ordering the proclamation of James "the Sixt king of Scotland and now also James the First king of England" (fol. 65).

The herald's book of precedence attributed to Philip Holland and begun ca.1605 opens with a listing of the companies and individual mourners who comprised the procession from White-hall to Westminster at Elizabeth's funeral, April 28, 1603 (V.a.213, fols. 2v–7v). The social order of the court is vividly evoked in the lists of mourners by rank and occupation, culminating in a diagram showing the queen's hearse. The inscription reads: "the liuely picture of her maiesties whole body in hir parliament Robes with a crowne on her heade and a Septure in her hand lynge on the corpes couered in purple veluet borne in a Chariot drawne by fower Horses Trapt in black veluet." The inner circle around the hearse consisted of six earls, six knights as pallbearers, twelve other noblemen, and an unspecified number of footmen, followed at near range in the entourage by "The Lady Marques of Northhampton Cheife mourner assisted by the Lord Treasurer and the Lord Admirall" and, in sequence, "Countesses, Ladies of honor, Viscoountesses, Earles daughters, Baronesses, and Maides of honor of the priuie Chamber" (fol. 7). A heraldic commonplace book compiled two decades later, ca.1625, also contains a copy of the hierarchy of processional mourners at Elizabeth's funeral, with the same diagrammatic representation of the royal hearse and its effigy (V.a.431, fols. 33v–36v).

As I hope to have conveyed through the particulars of the foregoing survey, Elizabeth I comes variously to life, action, and expression in the Folger manuscript holdings that are a rich legacy of her age to ours and an incomparable, continuing demonstration of her still vibrant historicity and interest.

1   A full listing of these can be found in the online finding aid for the Loseley papers: http://shakespeare.folger.edu/other/html/dfoloseley.html. Transcriptions of L.b.33 and L.b.109 are published in Bergeron, "Elizabeth's Coronation Entry (1559)," 4, 5.

2   A transcription of Folger MS V.b.72 is published in Arnold, *Wardrobe*, 335–50.

3   One commonplace book of the period, V.a.173, contains extracts from Elizabeth's Latin speeches at Cambridge University (1564) and Oxford University (1566); another commonplace book of the period, V.b.214, additionally contains her 1592 Latin speech at Oxford (fols. 67v–68r).

4   Langham is a pseudonym for William Patten. In addition to its original printing (STC 15190.5), Langham's *Letter* has seen several modern editions.

5   Folger MS X.d.172 is one of three surviving manuscripts of the Harefield entertainment. Robert Krueger believes it may be one of "several scribal copies" ordered by Davies. See Krueger, ed. *Poems of Sir John Davies*, 437–438. Besides Elizabeth, the 31 women are specified as follows in the text: "the Countesse of Derbye dowagre," "Lord Derbyes wife," "La: Worcester," "La: Warwicke," "La: Scroope," "Mrs neuill," "Mrs Thyme," "Mrs Hastings," "Mrs Bridges," "La: Scudamour," "La: Francis," "La: Kneuette," "La: Susan Vere," "Mrs Vauissour," "La: Southwell," "La: Anne Clifford," "Mrs Hyde," "La: Kildare," "La: Effingham," "La: Pagette," "Mrs Kiddermister," "Mrs Strangwidge," "Mother of the maydes," "La: Cumberland," "Lad: Walsingham," "La: Newton," "Mrs Wharton," "La: Digbye," "[La: Radc]liffe," "La: Dorothye," and "Mrs Anselowe."

6   Another legal document, Z.c.41(1), casts a sidelight on the fortunes of Leicester's vast landholdings after his death in November 1588. In this contemporary copy, under date of February 9, 1590, Anne Gresham, widow of Sir Thomas Gresham, leases to the queen for four years the manor of Cauntercelly, the manor and castle of Brentles and other land in Brecknockshire, formerly in the possession of the earl of Leicester by the queen's letters patent of June 19, 1566, to pay off a debt of 260 pounds.

7   Steven May asserts that though "ten versions of all or parts of Essex's poem have survived, only the Folger text confirms Essex's claim to its composition and provides a complete text of his work." Further, he identifies Aggs as probably "John Agges who became a Yeoman Warder at the Tower in 1606. . . . What he was doing there in February of 1601 I cannot determine, but it seems reasonable to conclude that he actually copied the Earl's penitential verses as they were written and was thus able to note precisely where Essex 'paused an howre or twaine' before continuing with his work." (From a written report in the Folger manuscript files.)

8   Copies of both of these letters are included in V.b.142 as well.

9   Lady Rich's letter appears in V.a.164 as well. Female petitioners' letters to Elizabeth comprise one of many potential areas of further study not included in the present overview: for two other examples, see Lady Wingfield's "poore . . . humble petition" submitted to the queen's "sacred regarde" (ca.1600?) on behalf of her husband, Sir Edward Wingfield (Winckfield) serving in Ireland; and the petition (1602) by Elizabeth (Burgh) Brooke and her three sisters, co-heirs of Robert, Lord Burgh, who died in infancy February 1601/02, to grant the estate to one of them (V.a.321, fols. 20v–21r, 87).

10 The list of distribution by prison occurs also in V.a.164. Another substantial Folger manuscript collection of documents about and from the earl of Essex and his relations with Elizabeth from early promise to ignominious end is included in V.b.214, fols. 60v–64v, 103–06, 198–200, 202–205v, 227–235, 262v–266), a commonplace book conjecturally identified in the Folger MSS card catalogue as a joint compilation by Thomas Scott of Eggerton and John Knatchbull, whose signatures occur on the next to last leaf of the volume. Copies of various Essex materials and letters made ca.1650 are contained in the voluminous collection of correspondence, much of it with Elizabeth, that is V.a.239.

11 Texts of these speeches figure in Sir Simonds D'Ewes, *The Journals of All the Parliaments during the Reign of Queen Elizabeth* (London: for John Starkey, 1682) and in Sir John Neale, *Elizabeth I and Her Parliaments*, 2 vols. (New York: St. Martin's Press, 1958).

12 These proclamations were printed as: STC 7995, STC 8014, STC 8016, and STC 8063.

13 M.b..2 is a typed transcription (ca.1910) of Yelverton 31/218, manuscripts in the possession of Lord Calthorpe, containing Anthony Babington's confession of treasonable dealings with Mary, Queen of Scots, and a plot to kill Queen Elizabeth, made to the examiners appointed by a special commission to try the conspirators involved in the plot.

14 To this grouping may be added M.c.42, a letter from Jacques Coyon de Matignon, Marshal of France, to M. de la Millure, at Bayonne, December 24, 1581, which makes mention of the proposed marriage between Elizabeth and the French heir apparent.

15 In X.d.428 (86) written a few days earlier, the earl of Shrewsbury tells his wife that the queen has hinted she will entrust Mary to his care. Several other letters in the Cavendish-Talbot Collection mention Mary in various contexts. Other Folger manuscripts dealing with her death and funeral are: G.b.7, V.a.347, V.a.466, V.b.74, V.b.277, and W.b.132 (14).

16 This is the copy-text used in *Elizabeth I: Collected Works* (hereafter *Works*), ed. Leah S. Marcus, Janel Mueller, and Mary Beth Rose (University of Chicago Press, 2000) for a modern English translation and in *Elizabeth I: Autograph Compositions and Foreign Language Originals* (hereafter *ACFLO*), ed. Janel Mueller and Leah S. Marcus (University of Chicago Press, 2002) for Elizabeth's original.

17 Occasionally the motive of address appears only to be profession of friendship and compliment, conveyed by letter as well as by messenger, as in X.d.138 (6), an Italian letter to Ferdinando de' Medici, Grand Duke of Tuscany, dated September 9, 1594, and subscribed in Italian by Elizabeth before appending her signature.

18 Compare V.a.321, fols. 33v–34, an English letter to the Ottoman Emperor, dated January 20, 1600/01, urging that two Scotsmen, Laurence Oliphant and Robert Douglas, victims of piracy and prisoners in Algiers, should be released. See *Works* for a modern English transcription of this letter. A mid-seventeenth century copy of a letter from the Ottoman Emperor "Mahomet" to Elizabeth, dated "att Constantinople in the 937th yeare of our most holy Prophett Mahomet" is preserved in V.a.239, fols. 56v–64v.

19 For a yet farther-flung circuit of trade, see V.a.321, fol. 34v–35, a copy of a letter in Italian on this very subject, addressed to Elizabeth by Emperor "Taicosama" of China in 1600.

20 Both letters, to Emperor Rudolf and Prince John George, have been provided with English translations under Folger custodianship.

21 This is the copytext used in *Works* for a modern English translation and in *ACFLO* for Elizabeth's French.

22 These are the copy texts used in *Works* for a modern English version and in *ACFLO* for Elizabeth's Latin. Another early copy of Elizabeth's Latin speech is V.b.214, fol. 67v.

23 Georgianna Ziegler notes that this narrative is indebted to William Camden's account.

24 fol. 64. "Life, what are you? A Queen has died; also, the Court of Virtue / Life, what are you? A Prince has died, and we all will die / Life, what are you? We cry 'Long live the King'; he will die. / Can Elizabeth, then, die? Say, Life, what are you?" "Death."

Chronological list of manuscripts at the Folger Library signed by Elizabeth I[1]

Compiled by Heather Wolfe

1   ca. 1550   Letter signed, to Sir Thomas Cawarden, assuring him of her good will and thanking him for care of certain property. Letter is possibly autograph. 2 fols. (L.b.4)

2   January 3, 1558/59   Warrant signed, directing Sir Thomas Cawarden to deliver to John Gresham and John Elyot, citizens of London, apparel required for setting forth pageants for the queen's coronation. Written from Westminster. With signet seal intact. (L.b.33)

3   August 8, 1562   Letter signed, to Philip of Hesse, recommending the queen's ambassador and relative, Henry Knolles. Written in the hand of her secretary, Roger Ascham, and signed by him. In Latin. (X.d.138 (1))

4   March 14, 1562/63   Letters patent, signed, to Jasper Seler, gent., subject of the Emperor, and Peter Ruse, merchant stranger. Grant of monopoly for the manufacture of white salt for 20 years. (Z.c.44 (3))

5   January 1, 1563/64   New Year's gift roll, signed. (Z.d.12)

6   June 1, 1564   Grant signed, to John Lumley, 1st baron Lumley, to collect £12,350, being the unpaid part of debt to the Crown from the State of Florence, and to pay the Queen £771, 17s., 6.d. per annum until all is collected. Lumley pledges Borne and 20 other Sussex manors and 2 in Salop [Shropshire], to the use of the Queen should he default in his annual payments. With fragment of great seal. (Z.c.35 (4))

7   January 1, 1564/65   New Year's gift roll, signed. (Z.d.13)

8   July 29, 1565   Letter of command, signed, to Roger North, 2nd baron North, and other Commissioners of Musters for Cambridgeshire, to take a muster of horses and geldings, and certify how many the county can provide for Her Majesty's service. With seal intact. (X.d.126)

9   February 12, 1565/66   Proclamation, signed, against excess in apparel. (Z.e.29 (1))[2]

10   February 17, 1565/66   Letter signed, to Philip II of Spain, on behalf of English merchants held in Spain since 1563. Written in the hand of her secretary, Roger Ascham, and signed by him. Written from Greenwich. In Latin. (X.d.138 (2))

11   June 22, 1568   Warrant signed, to Sir Ambrose Cave, chancellor of the Duchy of Lancaster, to inquire into an estate of the manor of More, Herts., taken away from William Heydon by Wolsey, and accordingly make restitution to his heirs. (X.d.83)

12	November 4, 1568	Letter of command, signed, to Sir Henry Sidney, Lord Deputy of Ireland, for Nicholas White to replace Thomas Stukeley as Seneschal of Wexford. (X.d.127)
13	November 5, 1568	Letters patent, signed, to Andrew van Loe, for a loan of £2142 to Sir Thomas Gresham on behalf of the Queen to be repaid April 20, 1569. Signed on dorse by privy council members. (Z.c.44 (8))
14	March 1, 1568/69	Proclamation, signed, against seditious books, for subjects to bring them to the bishop for him to keep and read. (X.d.85)
15	August 3, 1569	Proclamation, signed, against pirates, for customs officers, etc., to exercise stricter vigilance. (X.d.86)
16	March 14, 1570/71	Passport, signed, from Greenwich, for Thomas Knevet of Norfolk, esquire. (Z.c.24 (23))
17	June 11, 1573	Proclamation, signed, against seditious books written against the Prayer Book, particularly directed against *An Admonition to the Parliament* (London, 1572). (X.d.87)
18	December 22, 1573	Letter signed, to Friedrich III, elector Palatine, recommending an ambassador. In Latin. (X.d.138 (3))
19	March 11, 1573/74	Deed of exchange, signed, with Thomas Heneage, Esq., Treasurer of the Chamber. Signed at bottom by Burghley and Mildmay. Sealed with her first great seal. (Z.e.30)[3]
20	October 1574	Instructions, signed, to Roger North, 2nd baron North, English ambassador to France, on the accession of Henri III. Signed at the end by Sir Francis Walsingham. 4 fols. (X.d.90)
21	January 1, 1574/75	New Year's gift roll, signed. (Z.d.14)
22	ca. 1575	Letter signed, to an unknown person, concerning Mary, Queen of Scots (only first portion survives). Also, a fragment with her sign manual. (X.d.294-295)
23	January 1, 1578/79	New Year's gift roll, signed. (Z.d.15)
24	April 8, 1580	Warrant signed, for delivery of attendants' clothing. With signet seal intact. (X.d.75 (6))
25	January 1, 1584/85	New Year's gift roll, signed. (Z.d.16)
26	ca. 1585	Presentation, signed, of Thomas Barrett, archdeacon of Exeter, to the living of Challeygh [Chilley, Devon?], vacant by the death of John Cole. Signed also by John Woolton, bishop of Exeter. (X.d.267)

27 July 15, 1590   Letter signed, to Christian of Anhalt, soliciting his cooperation in the interest of Protestant unity and introducing a trusted ambassador, Horatio Pallavicino, who will treat with Henri IV of France and then proceed to Germany. In Latin. (X.d.138 (4))

28 November 25, 1590 Letter signed, to Christian of Anhalt, imploring his support for Pallavicino's diplomacy. In Latin. With signet seal intact. (X.d.138 (5))

29 January 29, 1591/92 Warrant signed, to John Fortescue, Master of the Wardrobe, to deliver a royal coat of arms to Thomas Knight, Rouge-Croix pursuivant. With an Elizabethan sixpence attached to the seal by a thread through a hole in the center. (V.b.55)

30 March 16, 1592/93 Autograph letter signed, to James VI, urging action against the earl of Bothwell's conspiracy against the crown of Scotland. (X.d.397)

31 September 9, 1594 Letter signed, to Don Ferdinand de Medici, grand duke of Tuscany, sending her friendly greetings. Written from Greenwich. In Italian. (X.d.138 (6))

32 ca. 1595   Autograph letter signed, to Henri IV of France, urging the importance of preserving the king's life rather than risking avoidable dangers. In French. 2 pp. (V.b.131)

33 December 19, 1597 Letter signed, to Prince John George of Anhalt, protesting against the edict expelling the Merchant Adventurers from German cities. Written in the hand of her secretary, Roger Ascham. With signet seal intact. In Latin. 8 pp. (V.b.181)

34 December 20, 1597 Letter signed, to Emperor Rudolf II, protesting against the imperial edict banning the Merchant Adventurers. In Latin. (X.d.138 (7))

35 January 1, 1598/99 New Year's gift roll, signed. (Z.d.17)

36 August 4, 1599   Letter of command, signed, to the earl of Nottingham, Lord Lieutenant of Surrey, requiring him to assemble horse and troop. 2 pp. (X.d.130)

37 June 28, 1602   Warrant signed, to the Treasurer of the Exchequer, to pay £2500 to Roger Aston for the king of the Scots, being part of an arranged gratuity. (X.d.99)

38 July 28, 1602   Letter of command, signed, to the High Sheriff of Warwickshire to raise horse and troop to serve as reinforcement in Ireland. (X.d.131)

---

1 These manuscripts are listed in the printed *Catalogue of Manuscripts of the Folger Shakespeare Library Washington D.C.*, 3 vols. and 1 supp. (Boston: G.K. Hall, 1971, 1988), under the subject headings "Great Britain. Sovereigns, etc., 1558–1603 (Elizabeth)" and "Elizabeth, queen of England, 1533–1603."

2 Formerly X.d.84.

3 Formerly V.b.141.

JVNO·POTENS·SCEPTRIS·ET·MENTIS·ACVMINE·PALLAS   ADFVIT·ELIZABETH·IVNO·PERCVLSA·REFVGIT·

HANS EWORTH QUEEN ELIZABETH CONFOUNDING JUNO·MINERVA and VENUS

Portraying Queens: the International Language of Court Portraiture in the Sixteenth Century[1]

Sheila ffolliott

TO CONTEMPLATE THE PORTRAITS OF ELIZABETH I, and the expectations they engendered in viewers "then," requires us to consider the roles such images—especially those of female sovereigns —played during Elizabeth's lifetime. Perhaps the most significant point regarding the Renaissance ruler portrait is that it was not intended simply as a likeness, but rather as a means to meld the individual person to the position of ruler.[2] We also look at Elizabeth's portraits "now," during the "Second" Elizabethan Age, through the filter of all manner of pictures of royal women inundating the media—including the current British monarch, who recently celebrated her Golden Jubilee, her late daughter-in-law, Princess Diana, as well as non-royal women in positions of authority, such as Margaret Thatcher.[3] This essay seeks to place the depiction of Elizabeth I (1533–1603) into the context of early modern women rulers, in particular as compared with her contemporary, Catherine de Médicis (1519–1589), queen regent of France. To do so it investigates the material conditions of portraits as objects, their production (from the standpoint of artist and sitter), certain aspects of their imagery, and their function, especially at court.

ELIZABETH THEN

Elizabeth's portraits have been well studied stylistically—especially within the English artistic tradition—and iconographically—in particular with regard to her anomalous situation as a female monarch.[4] Interest in her uniqueness within English culture, moreover, was central to New Historicism, that current of literary scholarship arising in the 1980s.[5] Insufficiently acknowledged is the fact that before, during, and after Elizabeth's lifetime many women ruled in Europe. Her sister sovereigns included several queens regnant, like herself, but the majority were regents, who ruled temporarily in the king's absence or when he was a minor.[6] In some respects, Elizabeth's portrayal resembles that of contemporary female rulers elsewhere. Portraits show all these queens individually or in family groups, attending to appropriate activities, at fêtes or ceremonies, hunting, in prayer, or as part of an allegory. Concerns over iconography in these depictions emerge from misogynist anxiety about woman's fitness to govern, spelled out in 1558 by John Knox in *The First*

H[ans] E[worth], attrib. *Elizabeth I and the Three Goddesses* (1569). RCIN 403446. The Royal Collection ©2002, Her Majesty Queen Elizabeth II.

Blast of the Trumpet.[7] In other respects, Elizabeth's portrayal differed: she was a Protestant and her imagery adapted to the changes occurring over her lengthy reign (1558–1603) as queen in her own right, primarily her transformation from marriageable princess, destined to rule and continue the Tudor Dynasty, to perpetual Virgin Queen in the 1580s.

In the early modern era, portraits in different formats and sizes played an important role in transnational court culture. Significantly, portraits themselves wielded power and were treated as if they were the very person they represented.[8] As Joanna Woodall has recently argued: "An understanding of portraits as direct substitutes for their sitters meant that the circulation of portraits could mirror and expand the system of personal patronage whereby power, privilege and wealth were distributed."[9] While we might imagine that the large-scale painted or sculpted portrait was the most visible and, therefore, the most highly prized form, in fact an inverse privileging obtained. Miniatures, medals, and cameos were more highly esteemed: in part, because they featured precious materials, but also because access to them could be limited and viewing created an occasion for intimacy. In his *Memoirs*, Mary Stuart's ambassador, Sir James Melville, related his experience with Queen Elizabeth in 1564 when, in the privacy of her chamber, she showed him a miniature portrait of Leicester that she drew from a small cabinet and unwrapped, after pretending she didn't want to show it. Melville asked Elizabeth to send the portrait to Mary because Elizabeth had "the original" (Leicester was standing in the room at the time), but the queen demurred.[10]

To confer authority, moreover, Elizabeth's own portrait appeared not only on seals and on coins but also in the margins of important documents and manuscripts. Similar depictions in the print media (woodcut or engraving) had the same effect but enjoyed a wider circulation.[11] Although he may have overstated the case, Roy Strong surmised that the portrait of Elizabeth serving as frontispiece to the *Bishops' Bible*, 1568 (see p. 36) "must have been seen by almost every subject."[12]

IMAGE CONTROL

Conceptually, portraiture occupied a paradoxical position in the Renaissance. As stated earlier, portraits were not regarded primarily as likenesses.[13] Woodall argues, nevertheless, that "portraiture had to be theorized as unmediated realism" even though "the *raison d'être* of these images was actually to represent sitters as worthy of love, honour, respect, and authority. It was not just that the real was confused with the ideal, but that divine virtue was the ultimate, permanent reality."[14] The specific challenge facing the portraitist of women rulers, therefore, was to furnish such an "ideal reality" for those who, according to patriarchal political thought, could never be ideal. With so much at stake, and with an increasing demand for portraits developing over the course of the sixteenth century, it is not surprising that Elizabeth recognized the necessity to regulate her image.[15] One way to exert control was to maintain a stable of preferred artists with official court positions and stipends. This was the norm on the Continent, as it had been for Henry VIII, who availed himself of the services of Hans Holbein to make pencil drawings, many of which served as patterns for painted portraits.[16] In France, Jean Clouet, in his capacity as *Peintre du Roi*, created similar drawings, called *crayons*, of important people at the court of Francis I. Tracings from these drawings, and later ones made by his son François and other artists, were the basis of many official portraits at the French court.[17] Catherine de Médicis collected and annotated these *crayons*, and they continued to serve her needs in producing portraits to send to relatives or as part of marriage negotiations.[18]

Elizabeth, probably for reasons of expense, chose not to support a large atelier.[19] Instead, her government proposed legal measures to control her representation, beginning in 1563 with a draft proclamation intended to prevent the production and distribution of depictions lacking quality.[20]

Hir Majestie perceiveth that a great number of her loving subjects are much greved, and take great offence with the errors and deformities allready comitteed by sondry persons in this behalf [i.e. royal portraiture], she straightly chargeth all hir officers and ministers to see the observation hereof, and as soon as maybe to reform the errors allready committeed, and in meantyme to forbydd and prohibit the showing and publication of such as are apparently deformed until they are reformed which are reformable.[21]

The proclamation provided for the production of approved model portraits for artists to copy—similar to the practice involving Holbein and Clouet—but it was never enforced. In 1575 the Painter Stainers' Company itself petitioned for assistance in maintaining standards.[22] Indicative of the ineffectiveness of these measures was the Privy Council's decision in 1596 empowering the Serjeant Painter, George Gower, to judge whether portraits of the queen in circulation were suitable; if not they should be destroyed.[23]

THE ARTISTS

Who portrayed Elizabeth? It is well known that England did not produce many native-born painters in the sixteenth century, but did nationality matter? Most court artists worked internationally. Flanders and France, particularly Fontainebleau, provided a haven for prospective court artists from throughout Europe: they could learn and practice an elegant—and increasingly international—Mannerist style much in demand.[24] Of Elizabeth's known portraitists, Nicholas Hilliard and John de Critz I (Serjeant Painter to James I) both spent time at Fontainebleau.[25] Lucas de Heere (who painted the *Allegory of the Tudor Succession*) was in the service of Catherine de Médicis before coming to England in 1567.[26] Once there, de Herre had as pupils Hans Eworth, de Critz, and Marcus Gheeraerts, and the latter two set up a joint workshop.[27] Gheeraerts, moreover—probable author of several portraits—trained in Flanders with Bernard van Orley, court painter to Margaret of Austria (1480–1530), Regent of the Netherlands.[28] The *Ditchley* and *Rainbow* portraits are attributed to his son, Marcus Gheeraerts II. On occasion, Elizabeth's portraitists depicted more than one queen. Federico Zuccaro (active in Flanders, Spain, and England, as well as in his native Italy) depicted Mary Stuart as well as Elizabeth I.[29] Women portraitists also circulated among courts, in general receiving appointments to a queen's household. Susanna Hornebolte, miniaturist, was First Gentlewoman to Anne of Cleves, and she later attended Catharine Parr.[30] The Italian painter Sofonisba Anguissola served as lady-in-waiting to Isabel de Valois, successor to Mary Tudor as wife of Philip II of Spain.[31] Flemish miniaturist Levina Teerlinc held appointments in both Mary's and Elizabeth's households.[32]

Nationality sometimes carried cachet. Catherine de Médicis sent her French master to portray Elizabeth, making a point by stating clearly at court that the local artists were not proficient.

Skilled painters, however, could emulate others' styles. Philip II requested that his Flemish court painter, Antonis Mor, imitate the style of the Italian Titian for his royal portraits, including that of Elizabeth's predecessor, Mary Tudor.[33]

IMAGERY

Dynastic symbols maintained the appearance of continuity in the face of the inevitable change characteristic of hereditary monarchy, wherein heirs replace their predecessors. In state portraiture —with the imperative to fuse person to position—supplanting often meant fitting the new ruler's personal traits and symbols to pre-existing prototypes. A shift in gender complicated the process, but since Elizabeth succeeded her elder sister, some of her portraits (The "*Darnley*" portrait and Quentin Massys II's *Portrait of Elizabeth I* in Siena), in Roy Strong's aptly dynastic terms, "are direct descendants of Mor's *Mary Tudor*.[34] As queens regnant, their portraits alone (frontal and iconic) graced the materials of state (seals, coins), whereas a queen regent's rule was always contingent upon the existence of a king, so its imagery emphasized connection.

Some images, however, feature the same symbols or similar formal composition but through subtle manipulation achieve different ends. One of the best known of Elizabeth's portraits is *The Rainbow Portrait* (ca. 1590) attributed to Marcus Gheeraerts the Younger.[35] The rainbow was the central feature of the *impresa* of Catherine de Médicis when she came to France as a young bride in 1533. As such, it replaced her individual identity and symbolized the conventional role of royal bride as bringer of peace. In Gheeraerts' portrait, although Elizabeth holds a rainbow, it does not replace her. The motto "*Non sine sole Iris*" (no rainbow without the sun) glosses the biblical symbol of peace and indicates that it would be impossible to achieve without the presence of the sun, i.e., the queen herself.

A different use of symbolical figures occurs in two similarly structured bi-partite narratives: the 1569 painting, *Elizabeth I and the Three Goddesses* (attributed to The Monogrammist HE) (see p. 165), and a 1560s tapestry design by Antoine Caron. In the painting, an iconic Elizabeth, crowned and holding orb and scepter, stands on a portico to demonstrate her authority to Juno, Minerva, and Venus. She, therefore, incorporates the qualities of all three goddesses, who, more normally, separately figured women in courtly iconography.[36] In France, for example, Juno or Minerva symbolized the queen, whether in triumphal entries, as was the case for Catherine de Médicis, or in medals or statuettes, as was the case for her cousin, Marie de Médicis, consort of Henri IV.[37] In courts with a King, Venus generally figured the mistress, though an interesting exception was Diane de Poitiers, mistress to Henri II. Ironically, because of her name, she subsumed the chaste Diana imagery later used for Elizabeth, the Virgin Queen.[38]

In Caron's tapestry design, *Receipt of Petitions*, Catherine de Médicis—referred to allegorically as Artemisia, an ancient widowed queen—appears, like Elizabeth, in a portico at left. Although formally the design resembles the similar depiction of Elizabeth, Catherine stands behind her son, the king.[39] In another Caron drawing, *The Book and the Sword*, Artemisia/Catherine oversees her son's education. In both these examples the queen's role is supervisory. She does not possess the sacral king's body, but acts on his behalf or makes certain that he receives appropriate education. Most female regents for minor sons were queen mothers.[40] As I have argued elsewhere, Caron drew upon Marian prototypes, in part because of the lack of formal prototypes for narratives with female protagonists, but also because of the Virgin Mary's eventual coronation.[41] In *The Petitions* note the Annunciation-like placement of the standing female in a portico with kneeling figure in front and the Adoration-of-the-Magi-like group of figures, one of whom genuflects before mother and child.

The Book and the Sword, on the other hand, resembles a Leonardo Madonna, e.g., *The Madonna of the Rocks*.[42] In this painting, Leonardo pioneered a compositional strategy that employs a system of interlocking gestures and glances to perform the human and symbolic relationships. The Madonna's outstretched left hand provides a canopy for her divine son, while her right secures John the Baptist's left shoulder and points him in the direction of his cousin, sitting on the ground near an angel. She alone organizes all connections and moves the narrative forward: John's prophecy, Christ's divinity and destiny. Similarly, in Caron's drawing it is Artemisia/ Catherine whose arms link the attributes of the two branches of learning while she shelters her son under the arch her body forms. She looks towards the side of letters, while her son holds the

book and, appropriately, looks towards the soldier. Artemisia and the Virgin, as mothers of important sons, play both protective and launching roles. They link the important actors.

By contrast, it has been argued that in Elizabeth's imagery she rather supplants Mary in her role as Virgin Queen in a Protestant country. Furthermore, for Catherine the imagery of the Book and Sword refers to the classical precepts for a balanced education, featuring letters and things military, while for Elizabeth these attributes take on a religious connotation, referring to her role as Protestant guardian of the Word.[43] These attributes, important in the iconography of Henry VIII, grace Crispin van de Passe I's engraved *Memorial Portrait of Elizabeth* (after Isaac Oliver).[44]

The emphasis on virginity was especially important to the imagery of Elizabeth. Because aristocratic and royal women bore male heirs necessary to continue the patriline, demonstrations

Antoine Caron. *Receipt of Petitions* from *Histoire d'Arthémise* (1560s), fol. 37. Cliché Bibliothèque nationale de France, Paris.

of chastity were important to all aristocratic and royal women, even when married. The case of Elizabeth, however, as Virgin Queen forever, is unique. *The Plimpton "Sieve" Portrait of Queen Elizabeth I*, now in the Folger Collection, demonstrates this important quality. Because of its association with the Vestal Tuccia, who proved her virginity by carrying water in a sieve, the device symbolizes chastity. This 1579 portrait is attributed to George Gower, appointed Elizabeth's Serjeant-Painter in 1581. As one of three similar portraits featuring a sieve, it illustrates as well the practice of replicating approved portraits because the depiction of her head corresponds precisely to an earlier portrait.[45] The sieve motif was used again in several other portraits painted in the early 1580s. Constance Jordan has interpreted the Italian inscription edging the sieve (which also appears in the portrait now in Siena), as "To earth the good, bad remains in the saddle."[46] Not conventionally associated with the sieve, the saddle alludes to the masculine nature of kingship—associated with horsemanship—and directs attention to the problem in attaching a female body natural to the male body politic. Jordan suggests that this disjuncture calls for an ironic reading of the inscription. In these portraits, therefore, Elizabeth, in female attire, assumes a properly decorous pose and holds the well-known symbol of chastity, with its subtle allusion to the ruler's being in the saddle and thus in control. Similarly, in another Caron tapestry design, Artemisia/Catherine de Médicis watches over her son's lesson in horsemanship , symbolic of the appropriate training for a future ruler; she herself does not ride.[47]

USES

In the sixteenth century, works of art provided the opportunity for courtly performance. The king or queen with an entourage visited artists' studios.[48] Within the palace, monarchs displayed portraits to important visitors, and courtiers participated in ceremonial presentations of new works and observed gift exchanges.[49] Diplomats often recorded these occasions because they served as a barometer for the constantly negotiated power relations at court. Their reports, and those by other courtiers or the artists themselves, tell us who was present, who did what, and who expressed what opinion. Portraits in particular figure in these chronicles of courtly life. In their absence they are objects of speculation, desire, and negotiation; in their presence, they can be events—as when displayed for the first time—or objects for examination and comment.

ABSENCE

With the understanding that portraits stood in for the person they represented, people spoke about/to the portrait as they might have spoken about/to the subject. In a letter to Elizabeth I of August 22, 1560, her ambassador writes of his interview with Mary Stuart, eighteen-year-old Queen of Scotland in her own right, and, as of one year, Queen consort of France. After professing her desire for amity with the English queen, Mary asks for her portrait, telling the ambassador:

Indeed they do all greatly praise her, and say that she is both a wise and very fair lady; and because the one of us cannot see the other, I will send her my picture, though it be not worth the looking on, because you shall promise me that she shall send me hers; for I assure you if I thought she would not send me hers, she should not have mine.[50]

Mary takes the opportunity to express an appropriately rhetorical modesty, via her assessment of her own portrait/herself. Her conventional language, moreover, indicates her desire for a likeness to corroborate the verbal portrait of Elizabeth's character.[51] This request illustrates Woodall's point about portraits being theorized as likenesses, although the "reality" they represent includes qualities worthy of admiration. Significantly, the Queen of France makes a demand of the ambassador, not just to test his influence with his sovereign, but also to make clear her expectation of reciprocity in this negotiation, and, by extension, in all others between these rival queens."[52]

Perhaps Mary was disingenuous and had already seen portraits of Elizabeth because at the same time Catherine de Médicis, her mother-in-law, had seen Elizabeth's portrait and had commented: "After what everyone tells me of her beauty, and after the paintings I have seen, I must declare that she did not have good painters."[53] In fact, when engaged in negotiations to marry Elizabeth to one of her sons, Catherine sent her own unnamed "French" painter to England to portray Elizabeth.[54] Nevertheless, Mary's statements are laced with attempts to jockey for position, conveniently displacing any personal remarks to portraits and artists.

PRESENCE

As a means of displaying loyalty, especially after plots against her life, Elizabeth's courtiers and diplomats wore or carried miniature portraits of their sovereign on their persons. These props facilitated their dealings. Sir Robert Cecil wrote to the Privy Council from Paris: "afterward he [the French King] passed the time in familiarity, both in discourse of the Queen and her Court showing to divers the picture I wear."[55] Such a miniature also played an important role at a soirée in honor of King Henri III held by his mother, Catherine de Médicis, at her Parisian palace in 1580, when marriage negotiations were carried on between Elizabeth and the king's younger brother.[56]

A letter from Lady Cobham, wife of the British ambassador, describes the occasion in detail.[57] During the evening, the king asked Lady Cobham if he could see "the Queen's picture," by which he intends a portrait of Elizabeth that he assumed she carried. She replied, however, that she "had made a vow that the first that should see it should be his mother." He pressed her nevertheless, and, holding her ground, she offered that the "picture was excellent" but demurred. After dinner, Lady Cobham continued, "the queen called me to her in the presence of the king and desired to see the picture; saying that I should not break my vow in showing it to her, because she was queen." The king, having failed in his quest to view the portrait, enlisted his wife's cooperation, so that the transaction remained one amongst women. Lady Cobham capitulated, saying, "Thereupon I showed it to her [Queen Louise], and [as] she was looking at it, the king suddenly took it from her, so that it was well viewed by both."

"The King said it was an excellent picture; the queen asked me if she were like it. I answered that she was."[58] To return to Woodall's point about portraits being theorized as likenesses, other reports from this time confirm that it is one of the main topics of conversation when examining portraits. Is this because of the tension between expectations that portraits were likenesses and the knowledge of people with experience, like Henry VIII, who perceived that the person (Anne of Cleves) did not look like the Holbein portrait?[59] The ideal situation involved both a painter and a witness, although this too left room for skepticism.[60]

What do these exchanges tell us? Did Elizabeth I see herself dealing with Catherine and not with the prospective bridegroom's brother? Because Lady Cobham is the agent, and Catherine was queen mother and not sovereign, can we conclude that the marriage discussion was thus on a less official plane? Did Elizabeth have more wiggle room, a strategy she used constantly at home when dealing with the marriage question?

Another remark of Lady Cobham's demonstrates clearly how portraits substitute for their subjects: "I told them her Majesty [Elizabeth] had commanded that whenever I came in the presence of them both, I should wish her there." After some exchanges about the excellence of both queens, she continued, "If . . . the queen, my mistress and your Majesty might meet, it then be truly said that two of the goodliest creatures and greatest queens in the world were together." Queen Louise protested (echoing the earlier rhetoric of Mary Stuart), saying that "as appeared by the picture, it might be true of my mistress [i.e., Elizabeth], but not in respect of herself. I answered that she much resembled my mistress . . . so the Queen thanked me for the good opinion I had of her." Like a true diplomat, Lady Cobham managed to flatter the French queen while praising her own queen Elizabeth, but when Louise, "asked me if I could find in my heart to part with the picture," Lady Cobham refused. She thus managed to retain the portrait (and her authority to represent the queen's interest) by answering that "the greatest comfort which I have, being absent from my mistress, is to behold it," and Queen Louise gave way.

Again, what did this verbal, but not material, exchange, signify? If the portrait had been presented as a gift, or if the exchange had been between men, not women, would it have meant a more serious acknowledgment of betrothal on the part of the bride? Did Lady Cobham's coyness simply reproduce Elizabeth's own way of deferring from a distance? What about the flattering comparison of female virtue, as embodied in Elizabeth's portrait and, according to Lady Cobham, Queen Louise herself? In all these cases, the portrait was the nexus.

ELIZABETH NOW

Space does not permit discussing the full range of issues informing the imagery of Elizabeth I and her contemporary queens. When we briefly survey the portrayal of Elizabeth II, whose reign now exceeds her eponymous predecessor by five years, we notice lingering traditions and adaptations to changes in situation over the years. Cecil Beaton photographed Elizabeth while a princess, setting her quite obviously into dreamy formal prototypes derived from eighteenth-century French artists, like Boucher. Portraits produced at the time of her Coronation in 1953 conform to type, especially her *State Portrait* by Sir James Gunn.[61] Featuring characteristics seen in Tudor royal portraiture, but standardized with the Stuarts, this image features the monarch, standing before a chair, her hand placed on a table, upon which rest the regal crown and sword. Julian Calder updated this portrait in a photograph made for Elizabeth II's Golden Jubilee. Unlike images of the first Elizabeth, featuring the "Mask of Youth" invented by Nicholas Hilliard in the 1590s to maintain the illusion of the monarch's youth, the photograph, as well as Lucien Freud's controversial *Portrait of Elizabeth II*, included in the Queen's Gallery exhibition celebrating the Golden Jubilee, reveal the effects of time on the current queen's appearance. Christopher Lloyd, Surveyor of the Queen's Pictures, has explained such changes in the following terms: "Modern artists [have difficulty in] sustain[ing] the traditions of royal portraiture . . . [in part because] the potency of formal portraiture has been greatly reduced."[62] Paparazzi, with the wide dissemination of their photographs on television and in tabloids, have invaded the privileged isolation of the royals that heretofore largely protected their control and dissemination of imagery of their choice.

1 For their advice, I would like to thank Mack P. Holt, Annemarie Jordan, Julia Marciari-Alexander, Martha McCrory, David Harris Sacks, and the editors of this catalogue.

2 Lorne Campbell, *Renaissance Portraits: European Portrait-Painting in the 14th, 15th, and 16th Centuries* (New Haven: Yale University Press, 1990), 1–2, discusses the imprecise nature of Renaissance terminology regarding portraiture. Sir John Davies used "counterfeit" in his poem about a portrait of Elizabeth I, "To Her Picture"; see *The Poems of Sir John Davies*, ed. Robert Krueger (Oxford: Clarendon Press, 1975), 77. The verb *counterfeit* sometimes meant portray, suggesting an imperative to produce a likeness. See also Joanna Woodall, ed. *Portraiture: Facing the Subject* (New York: St. Martin's Press, 1997), 1. For the requirements of the State Portrait, see Marianna D. Jenkins, *The State Portrait, its Origins and Evolution* (New York: College Art Association of America, 1947). Much later scholarship depends upon Ernst Kantorowicz, *The King's Two Bodies: A Study in Mediaeval Political Theology* (Princeton: Princeton University Press, 1957), and Marie Axton, *The Queen's Two Bodies: Drama and the Elizabethan Succession* (London: Royal Historical Society, 1977). See also Roy C. Strong, *The Portraits of Queen Elizabeth I* (Oxford: Clarendon Press, 1963), 34.

3 For a discussion of how issues facing women in positions of power in the Renaissance continue to affect women in public life, see Carole Levin and Patricia A. Sullivan, "Women and Political Communication: From the Margins to the Center," in *Political Rhetoric, Power, and Renaissance Women*, edited by Carole Levin and Patricia A. Sullivan (Albany: State University of New York Press, 1995), 275–82.

4 Strong, *Portraits*, attempted to attribute the portraits to artists and to organize them into formal types; see also Erna Auerbach, *Tudor Artists: A Study of Painters in the Royal Service and of Portraiture on Illuminated Documents from the Accession of Henry VIII to the Death of Elizabeth I* (London: University of London, Athlone Press, 1954); Frances A. Yates, *Astraea: The Imperial Theme in the Sixteenth Century* (London: Routledge and Kegan Paul, 1975); Maurice Howard, *The Tudor Image* (London: Tate Gallery, 1995); David Howarth, *Images of Rule: Art and Politics in the English Renaissance, 1485–1649* (Berkeley: University of California Press, 1997); but see *Dissing Elizabeth: Negative Representations of Gloriana*, ed. Julia M. Walker (Durham: Duke University Press, 1998).

5 A founding New Historicist text is Stephen Greenblatt's *Renaissance Self-Fashioning: from More to Shakespeare* (Chicago: University of Chicago Press, 1980); see also Louis Adrian Montrose, "*A Midsummer Night's Dream* and the Shaping Fantasies of Elizabethan Culture: Gender, Power, Form," in *Rewriting the Renaissance: The Discourses of Sexual Difference in Early Modern Europe*, ed. Margaret W. Ferguson, Maureen Quilligan, and Nancy J. Vickers (Chicago: University of Chicago Press, 1986), 65–87, and "Idols of the Queen: Policy, Gender, and the Picturing of Elizabeth I," *Representations*, 68 (1999): 108–61; and Susan Frye, *Elizabeth I: The Competition for Representation* (New York and Oxford: Oxford University Press, 1993).

6 For a discussion of several of these rulers, see the catalogue essay on "Foreign Relations."

7 These aspects inform the exhibition *Women who Ruled: Queens, Goddesses, Amazons in Renaissance and Baroque Art* and catalogue, ed. Annette Dixon (London: Merrell Publishers Ltd. in association with the University of Michigan Museum of Art, 2002). For a discussion of Knox, see the current catalogue, p. 113

8 See Bernard Denvir, *From the Middle Ages to the Stuarts: Art, Design, and Society, before 1689* (London; New York: Longman, 1988), 124. For a general discussion on this theme, see David Freedberg, *The Power of Images: Studies in the History and Theory of Response* (Chicago: University of Chicago Press, 1989).

9 Woodall, *Portraiture*, 3; with regard to female portraiture, the idea that outer beauty reflected inner virtue, see David Alan Brown, *Virtue and Beauty: Leonardo's Ginevra de' Benci and Renaissance Portraits of Women* (Washington, DC: National Gallery of Art, 2001).

10 James Melville, *Memoirs*, 2nd ed. (Edinburgh: Ruddimans, 1735), 97; see also the discussion by Patricia Fumerton, "Secret Arts: Elizabethan Miniatures and Sonnets," in *Cultural Aesthetics: Renaissance Literature and the Practice of Social Ornament* (Chicago: University of Chicago Press, 1991), 67ff.

11 Strong notes also that, as a category, documents bear the greatest number of illuminated portraits of the queen (*Portraits*, 31).

12 Strong, *Portraits*, 30; similarly, he noted also the wide circulation of her portrait in the initial C in John Foxe's *Actes and Monuments*. See also John King, *Tudor Royal Iconography: Literature and Art in an Age of Religious Crisis* (Princeton: Princeton University Press, 1989).

13 Regarding the mimetic function of the portrait in sixteenth-century France, see Robert D. Cottrell, *Brantôme: The Writer as Portraitist of His Age* (Geneva: Droz, 1970), 59.

14 Woodall, *Portraiture*, 3.

15 Roy Strong, *The English Renaissance Miniature* (London: Thames and Hudson, 1983), 81. The necessity to regulate came "as a result of dawning awareness that it [her image] could be manipulated as a focus of loyalty to the state" (Strong, *Miniature*, 82).

16 Oskar Bätschmann and Pascal Griener, *Hans Holbein* (Princeton: Princeton University Press, 1997), 134.

17 *Les Clouet & La Cour des Rois de France de François IER à Henri IV*, ed. Jean Adhémar (Paris: Bibliothèque Nationale, 1970), 13, and Alexandra Zvereva, *Les Clouet de Catherine de Médicis: chefs-d'oeuvre graphiques du Musée Condé* (Paris: Somogy, 2002).

18 Adhémar mentions that Catherine de Médicis had 500 *crayons* in her collection; he notes that Elizabeth too possessed a collection of *crayons*—stored in a cabinet, each kept between two leaves of silk paper—which she showed one day to a French ambassador. She also had a collection of drawings by Holbein, bought by Edward VI in 1550 (now at Windsor), (*Les Clouet*, 9, 12).

19 Strong, *Miniature*, 81. Her predecessors also spent more to maintain household painters.

20 Strong, *Portraits*, 6; in this case, lack of "quality" refers to what is presumed to be the artist's inability to produce an appropriately flattering portrayal.

21 *Archaeologia*, II, 169ff.; quoted from Bernard Denvir, *From the Middle-Ages to the Stuarts* (London; New York: Longman, 1988), 124–25.

22 Their petition decried "the low standard of workmanship by those insufficiently trained as painters 'as well as counterfeyting your Majesties picture and the pictures of noble men and others'" (Strong, *Miniature*, 81).

23 Strong, *Portraits*, 5; "They had been, it is stated, 'to her great offence,'" which points to Elizabeth's own strong opinions (Strong, *Miniature*, 82).

24 See also Strong, *Portraits*, 14.

25 Christopher Foley, "Jacob de Critz" in *The Dictionary of Art*, ed. Jane Turner (New York: Grove's Dictionaries, 1996), 8:165–66.

26 ca. 1570, at Sudeley Castle, Gloucestershire.

27 Carl van de Velde, "de Heere," in *The Dictionary of Art*, ed. Jane Turner (New York: Grove's Dictionaries, 1996), 14:296–97.

28 William Scrots, who painted Edward VI, had also been her court painter. The Elizabeth portrait is at Welbeck Abbey, Nottinghamshire. Els Vermandere, "Marcus Gheeraerts," in *The Dictionary of Art*, ed. Jane Turner (New York: Grove's Dictionaries, 1996), 12:513–15.

29 Liana de Girolami Cheney, "Federico Zuccaro," in *The Dictionary of Art*, ed. Jane Turner (New York: Grove's Dictionaries, 1996), 33:718–21.

30 Strong, *Miniature*, 44.

31 Ilya Sandra Perlingieri, *Sofonisba Anguissola: The First Great Woman Artist of The Renaissance* (New York: Rizzoli, 1992).

32 Mary Edmonds, "Levina Teerlinc," *The Dictionary of Art*, ed. Jane Turner (New York: Grove's Dictionaries, 1996), 30: 411–12.

33 Joanna Woodall, "An Exemplary Consort: Antonis Mor's Portrait of Mary Tudor," *Art History* 14 (1991):192–224.

34 Strong, *Portraits*, 15.

35 The portrait is at Hatfield House. For further discussion of this theme, see Sheila ffolliott, "Make Love not War: Images of Peace through Marriage in Renaissance France," in *Peace and Negotiation: Strategies for Coexistence in the Middle Ages and Renaissance*, ed. Diane Wolfthal (Tempe, Arizona: ACMRS, 2000), 213–32.

36 Karen Hearn, "Elizabeth I and the Three Goddesses," in *Dynasties: Painting in Tudor and Jacobean England, 1530–1630*, ed. Karen Hearn (New York: Rizzoli, 1996), 73–74. Sarah B. Pomeroy, in *Goddesses, Whores, Wives, and Slaves: Women in Classical Antiquity* (New York: Schocken Books, 1975), made the important point that while the Greek gods regularly embodied several traits, the goddesses were limited to a single specialty.

37 One, among many, examples of Catherine de Médicis as Juno occurs in the royal entries; see Victor Graham and W. McAllister Johnson, *The Royal Tour of France by Charles IX and Catherine de Médici: festivals and entries, 1564–1566* (Toronto: University of Toronto Press, 1974), 202; similarly a statuette by Matthieu Jacquet, ca. 1600 (Baltimore, Walters Art Museum) depicts *Marie de Médici as Juno*.

38 Philippa Berry, *Of Chastity and Power: Elizabethan Literature and the Unmarried Queen* (London and New York: Routledge, 1989).

39 For an analysis of the *Petitions*, see Sheila ffolliott, "Women in the Garden of Allegory: Catherine de' Médici and the Locus of Female Rule," in *Villas and Gardens in Early Modern Italy and France*, ed. Mirka Benes and Dianne Harris (Cambridge: Cambridge University Press, 2001), 207–24.

40 French and Italian regents after Elizabeth's death appeared jointly with their children in painted and engraved portraits and in medals. For examples, see *Women Who Ruled*, ed. Annette Dixon, 131–35.

41 This discussion derives from a paper I delivered to the 1996 Berkshire Conference.

42 Versions in London, National Gallery, and Paris, Louvre.

43 Robert J. Clements, "Pen and Sword," in *Picta Poesis: Literary and Humanistic Theory in Renaissance Emblem Books* (Rome: Edizioni di Storia e Letteratura, 1960), 145.

44 See King, *Tudor Royal Iconography*, chapter 2 and 264–65.

45 Roy Strong, *Gloriana: The Portraits of Queen Elizabeth I* (New York: Thames and Hudson, 1987), 95, demonstrated that her head replicates the "Darnley" Portrait, now London, National Portrait Gallery; see also William L. Pressly, *A Catalogue of Paintings in the Folger Shakespeare Library* (New Haven: Yale University Press, 1993), 329–31.

46 Constance Jordan, "Representing Political Androgyny; more on the Siena Portrait of Queen Elizabeth I," in *The Renaissance Englishwoman in Print: Counterbalancing the Canon*, ed. Anne M. Haselkorn and Betty S. Travitsky (Amherst: University of Massachusetts Press, 1990), 166.

47 For more on horsemanship and male rule, see Sheila ffolliott, "Once Upon a Tapestry: Inventing the Ideal Queen," in *Images of a Queen's Power: The Artemisia Tapestries*, by Candace Adelson and Sheila ffolliott (Minneapolis: Minneapolis Institute of Arts, 1993), 13–19.

48 Benvenuto Cellini, *The Autobiography*, trans. George Bull (London and New York: Penguin, 1996), 259–60, describes a visit by Francis I and his entourage. Pierre de Bourdeille, seigneur de Brantôme, *Oeuvres Complètes* (Paris: Foucault, 1822–23), V: 33–34, describes a visit of Catherine de Médicis to the studio of Corneille de Lyon.

49 Cellini, *Autobiography* 298–300, describes the initial presentation of his silver *Jupiter* candlestick in the Galérie François I.

50 *Calendar of State Papers, Foreign Series, from the Reign of Elizabeth I, 1560–61*, ed. Joseph Stevenson (London: HMSO, 1865), "Throck-morton to the Queen," (251).

51 Brown, "Introduction," in *Virtue and Beauty*, 18–19.

52 See Christopher Lloyd and Vanessa Remington, *Masterpieces in Little: Portrait Miniatures from the Collection of Her Majesty Queen Elizabeth II* (London: Royal Collection Enterprises Ltd., 1996), 62; see also Strong, *Portraits*, 24.

53 Gustave Lebel, "British-French Artistic Relations in the XVIth Century," *Gazette des Beaux-Arts* 33 (1948):278.

54 Lebel, 278.

55 Auerbach, *Tudor Artists*, 103.

56 As I have argued in a paper presented to the 2002 Renaissance Society of America meeting.

57 *Calendar of State Papers, Foreign Series, . . . Elizabeth I, 1579–80*, ed. Arthur John Butler (London: HMSO, 1904), #189: "Lady Cobham at the French Court, Feb.? 1580," 174–76.

58 Edmond Bonnaffé, *Inventaire des Meubles de Catherine de Médicis en 1589: Mobilier, Tableaux, Objets d'art, Manuscrits* (Paris: Chez Auguste Aubry, 1874), 58, lists a miniature of Elizabeth in an ebony frame.

59 Bätschmann and Griener, *Holbein*, 192.

60 As part of marriage negotiations, Catherine de Médicis sent Elizabeth *crayons* of her son Henri. See *Lettres de Catherine de Médicis*, ed. Hector de la Ferrière (Paris: Imprimerie Nationale, 1891), IV:52.

61 At Windsor Castle.

62 Christopher Lloyd, in *Art Quarterly of the National Art Collections Fund*, Summer 2002.

GLORIANA

Benjamin Britten

Re-inventing Elizabeth I:
Memories, Counter-memories, Histories
Barbara Hodgdon

GLORIANA. BELPHOEBE. CYNTHIA. DIANA. THE VIRGIN QUEEN. Who is Elizabeth I? What is she? Today, hers is a name that identifies an historical figure who comes into view primarily as a site or locus of memories and counter-memories, deriving her authority from multiple collaborations with history. Resplendent in white, a tiara on her head, backed by a gossamer ruff outlined in pearls, she stands, as in the ca.1592 Ditchley portrait by Marcus Gheeraerts the Younger, on the map of Oxfordshire, "halfway," Susan Frye writes, "between England and God."[1]

But the face that looks out from the gown, in Susan Herbert's recent rendering from The Cat's Gallery of Art, is that of a ginger cat. Elsewhere, her figure graces a Barbie doll or a Celebri-Duck— oddly evoking the Victorian consensus that Sir Francis Drake and the Armada conferred greatness on her reign—collectibles produced for a commercial marketplace that harks back to her own Age of Commodity and Expansion. Stamped on egg warmers, teapots (again with Drake), tea cozies, tea towels, and pomander balls, her face and body warm the tea, dry the good china, scent the cupboards, imparting royal sanction to domestic chores. In several biographies written for children, she becomes a perfect role model: a daughter who followed in her father's footsteps, a devoted student preparing for her future role, even a spokesperson for Grrrl power.[2] Figuring her as "manag[ing] history's greatest corporate turnaround," *Elizabeth,CEO*'s jacket blurb promises to condense her leadership wizardry into ten lessons—strategies for communicating a vision of excellence, nurturing creativity, turning crisis into triumph, and creating common cause without tyranny—that today's business leaders can employ in their own quests for excellence and supremacy.[3] And in the computer game *Civilization III*, a player can become Elizabeth and so gain practice in ruling "a society characterized by commercialism and enterprise."[4] She returns in other guises as well, most recently in a Summer 2002 London Dungeon exhibit of "Hell's Belles," where posters in the tube, captioned "Elizabeth the Worst?" show her with staring eyes, peaked nose, and pursed mouth, a frothy red fright wig atop her head, her neck encircled with a ruff, an image reminiscent of her early modern caricature as a chicken with pointed beak, an exemplum of "pride, as exhibited in new fashions of apparel," one of seven "monstrous foules" arrayed in "flaunting ruffes" from William Woodwall's

Benjamin Britten. *Gloriana: an opera in three acts* (London, 1953). M1503 B86 G5, front cover.

privately produced manuscript, *The Acts of Queene Elizabeth Allegorized* (ca.1595).[5] And in a Target ad, printed shortly after the release of "her" latest biopic, Shekur Kapur's *Elizabeth* (1998), the ruff (sign par excellence of her Age) transforms into an air filter ($9.99) circling the neck of a red-haired model resembling Cate Blanchett, that film's star actor.[6]

These, her impromptu reappearances, represent mass culture's ways, to appropriate Stephen Greenblatt's phrase, of speaking with the dead. What these artifacts and images suggest is that Elizabeth's "real" identity disappears in a play of visible, material signs—red hair, whitened face, heart-shaped ruff, pearls, black and white gowns. Among these, costume is perhaps her most stable signature, which acts like a screen: to fashion "Queen Elizabeth" is, above all, a matter of fashion. Moreover, just as the mystified medieval doctrine of the king's two bodies—mortal and immortal—attests that the represented body is not the same as the material body, Elizabeth's contemporary embodiments offer instances of how, as Peggy Phelan writes, the real is read through representation, the representation through the real.[7] Perhaps as much as anything else, present-day re-appearances of Elizabeth I show how history repeats itself as something other than itself through a series of performances that stand in for an elusive entity that they aspire to embody, if not replace. Two late twentieth-century Elizabeths, bringing her into view as a figure of display, suggest how the Elizabethan body, and the gossip surrounding it, can lie like truth—or history.

At the seventy-first Oscars ceremony on March 21, 1999, "Queen Elizabeth" appeared on stage to introduce *Shakespeare in Love* (Marc Norman and Tom Stoppard, 1998), nominated for a number of awards. Everything about her was authentic—red hair, standing ruff, jeweled gown—except that the face under the heavy white make-up was unmistakably black and the voice announcing, "I am the African Queen. Some of you may know me as the Virgin Queen, but I can't imagine who," was instantly recognizable as that of Whoopi Goldberg. Perhaps one of the most outrageous Elizabethan masquerades within a long history that includes *Monty Python*'s John Cleese, Miranda Richardson's travestied "Queenie" in *Blackadder II*, and Quentin Crisp's alluringly authentic fetish-Elizabeth from Sally Potter's *Orlando* (1994), Goldberg's apparition, foreclosing on "the real," shadowed another, arguably more reputable surrogate, *Shakespeare in Love*'s queen, Judi Dench. Seen first attending a performance of Shakespeare's *Two Gentlemen of Verona*, she sits imperiously on her state, alternately bored (snoring during "romantic" soliloquies) and delighted (laughing uproariously at Will Kemp and his dog); she then becomes a fairy-godmother to Will Shakespeare and his lover Viola de Lesseps, enabling Shakespeare to win a £50 wager that allows him to join the Chamberlain's Men and, by protecting Viola's disguise as Thomas Kent, prevents the entire cast of *Romeo and Juliet* from being arrested for letting a woman perform on the public stage. Fixing Viola with a stern look, she remarks, "I know something of a woman in a man's profession, yes, by God, I do know about that." Leaving the theater, she encounters a large puddle; hesitating, she then splashes through it, muttering, "Too late; too late," as waiting courtiers sweep their cloaks into the mud.

Drawing Elizabeth's historicity from mise-en-scène (an "authentic" replica of the Rose Theatre, historical locations), from knowledge about the queen's patronage of playwrights and poets, and from famous shards of gossip (Sir Walter Raleigh laying his cloak before her), *Shakespeare in Love*'s Elizabethan fantasy exemplifies the kind of bricolage or patchwork characteristic of contemporary narratives housing her popular memory. Yet insofar as both Goldberg's improvisatory riff and Dench's performance of an aging queen show her as an authoritative author of her self, a consummate performer, they not only preserve Elizabeth's iconography but also gesture beyond the most familiar story about her, one that maps a complex relationship among official history, censorship, and interpretation to condense her figure into the heroine of a romantic liaison with Robert Devereux, the earl of Essex. Although traces of that myth appeared in fragmented form in John Webster's *The Devil's Law Case* (1619–20) and John Ford's *The Broken Heart* (1627–31), it took about fifty years to cook into narrative, becoming most fully elaborated in *The Secret History of the Most Renowned Queen Elizabeth and the Earl of Essex, by a Person of Quality* (1680), exemplary of a genre of pseudo-memoirs focused on women's interior experience and on their role as agents behind the scenes of great events.[8] If *Secret History* is the first retelling to establish marriage as the structuring absence of Elizabeth's anguished inner life, the visions and re-visions of her romantic history that follow consistently dramatize a clash between her political and erotic mythologies and circulate ghosted strands of gossip as serious memory to figure Elizabeth's history as a means for exploring the problematics of power located in a body coded exclusively by desire.

Viewed through the lenses of twentieth-century cinema and television, Elizabeth I is a circum-Atlantic reinvention[9] who comes to prominence in 1912, in Sarah Bernhardt's portrayal in *Queen Elizabeth* (1912), which opened at New York's Lyceum theater before being screened at London's Palace Theatre, to immense box-office success. At mid-century, shortly before World War II, Elizabeth again takes on America (and Hollywood) as Bette Davis's exemplary monarch; by the early 1970s, Glenda Jackson's portrayal in *Elizabeth R* (aired initially on BBC-TV and in 1972 on PBS's Masterpiece Theatre) aligned with the high moment of the "New Feminism," reifying the claims made by the seventeenth-century *Secret History* that women's private experiences exert political effects and that the two spheres of social reality were inseparable. In each retelling, royal history becomes a space of play, emerging in these visions and revisions of Elizabeth as flickers and flashes of meanings layered onto the present. Any history, of course, is always self-interested: as the authors of *1066 and All That* put it, "History is what you remember," and what and how one remembers depends, as with Shakespeare's Falstaff, on the teller and her or his own moment; in one sense, and especially within mass culture representations, all history is contemporary history. Moreover, in this genealogy of Elizabethan re-performances, each of which attempts to restore her behavior and personality through a kinetic vocabulary of body, gesture, and language and in which each retelling simultaneously raids and reconfigures the previous one, "Elizabeth" becomes a succession of surrogates, never performed the same way twice but reinvented and recreated with each appearance. And, like any genealogy, such performances not only document the historical transmission and dissemination of history and culture but also are designed to repossess a heritage, to make it our own.[10]

As the first in this hereditary line, Bernhardt's portrayal stands somewhat apart from later traditions of cinematic realism that strive to depict "Elizabeth herself," for her film makes no attempt to keep the performing body hidden beneath that of the historical person: instead, her costumes owe more to Parisian haute couture than to Elizabethan models; conflating grande dame and queen, her image says that while royalty may not be reproducible, it can be represented by a famous actor, who, like the legend she portrays, lives for the eyes of her subjects—or fans. *The Private Lives of Elizabeth and Essex* (dir. Michael Curtiz, 1939), starring Bette Davis and Errol Flynn, not only evoked Edward VIII's 1936 abdication to marry Wallis Simpson, which made amorous liaison a trope for conflict within monarchy, but also appealed to a haut-bourgeois fascination with royal and aristocratic lives that has its counterpart in present-day retellings of Princess Diana's private life. Ideally attuned to viewers' pleasure, *Lives* produced Elizabethan history as a terrain where sociopolitical conflicts are governed by emotion in a world enhanced by Technicolor glamour, giving Tudor rule flamboyant authenticity. Blatantly hedging one history to make another, its finale, where Essex's declaration that he must be executed in order for England to survive, becomes tantamount to cementing the Anglo-American alliance Winston Churchill had already described in terms of America's lend-lease agreement with Britain, as a new Magna Carta. Indeed, *Lives* represents, at mid-century, the culmination of a mass culture Elizabethan imaginary condensed so as to refashion—and re-masculinize—an American hero across the body of an English Queen.

According to Curtiz's film, scripted from Maxwell Anderson's 1930 verse drama, *Elizabeth the Queen*, Elizabeth herself chooses to "go down in history" while remaining caught in desire. Although a similar premise circulates throughout *Elizabeth R*, what the television series makes patently clear is that going down in history does not suggest that she did it lying on her back: indeed, the nine episodes refashion her romantic pedigree, nearly erasing the Essex story and instead looking back to her long-standing relationship with Robert Dudley, the earl of Leicester, as the lifelong attachment shaping her private as well as public persona and reading forward to divest her from the sedimented meanings of sexual repression mobilized by *Lives*. Here, too, Glenda Jackson's performance not only stands inside the queen's iconography but also presents its critique to position Elizabeth as an emergent feminist subject and as the subject of feminist inquiry. Certainly one of *Elizabeth R*'s primary pleasures derives from rereading old stories through a layering or proliferation of scenarios that give her history the status of a palimpsest, especially because recasting Elizabeth's own words as a performative score remediates their representational authority, opening her to potential renegotiations of meanings. Still, unlike earlier versions of her myth, this retelling is less a cultural fantasy than an attempt to render an historical account of gendered imagination. Perhaps most strikingly, in setting up a profound contradiction between her ability to fashion herself and her extreme vulnerability to others' constructions and manipulations of her, *Elizabeth R* succeeds in clearing a representational space in which the memories and motifs of romance are less the material of private desire than of public narrative—a space where "romance" might be redefined as a term that harnesses sexual to social histories, rejoining the personal to the political.

Elizabeth R moves decisively towards showing her brilliance as a strategist adept at winning the hearts of her people, anticipating *Elizabeth: CEO*'s portrayal of her as a great communicator and as "Queen of the bottom line." Kapur's *Elizabeth*, with Cate Blanchett her most recent surrogate, gestures in that direction, notably in a sequence juxtaposing her struggle to find words with her appearance at Parliament, where she wittily deflects the question of marriage and (with Walsingham's manipulative aid) passes the Act of Uniformity legislating a common prayer book to unite Catholic and Protestant factions in a common purpose which, as she puts it, "makes common sense, a most English virtue." Religious division grounds the film's interest in the instabilities and terrors preceding and surrounding her reign, established in the opening where, under Mary's rule, Protestant heretics are shown having their heads brutally shaved and then being burned at the stake. Situating its narrative within a post-Reformation conflict that, four years following the film's release, seems once again topical, *Elizabeth* clearly is something other than the usual mythic biography of an Elizabethan Golden Age—the type of period film characterized by Fredric Jameson as symptomatic of a society "condemned to seek the historical past through [its] own popular images and stereotypes about the past, which itself remains forever out of reach."[11] To be sure, since film is one of the arenas in which the culture practices sexualities, the romance narrative (again with Robert Dudley) still features prominently, even including scenes of Elizabeth and Dudley making love. Overall, however, the narrative demystifies romance by interweaving it with a thriller-like tale of conspiracy and multiple betrayals to reveal Elizabeth shaping her own image in two realms—one of theatricalized sexuality, the other of theatricalized power—spheres that, finally, as in the Jacobean theatre, are seen to be one and the same. And although this also is not the usual chocolate-box period story of a woman in a frock, costume—the most conspicuously charged material for writing a politics of the performing body—still matters.[12] Here, Elizabeth's costumes map her change from a carefree young beauty in a low-cut dress with pink flounces at her shoulders to a Queen, her gowns coding her sexuality and power into a contradictory aesthetic in which stiff cuffs and ruffs highlight dark velvets or soft silks and tightly laced bodices suggest the constraints of office.

The film's trajectory is modeled around the idea that history is about the choices one makes—in Elizabeth's case, her choice between personal life and a career—a terrain that takes comic form in television's *Ally McBeal* or *Sex and the City* and is synchronous with the dilemma of self-compartmentalization facing present-day professional women.[13] But in stressing Elizabeth's extreme vulnerability and further emphasizing the influences exerted on her by four men—Dudley, her lover; William Cecil, later Lord Burghley, her trusted advisor; Norfolk, the Northern Catholic lord plotting her assassination; and Francis Walsingham, here a curiously reconfigured "spymaster"—her history becomes a story of male politics, a postmodern fairy tale of Beauty and the Beasts. Stressing her entrapment, frequent high-angle long shots observe Elizabeth from a God's eye perspective that diminishes her figure amidst the overwhelming size and weight of cold stone spaces, places of national memory that spell out "history" and "England," as though location shooting might convey the movement of history as well as its re-performance. Consistently, such shots rob her of power, making her doubly subject, to the men surrounding her and to the filmmaker's camera. Yet it also is the case that all of them—lover, advisor and enemy alike—need Elizabeth to be a woman in order to forward their own objectives, plot their own statecraft. Indeed, perhaps the most lasting cultural work the film accomplishes toward engendering a "new" Elizabeth is to refigure the significance of her femininity, for after all, the male posturings around her depend absolutely upon her being at the center of things; this was, simultaneously, both the source of her power and the continuing political problem of her reign: that everything depended upon her.

Elizabeth's finale traces her journey towards discovering what Susan Frye calls "a conceptual space from which she could govern," one that enables her to construct "an autonomous self."[14] Having rid England of her enemies in a sequence (not incidentally, raiding Francis Ford Coppola's *The Godfather* [1972]) that juxtaposes shots of the arrest and execution of those who have betrayed her to ones detailing her resolve, she appears, Walsingham beside her, in a chapel before a statue of the Virgin Mary. To her questions—"What do I do now? Am I to be made of stone?"—his reply "All men need something greater than themselves to look up to and worship. They must be able to touch the divine here on earth"—cues Elizabeth's gaze at the statue, "She had such power over men's hearts," and Walsingham's answer, "They have found nothing to replace her," introducing what becomes, in the film, a stunning visual rendering of Elizabeth's escape from one identity and transformation into another. The camera booms up to the statue's face, looking down; in the next shot, Elizabeth lifts her head in close-up, Queen replacing Virgin across the cut. Like Shakespeare's Cleopatra, with whom she shares a notorious representational history, Elizabeth rejects "inward truth" for "outward seeming" to construct her own hieratic self-image; like Cleopatra, too, costume is the performative sign that masks one self in another in two further transformations. In the first, where Elizabeth's women cut her hair, editing generates the sense that they are literally cutting her apart, divesting her of a former self and identity, and this is enhanced by flashbacks of Elizabeth's past seen in reverse chronology, an erasure of memory that replays history, takes her back to her beginnings: as she says, "I have become a virgin." A shot of white make-up being spread on her hand prepares for a close-up of Elizabeth, her rudely cut hair echoing the image of the Protestant heretic in the film's opening, drawing together Queen and martyr and (again, not incidentally) overtly evoking one of cinema's most famous transformative moments, that where Jeanne Falconetti has her head shaved in Carl Dreyer's *La Passion de Jeanne d'Arc* (1928). The second transformation is not detailed (Can cinema represent the making of a saint?): all rests on appearance; all is for us. From within a curtain-framed white space, Elizabeth seems to materialize out of the ether,

descending from heaven's gate: transformed into a moving sculpture, she descends a flight of steps, her court parting and kneeling in awe at her approach. Pausing briefly before Cecil, she holds out her hand—"Observe, Lord Burghley, I am married to England"; as she walks forward, only a brief insert shot of Dudley, a last fleeting memory, interrupts her progress toward the camera and the throne. As a *Te Deum* sounds, she completes her procession, looking straight out in close-up, backed by her motto, "Video et taceo" (I see and am silent), her face a white mask, fixed, immobile, transfigured into a venerated icon through a miraculous (cinematic) spectacle of re-birth.

The World Would Never Be the Same. *Elizabeth*'s tag line rather neatly turns back on itself to hint at the film's own position in the long chain of Elizabethan surrogates. Hers is, after all, a body to be played with, simultaneously immortal and mortal, icon and iconoclast; the trajectory of her history from one provisional embodiment to another consistently demonstrates what Susan Frye has so aptly called a competition for representation. Giving Orlando and his heirs the deed to his property, Quentin Crisp's Elizabeth mandates her conditions: "Do not fade. Do not wither. Do not grow old." Those words might even more appropriately mark the successive re-performances of Elizabeth I's body within popular cultural memory, each capable of engendering yet another embodiment of the queen described in her most recent publicity as "Formidable. Untouchable. Unbeatable. Fearless. Solitary. Supreme."

Popular culture items from the twentieth century.

1 Susan Frye, *Elizabeth: The Competition for Representation* (Oxford: Oxford University Press, 1993), 114.

2 See Abigail Frost, *Children of History: Elizabeth I* (New York and London: Marshall Cavendish, 1989); Francine Sabin, *Young Queen Elizabeth* (London: Troll Associates, 1990); Catherine Bush, *World Leaders Past and Present: Elizabeth I* (London and New York: Burke Publishing Co., Ltd., 1985).

3 Alan Axelrod, *Elizabeth,CEO: Strategic Lessons from the Leader Who Built an Empire* (Paramus, NJ: Prentice Hall Press, 2000).

4 The computer game, "Civilization III," is created by Sid Meier, published by Infogrames Entertainment, 2001. I am grateful to Lizzie Frye for this reference.

5 See also Francis M. Kelly, "Queen Elizabeth and Her Dresses," *The Conoisseur* 113 (1944), 71–79, esp. 78–79.

6 Ad printed in the *New York Times Magazine*, 11 April 1999, 76.

7 Peggy Phelan, *Unmarked: The Politics of Performance* (London: Routledge, 1993), 2.

8 Here, and in the discussion of the films (except for Kapur's *Elizabeth*), I draw on my "Romancing the Queen" in *The Shakespeare Trade: Performances and Appropriations* (Philadelphia: University of Pennsylvania Press, 1998), 110–70.

9 See Joseph Roach, *Cities of the Dead: Circum-Atlantic Performance* (New York: Columbia University Press, 1996).

10 For the idea of a genealogy of performance, see Roach, *Cities of the Dead*, 25.

11 Fredric Jameson, "Postmodernism and Consumer Society," in *The Cultural Turn: Selected Writings on the Postmodern, 1983–1998* (London: Verso, 1998), 8–10.

12 See Carol Chillington Rutter, *Enter the Body: Women and Representation on Shakespeare's Stage* (London: Routledge, 2001), xvi.

13 For another reading of Kapur's film, see Courtney Lehmann, "Crouching Tiger, Hidden Agenda: How the Renaissance is Taking the Rage out of Feminism," *Shakespeare Quarterly* 53:2 (Summer 2002):260–79.

14 Frye, *Elizabeth I*, viii, 147.

Selected Readings

Arnold, Janet. *Queen Elizabeth's Wardrobe Unlock'd*. Leeds: Maney, 1988.

Berry, Philippa. *Of Chastity and Power: Elizabethan Literature and the Unmarried Queen*. London; New York: Routledge, 1989.

Cole, Mary Hill. *The Portable Queen: Elizabeth I and the Politics of Ceremony*. Amherst: Univ. of Massachusetts Press, 1999.

Dobson, Michael and Nicola Watson. *England's Elizabeth: the Virgin Queen in National Mythology*. New York: Oxford Univ. Press, 2002.

Doran, Susan. *Elizabeth I and Foreign Policy 1558–1603*. London; New York: Routledge, 2000.

———. *Elizabeth I and Religion 1558–1603*. London; New York: Routledge 1994.

———. *Monarchy and Matrimony: the Courtships of Elizabeth I*. London; New York: Routledge, 1996.

Elizabeth I. *Collected Works*. Ed. Leah S. Marcus, Janel Mueller, Mary Beth Rose. Chicago: Univ. of Chicago Press, 2000. (See also revisions in the paperback edition, Univ. of Chicago Press, 2002.)

———. *Autograph Compositions and Foreign Language Originals*. Ed. Janel Mueller and Leah S. Marcus. Chicago: Univ. of Chicago Press, 2003.

———. *Queen Elizabeth I: Selected Works*. Ed. Steven W. May. Washington, D.C.; New York: Folger Shakespeare Library and Washington Square Press, 2003 (forthcoming).

Ellis, Steven G. *Ireland in the Age of the Tudors, 1447–1603*. London; New York: Longman, 1998.

Frye, Susan. *Elizabeth I: the Competition for Representation*. New York: Oxford Univ. Press, 1993.

Hackett, Helen. *Virgin Mother, Maiden Queen: Elizabeth I and the Cult of the Virgin Mary*. New York: St. Martin's Press, 1995.

Haigh, Christopher. *Elizabeth I*. 2nd ed. London: Longman, 1998.

Hammer, Paul E. J. *The Polarization of Elizabethan Politics: the Political Career of Robert Devereux, 2nd Earl of Essex, 1585–1597*. Cambridge: Cambridge Univ. Press, 1999.

Johnson, Paul. *Elizabeth I: a Study in Power and Intellect*. London: Futura, 1976.

Jones, Norman L. *The Birth of the Elizabethan Age: England in the 1560s*. Oxford: Blackwell, 1993.

King, John N. *Tudor Royal Iconography: Literature and Art in an Age of Religious Crisis*. Princeton: Princeton Univ. Press, 1989.

Levin, Carole. *The Heart and Stomach of a King: Elizabeth I and the Politics of Sex and Power*. Philadelphia: Univ. of Pennsylvania Press, 1994.

———. *The Reign of Elizabeth I*. Hampshire; New York: Palgrave, 2002.

MacCaffrey, Wallace. *Elizabeth I*. London: Edward Arnold, 1993.

Montrose, Louis Adrian. "'Eliza, Queene of shepheardes,' and the Pastoral of Power." *English Literary Renaissance*, 10 (1980):153–82.

———. "Idols of the Queene: Policy, Gender, and the Picturing of Elizabeth I." *Representations*, 68 (1999): 108–161.

Mullett, Michael A. *Catholics in Britain and Ireland, 1558–1829*. New York: St. Martin's Press, 1999.

Neale, J. E. *Elizabeth I and Her Parliaments, 1584–1601*. (London: Jonathan Cape, 1957).

———. *Queen Elizabeth I: a Biography*. New York: Doubleday, 1957.

Nichols, John. *The Progresses and Public Processions of Queen Elizabeth*. 3 vols. London: J. Nichols & Sons, 1823.

Ridley, Jasper. *Elizabeth I: the Shrewdness of Virtue*. New York: Viking, 1988.

Rodríguez-Salgado, M. J. et al. *Armada, 1588–1988*. London; New York: Penguin Books in association with the National Maritime Museum, 1988.

Shell, Marc. *Elizabeth's Glass: with "The Glass of the Sinful Soul" (1544) by Elizabeth I, and "Epistle Dedicatory" and "Conclusion" (1548) by John Bale*. Lincoln: Univ. of Nebraska Press, 1993.

Somerset, Anne. *Elizabeth I*. New York: St. Martin's, 1991.

Starkey, David. *Elizabeth: Apprenticeship*. London: Chatto, 2000.

Strong, Roy. *The Cult of Elizabeth: Elizabethan Portraiture and Pageantry*. London: Thames & Hudson, 1977.

———. *Gloriana: the Portraits of Queen Elizabeth I*. London: Thames & Hudson, 1987.

———. *Portraits of Queen Elizabeth I*. Oxford: Clarendon Press, 1963.

Trevor-Roper, Hugh. *Queen Elizabeth's First Historian: William Camden and the Beginnings of English 'Civil History.'* Neale Lecture in English History. London: Jonathan Cape, 1971.

Walker, Julia M., Ed. *Dissing Elizabeth: Negative Representations of Gloriana*. Durham: Duke Univ. Press, 1999.

———. "Reading the Tombs of Elizabeth I." *English Literary Renaissance*, 26 (1996): 510–30.

Watkins, John. *Representing Elizabeth in Stuart England*. Cambridge: Cambridge Univ. Press, 2002.

Wilson, Elkin Calhoun. *England's Eliza*. Cambridge: Harvard Univ. Press, 1939; rpt. New York: Octagon, 1966.

Wormald, Jenny. *Mary, Queen of Scots: Politics, Passion and a Kingdom Lost*. London: Tauris, 2000.

Yates, Frances A. *Astraea: The Imperial Theme in the Sixteenth Century*. London: Routledge, 1975.

Ziegler, Georgianna. "England's Savior: Elizabeth I in the Writings of Thomas Heywood." *Renaissance Papers* (1980): 29–37.

Index of Historical Personages